Relati

Relational Depth

New Perspectives and Developments

Edited by

Rosanne Knox

David Murphy

Sue Wiggins

Mick Cooper

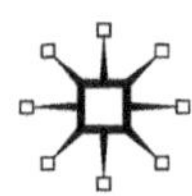

First published 2013 by
PALGRAVE MACMILLAN

Palgrave Macmillan in the UK is an imprint of Macmillan Publishers Limited, registered in England, company number 785998, of Houndmills, Basingstoke, Hampshire RG21 6XS.

Palgrave Macmillan in the US is a division of St Martin's Press LLC, 175 Fifth Avenue, New York, NY 10010.

Palgrave Macmillan is the global academic imprint of the above companies and has companies and representatives throughout the world.

ISBN: 978–0–230–27939–1

This book is printed on paper suitable for recycling and made from fully managed and sustained forest sources. Logging, pulping and manufacturing processes are expected to conform to the environmental regulations of the country of origin.

A catalogue record for this book is available from the British Library.

A catalog record for this book is available from the Library of Congress.

10 9 8 7 6 5 4 3 2 1
22 21 20 19 18 17 16 15 14 13

Printed and bound in Great Britain by
CPI Antony Rowe, Chippenham and Eastbourne

Contents

Foreword

It is interesting to see the growing interest in the notion of relational depth. From the outset I have asserted that there is nothing new in the concept, but that it merely emphasizes the importance of taking seriously the 'therapeutic conditions' of empathy, unconditional positive regard and congruence. A person-centred therapist should expect themselves to provide all these qualities and in high degree. Only then is the power of person-centred therapy realized because it offers a quality and depth of relationship unique in therapy and quite possibly unique in the life experience of the client.

Forty years ago, Rogers supervised my therapy with profoundly traumatized hospital patients. He loved that kind of work for the commitment and creativity it demanded. Many years earlier, he had worked with the same population (Rogers and Wallen, 1946) and it was only 10 years previously that he had invested 166 sessions with Jim Brown, among other patients, in Mendota State Hospital (Farber et al., 1996; Rogers, 1967). One of the interesting findings in this study was the division among the therapists in regard to their willingness to be congruently present (McLeod, in press) – a critical issue in working with this population. Some therapists could invest themselves fully in relationship but others were reluctant to move beyond their comfort zone.

In supervising my own work, Rogers showed an excited involvement, sometimes asking me to phone him later that evening to report on what had happened in a potentially crucial encounter with a patient. It is strange to compare this involved, excited figure with the nondirective caricature as he is sometimes depicted.

For me, the crucial issue in therapy, especially with hard-to-reach clients, is the huge personal *challenge* posed by relational depth for both the client and the therapist. I often remember clients and patients giving me that long, cold stare that says: 'I guess I am maybe going to go where I'm too scared to go.' Relational depth is not the same as the *therapeutic alliance* – it is not merely about establishing enough contact and trust such that the client allows the therapist to perform their work – it is about establishing such a powerful contact at a range of depths that the client feels *joined* by the therapist. This joining will make it possible for them to go to places within themselves that they have previously had to avoid. This joining will also allow them to experience relationship as the most nutritious environment for growth. But the fear is also real. Many would have been damaged in relationship and others, such as the traumatized client, know that to bring themselves closer to the existential impact of the trauma might destroy them. In holding the stare of the client or patient as they make their decision, you taste their fear.

Relational depth poses challenges for the therapist as well as the client. It is not just the challenge of being so close to the client's fear or despair, it is the developmental challenge of becoming a person who can offer an encounter at depth, not merely with some clients, but with every person who comes through their door. Development is not just about expanding knowledge and experience – it is about expanding the person.

The notion of relational depth carries a strong research challenge into the future, and some of that is represented in this book. There is an essential interplay between theory building and research. All my theoretical suggestions have been based on direct observation of clients and indirect reports of trainees and colleagues, supplemented and enhanced by the theoretical writings of others. That observation and sifting is a scientific endeavour. In just the same fashion as the qualitative researcher, our observation and sifting reflects the sometimes explicit and often implicit ideas we carry into the material. Yet, we have a genuine curiosity to get beyond these presumptions, because there is potentially much more delicious learning to be obtained if we can take a range of perspectives on our data. One lateral shift that proved priceless for me was when I got over the presumption that a good therapeutic relationship epitomized openness on the part of both parties. When I became aware of the immensity of the *unspoken relationship* between client and therapist, even in a good therapeutic relationship, I was able to ask the subsequent question: Under what circumstances do the parties reveal more about their experiencing of each other and their relationship? It was this question that led to a realization of the importance of relational depth. On another scientific enterprise, I listened to many tapes of my sessions and realized that I paid much better attention to my clients' 'growthful' statements than their 'not for growth' utterances. That changed my whole practice. I began to listen to the *whole* of my client – and the whole of my client began to come to the therapy.

But we also need the help of others as researchers. There was one point in our 2005 book (Mearns and Cooper, 2005) about which I felt uncomfortable. It was the idea that in the therapeutic relationship, the depth of relationship would be experienced by *both* people. There was logic in that, and yet it didn't really fit with my therapy experience with clients. Unfortunately, I did not focus on my dissonance – so often the seed of scientific learning. It was the second time I had made the same mistake over the same point. The other opportunity had been over the Rogers–Buber debate (Kirschenbaum and Henderson, 1989, pp. 41–63), where Rogers suggested that the therapeutic relationship he was describing was the same as Buber's notion of the I-Thou. Buber disagreed, asserting that the I-Thou relationship could not pertain where there was a power difference between the parties. Both these great writers were important to me (Buber's writing was my first diversion from a life studying maths and physics), and I should have paused awhile and asked that frequently productive scientific question – What if both are true? That would surely have led to the realization that the I-Thou relationship might exist for both client and therapist, but might be experienced *differently* by them. At times like this, when the personal scientific process fails, it is important that we have the empirical work. In an interesting piece of research by McMillan and McLeod (2006), they suggested that while the therapist tends to see relational depth in terms of the relationship, the client's frame of reference is rarely the relationship – it is more often their own process. The client's experience of what the therapist might call 'relational depth' is more in terms of the increase in freedom of expression they experience. So, I was able to learn from the empirical work of colleagues and incorporate that learning into the next book (Mearns and Thorne, 2007, pp. 64–5). Rogers and Buber were not so fortunate.

Advancing our understanding involves us in a dialogue between our own learnings to that point and the insights of others. In this book, *Relational Depth: Contemporary Perspectives and Developments*, we are offered a wealth of insights on the challenging issue of relational depth.

Dave Mearns
May 2012

References

Farber, B.A., Brink, D.C. and Raskin, P.M. (1996) *The Psychotherapy of Carl Rogers.* New York: Guilford Press.

Kirschenbaum, H. and Henderson, V.L. (1989) *Carl Rogers: Dialogues.* Boston, MA: Houghton Mifflin.

McLeod, J. (in press) Research on person-centred counselling. In D. Mearns and B. Thorne with J. McLeod, *Person-centred Counselling in Action* (4th edn) (Chapter 10). London: Sage.

McMillan, M. and McLeod, J. (2006) Letting go: The client's experience of relational depth. *Person-Centered and Experiential Psychotherapies*, 5, 277–92.

Mearns, D. and Cooper, M. (2005) *Working at Relational Depth in Counselling and Psychotherapy*. London: Sage.

Mearns, D. and Thorne, B. (2007) *Person-Centred Counselling in Action* (3rd edn). London: Sage.

Rogers, C.R. (ed.) (1967) *The Therapeutic Relationship and its Impact: A Study of Psychotherapy with Schizophrenics*. Madison, IL: University of Wisconsin Press.

Rogers, C.R. and Wallen, J.L. (1946) *Counselling with Returned Servicemen*. New York: McGraw-Hill.

Acknowledgements

Mick Cooper
Many thanks to colleagues in the relational depth research field who contributed their reports, comments and critical reflections to Chapter 5: Rosanne Knox, David Murphy, Sue Wiggins, Ambika Erin Connelly, John Leung, Eleanor Macleod, Gillian Morris and Rob Omielan.

Sue Wilders
With thanks to Sam Robinson for extensive editing help and ideas, and to Jerold Bozarth for comments on the draft and editing suggestions for Chapter 15.

Gill Wyatt
I would like to thank the following people who took part in the research for Chapter 8. Their contribution has been invaluable to this chapter and the development of the ideas in it: Alan Coulson, Jan Inglis, Janet Hills, Colin Lago, Mhairi McMillan, Peter Schmid, Gill Westcott, Lynn Wethenhall, Gail Parfitt, Rose Cameron, Ian Holmes-Lewis, Peggy Natiello, Dave Key, Irmgard Fennes, Jerold Bozarth, Paul Wilkins, Makiko Mikuni.

Colin Lago and Fevronia Christodoulidi
We would like to thank Shukla Dhingra and Sheila Mudadi-Billings for their input in Chapter 9.

Introduction: the in-depth therapeutic encounter

Rosanne Knox, Sue Wiggins, David Murphy and Mick Cooper

> I really, by her presence, I guess ... and maybe she just experienced me differently that day. You know, in her whole being ... There was something more about her presence in the room ... um, a way of being. Something changed, that day for me. And for her. I really felt that she was there. And understood what I meant ... and how I felt. (client, from Knox, 2011)

The origins and developments of relational depth

Psychotherapy and counselling of all persuasions are carried out in the context of the relationship between those seeking help and those providing help. Whether it is in a dyad or with a couple, family or small group, the relationship between therapist and client is critically involved in the process of recovery and growth. In 1996, Dave Mearns first used the term 'relational depth' to emphasize the potential role and value of the depth of relating in counselling and psychotherapy. Since then there has been a resurgence of interest in the relational aspects of therapy across the spectrum of therapeutic approaches. The concept of relational depth was more fully explored and developed by Mearns and Cooper (2005) in *Working at Relational Depth in Counselling and Psychotherapy*; a book that, while perceived by some as controversial (see Wilders, Chapter 15, this volume), has proved pivotal in bringing the relationship to the forefront of person-centred and experiential therapy practice, theory and research. The debates that have emerged as a consequence of this increased interest in relational factors have marked the beginning of what we feel is an important, exciting journey towards a deeper understanding of the therapeutic relationship at the core of the therapeutic process. It is a journey that we have found sometimes surprising, often humbling, and always inspiring; and it is far from over, there is much more yet to learn. We invite you to join us on that journey as we explore a rich mix of theoretical developments, practice experience and empirical evidence, from the perspectives of theorists, practitioners, researchers and, perhaps most importantly, clients themselves.

Evolving definitions

In the original conceptualization of relational depth, Mearns and Cooper (2005, p. 36) offered the following definition:

> A feeling of profound contact and engagement with a client, in which one simultaneously experiences high and consistent levels of empathy and acceptance towards the Other, and relates to them in a highly transparent way. In this relationship, the client is experienced as acknowledging one's empathy, acceptance and congruence – either explicitly or implicitly – and is experienced as fully congruent in that moment.

Underlying this description is Rogers' ([1957]1990, p. 221) theory of personality change and the six conditions that he proposed were both necessary and sufficient for change to occur:

1. Two persons are in psychological contact.
2. The first, whom we shall term the client, is in a state of incongruence, being vulnerable or anxious.
3. The second, whom we shall term the therapist, is congruent or integrated in the relationship.
4. The therapist experiences unconditional positive regard for the client.
5. The therapist experiences an empathic understanding of the client's internal frame of reference and endeavors to communicate this experience to the client.
6. The communication to the client of the therapist's empathic understanding and unconditional positive regard is to a minimal degree achieved.

With the focus on what Rogers called the three 'core' conditions of empathy, congruence and unconditional positive regard, the description of relational depth emphasized the importance of the integrative nature of these conditions; the suggestion being that when offered together in high degree it would be more accurate to describe them as different facets of a single variable, namely 'relational depth'. While Rogers' conditions have been the primary focus of person-centred theorists and practitioners over the years, the concept of their unification in relational depth is relatively new.

Two aspects of relational depth

There are a number of issues that inform the debates in the field of relational depth theory. For example, taking a closer look at Mearns and Cooper's definition above, we can see that two distinct aspects of relating have been incorporated into the phenomenon of relational depth. The first describes an ongoing, sustained deep relationship, one in which the therapist is congruent and consistently experiences high levels of unconditional positive regard, successfully communicated through empathic understanding, and in which the client acknowledges receiving the conditions. In such a relationship, the therapist is experienced by the client as genuine and caring, as shown by the following description from a research participant:

> And also that he's not faking it, the relationship is genuine, that he's not ... he's not just pretending to be there with me, he's not pretending to like me. I know it's not accepting just in the session. I have this sense that he would be the same with me, or with anyone else. He's that kind of person, he isn't just putting it on. (client, from Knox, 2011)

Since Rogers ([1957]1990) first proposed the therapeutic relationship conditions of empathy, unconditional positive regard and congruence, the enduring relationship has been the focus of much research. However, Rogers (1959) also commented on there being specific moments in the relationship that were important in leading to change. Here, this relates to the second aspect of the relational depth phenomena and refers to specific, identifiable *moments* of profound engagement and connectedness. The following is an example of a client's description of such a moment:

> The pace of the meeting seemed to slow ... I got to a point where I was speaking where I thought, 'Yeah, I'm going to do it, I can't go back,' and I spoke very openly ... Yeah, the environment we were in, the circumstances, the close – it was as if we were one. As if ... almost as if I was talking to that being that is within me, anyway. (client, from Knox, 2011)

Relational depth theory acknowledges both of these distinct, but interrelated aspects, and each are addressed in the following chapters. In recent years, however, research has primarily concentrated on specific *moments* of encounter, and this will be the principal focus for the research chapters in this book.

Theoretical developments

Since the publication of Mearns and Cooper's (2005) original text, a growing number of theorists and practitioners have been discussing the notion of relational depth, and in 2006 a special issue of *Person-Centered and Experiential Psychotherapies* was dedicated to the subject, exploring the notion from a variety of perspectives. Mearns collaborated with Peter Schmid on two papers (Mearns and Schmid, 2006; Schmid and Mearns, 2006), bringing together his own work on relational depth and Schmid's (2003) description of an 'encounter relationship'. Schmid and Mearns (2006, p. 174) described person-centred psychotherapy as an 'in-depth co-creative process of personalization', arguing that it is the therapist's task to be 'the person that he or she is'

(p. 181), and to 'stand firm as a person and face the client as a person'. They proposed that for the therapist *being-counter* to the client is just as important as *being-with*, as it is the former that provides the foundation for dialogue and relational depth.

From within this conceptualization, relational depth can be considered a particular form of relating that comes about when there is a true encounter between client and therapist. This form of relating might be seen in any therapeutic approach, in any helping situation and perhaps in any relational context where each person is relating authentically with the other. While, currently, the major developments in this field have come from within person-centred psychology, the phenomenon is by no means confined to the person-centred approach to psychotherapy. However, it is fair to say that an experience of relational depth is probably more likely when the relationship component of any encounter is considered to be of worth in its own right.

Empirical evidence

The past few years have also seen a growing body of research into different aspects of relational depth. In an effort to extend our understanding of the phenomenon, studies have been undertaken from the therapist's perspective (Cooper, 2005) and the client's perspective (MacLeod, 2009; McMillan and McLeod, 2006; Knox, 2008, 2011; Omielan, 2009) and from both sides of the therapeutic dyad (Leung, 2009; Murphy, Chapter 14, this volume; Wiggins, Chapter 4, this volume). Fortunately, there has been an unusually strong spirit of coordination by researchers in the field, so that the overall knowledge base has been building in a robust and cohesive manner; for example, Knox's (2008) qualitative study into clients' experiences of the moment of relational depth was followed by Wiggins' (2011) quantitative study into the same aspect, lending weight and validity to the findings of each. Following on from the studies into clients' and therapists' individual experiences of relational depth, work is now underway to investigate the synchrony of experiencing high levels of relational connection by both clients and therapists towards each other (Cooper, 2012). An in-depth review of the emerging evidence on relational depth is given by Cooper in Chapter 5. This review is comprehensive but we urge interested readers to develop opportunities to build on the research in the field of relational depth theory.

Controversies

The concept of working at relational depth has not been without controversy. The notion has been debated within the person-centred community, being perceived by some as directive, unhelpful to the person-centred practitioner, and as a contradiction to classical client-centred counselling as described by Rogers. Brodley (2006) and Wilders (2007, Chapter 15, this volume) have questioned how the notion of working at relational depth sits with a person-centred approach that holds nondirectivity at its core. They have argued that working at relational depth, as it was described by Mearns and Cooper (2005), necessitates a directive stance on the part of the therapist. In responding to these critiques, Mearns (2007) suggested that their differing views might in part stem from the fact that he himself knew Rogers later on in Rogers' career, when Rogers' therapy could certainly be described as relational. However, Mearns was clear in his view that there is nothing in the notion of working at relational depth that conflicts with the person-centred approach. Cooper's (2007) response to the above critiques has focused around individual clients' wants, arguing that different clients want and need different styles of therapy at different times – such that, for some, a more interactional stance may be quite appropriate at particular points in therapy. He also argued that relational depth is not described as something that therapists should 'make' happen (even if they could), but as something that they might learn to open themselves more fully to. As further discussed by Knox (Chapter 2, this volume), this view would also seem to be borne out by clients, who, according to research, see themselves as the decision makers in enabling moments of relational depth to occur. As one research participant described it:

> I think it's – 60% was me, my need, my desire, my ... and 40% was the environment my counsellor had contributed to, the environment, the trust that we had, the acceptance. (client, from Knox, 2011)

A key factor that has been opened up as a result of developments in relational depth theory is this focus on the collaborative, bidirectional aspects to the therapeutic relationship. This has been important as, until this development, the theoretical construct of the therapeutic alliance has been the principal focus of psychotherapy research. This is largely due to its focus on the collaborative features of the relationship where Rogers' (1957) conditions have been researched as more unilateral phenomena (Murphy et al., 2012).

Related concepts

The notion of relational depth, although developed within the person-centred approach, has relevance for a wide range of therapeutic approaches or relational helping in other professional disciplines. While the terminology may vary, the depth of relating between client and therapist is, to some extent, acknowledged within all the major schools of therapy. In what we believe is a helpful atmosphere of increasing dialogue, the similarities and connections in theoretical perspectives are being made. Rogers' famous dialogue with the

German existential philosopher Martin Buber, who developed the concept of an I-Thou relationship (1970), has provided an invaluable resource for developing our understanding of the ways in which the therapeutic relationship proposed by Rogers and the I-Thou relation proposed by Buber have much in common. The Gestalt therapist Hycner (1991) has drawn on the work of Buber (1970) and Friedman (1985) to develop a dialogical approach with the aim of facilitating a mutual encounter. Existential-humanistic therapists have also emphasized the importance of the client's presence and openness to the therapist, and encourage the articulation of the 'lived moment' of the therapeutic encounter (Bugental, 1978; May, 1958; Yalom, 2001). The transpersonal therapist Rowan (Chapter 16, this volume) has written of a moment of profound engagement as 'linking'; and in the psychoanalytical field there are similarities that can be drawn with Stern's (2004, p. 77) description of moments of meeting, Ehrenberg's intimate edge (1992, p. 34) 'at the growing edge of the relationship', and Bion's (1967) notion of intuition. All this suggests the importance of recognizing the relational in therapy. This is particularly pertinent, as the more technological interventionist approaches to therapy, which have featured prominently in recent years within the healthcare sector, are perhaps also having to redefine their helpful and active ingredients. For example, recent developments in third and fourth generations of cognitive behavioural therapy have seen the introduction of relational aspects to therapy through terms such as 'acceptance and commitment', 'compassion focused' and 'mindfulness', which point towards the central role of interpersonal relating in the therapeutic space. As relational depth theory continues to develop, these approaches are also likely to find a connection to and role for deep relating in therapy.

Aims of the book

Relational depth is not simply another way of describing a strong therapeutic alliance. It is not just a collaboration of shared goals and objectives, or a working partnership, it is something very different. But the field of relational depth theory is still relatively new. We anticipate that, through an ongoing programme of research and theoretical development, an understanding of relational depth will be adapted as new findings and thoughts are developed. As such, rather than aiming to offer a homogeneous, definitive and prescriptive definition of relational depth, this book aims to explore the meaning and experience of relational depth from a multiplicity of perspectives, asking questions such as: What is it like for therapists to experience relational depth with clients? Is it something therapists should be striving for, preparing for, or simply not preventing? Does relational depth have a therapeutic value? Is there any evidence to show that relational depth might contribute to a positive outcome for the client?

Our understanding of relational depth in therapy is deepening on a daily basis, both in terms of theoretical developments and refinements and, perhaps more importantly, in terms of what clients themselves think. In putting together the chapters for this book, we have extended our knowledge further into the notion of relational depth, and we have found more and more doors opening up to reveal different areas of inquiry and new links to theory in specific fields or practice. Our aim for this book has been to gather together all these developments in theory, practice and research that have occurred since the original Mearns and Cooper (2005) book. These developments are supported by vivid descriptions of experiences of relational depth described by the clients and therapists involved, and ultimately lay the ground for further developments and learning around the concept of relational depth.

The chapters

Part I: Experience and evidence of relational depth

There seems little doubt that both clients and therapists experience moments of deep relational connection and they often describe the therapeutic relationship as having a deep and meaningful purpose. Consequently, we have opened the book with a short series of case examples. Each of the examples, as one would expect, is unique in the phenomenological experience of relational depth described. They show the pattern of intensity of relating that seems to be present in such moments. The opening chapter acts as a foundation stone for the research and theory that is presented later in the book. As much of Rogers' work was grounded in the knowledge he developed from his own experiences, we hope that, in providing these examples, it creates a point of contact for readers who have themselves experienced relational depth.

The chapters in Part I provide evidence of the ways in which relational depth is experienced by both therapists and clients. Drawing on her research into clients' experiences, Rosanne Knox discusses clients' perceptions of the moments themselves, their impact and long-term effects, and how the moments emerged. Based on this evidence, Rosanne then proposes a model of meeting at relational depth. Chapter 3 sees Eleanor Mcleod reviewing the findings of research into experiences of relational depth with clients with learning difficulties, and looks at the factors perceived by therapists as facilitating, deepening and impeding relational depth with this client group. In Chapter 4, Sue Wiggins takes us through the research journey that has led to the development of the Relational Depth Inventory, giving an insight into the background and components of relational depth as a measurable construct. In Chapter 5, the final chapter in Part I, Mick Cooper brings together the evidence to produce a systematic account of what we know so far, and what areas are proving to be fruitful avenues for further study.

Part II: Relational depth in context

This part looks at relational depth within the context of a range of different settings from the perspective of practitioners within their respective fields. In Chapter 6, Sue Hawkins discusses the process of working at relational depth work with children and young people. Theoretical issues are explored through Sue's work with young offenders, emphasizing the particular importance of working at relational depth for this client group. David Murphy and Stephen Joseph then discuss, in Chapter 7, their experiences of working at relational depth with trauma clients, and explore how this can create the therapeutic space for posttraumatic growth to occur.

While the possibilities for working at relational depth in one-to-one therapy settings might be relatively easy to imagine, a frequently asked question is how this might work in groups. In Chapter 8, Gill Wyatt offers an answer to this important question by drawing on aspects of complexity, chaos and systems theory to deepen and expand our understanding of relational depth within the setting of groups. Gill addresses the practical applications arising from the development of the concept of relational depth, and explores the benefits to the group culture and environment of being able to work at relational depth at a group level and at the individual level.

Another interesting question is how far relational depth can be achieved with clients whose backgrounds are very different to our own as therapists. The challenges and complexities faced by therapists when working with clients from different and diverse communities are explored in Chapter 9 by Colin Lago and Fevronia Christodoulidi, who steer us through a landscape of potential barriers that can stand in the way of satisfactory 'transcultural' therapeutic progress.

A vital component of any effective therapy is, of course, that of supervision, but what is the relevance of the concept of relational depth to this aspect of therapy? Elke Lambers addresses this subject in Chapter 10, exploring the meaning for the supervision dyad itself, and how the supervision relationship can support the supervisee in their capacity to relate at depth to their clients. Chapter 11, the final chapter in Part II, looks at the subject of training and professional development. Mick Cooper presents a series of self-development exercises that can help therapists to enhance their experiential capacity to meet clients at relational depth.

Part III: Related perspectives

The last part explores how the notion of relational depth sits within the wider field of person-centred and experiential psychotherapies, discussing it in relation to a range of closely connected concepts. In Chapter 12, Peter Schmid examines the notion of therapy as 'dialogue', from an anthropological, epistemological, ethical and political stance, and discusses how the concept of relational depth relates to a dialogical understanding of psychotherapy. Schmid's exposition of a dialogical therapy is as an intrinsically relational therapy and places relational depth at the heart of the person-centred approach.

Taking a slightly different perspective, Shari Geller proposes in Chapter 13 that therapeutic presence is, in fact, a relational experience that then deepens a relational depth encounter. Shari goes on to explore the different aspects of therapeutic presence as grounded in two studies: a qualitative study of therapeutic presence and a study on the development of a presence measure. Focusing on the notion of mutuality, the proposal made by David Murphy in Chapter 14 is that it is the mutual experiencing of Rogers' therapeutic conditions by both therapist and client that lays the ground for relational depth encounters to occur.

We have openly acknowledged that there have been challenges to the development of the notion of working at relational depth, and it is important that these challenges are heard and understood so that colleagues in the field may come to their own conclusions. In Chapter 15, Sue Wilders raises the question of how the notion of working at relational depth is able to sit comfortably with an underlying belief in nondirectivity. The integral and transpersonal therapist John Rowan argues in Chapter 16 that there is a strong connection between working at relational depth, as described by Mearns and Cooper (2005), and the phenomenon of 'linking' as described by Budgell (1995), and suggests that relational depth can be located in what he describes as the 'transpersonal realm'.

Finally, in conclusion to the book, Chapter 17 looks at the advances in our understanding of relational depth, and plots the future potential for further research on and development of the construct.

References

Bion, W.R. (1967) *Second Thoughts*. New York: Jason Aronson.

Brodley, B. (2006) Regarding Baker, Johnston and Wenner 'Relational depth: How do we assess it?' *Person-Centred Quarterly*, November, 13–14.

Buber, M. (1970) *I and Thou*. New York: Scribner's Sons.

Budgell, R. (1995) Being touched through space. Dissertation, School of Psychotherapy and Counselling, Regents College, London.

Bugental, J. (1978) *Psychotherapy and Process*. New York: McGraw-Hill.

Cooper, M. (2005) Therapists' experiences of relational depth: A qualitative interview study. *Counselling and Psychotherapy Research*, 5(2), 87–95.

Cooper, M. (2007) Thoughts and feelings on the relational depth debate. *Person-Centred Quarterly*, May, 14–15.

Cooper, M. (2012) Clients' and therapists' perceptions of intrasessional connection: An analogue study of change over time, predictor variables, and level of consensus. *Psychotherapy Research*, 22(3), 274–88, DOI:10.1080/10503307.2011.647931.

Ehrenberg, D. (1992) *The Intimate Edge: Extending the Reach of Psychoanalytic Interaction*. New York: W.W. Norton.

Friedman, M. (1985) *The Healing Dialogue in Psychotherapy*. New York: Jason Aronson.

Hycner, R. (1991) *Between Person and Person: Towards a Dialogical Psychotherapy*. Highland, NY: Gestalt Journal Press.

Knox, R. (2008) Clients' experiences of relational depth in person-centred counselling. *Counselling and Psychotherapy Research*, 8(3), 182–8.

Knox, R. (2011) Clients' experiences of relational depth. Unpublished PhD dissertation, University of Strathclyde, Glasgow.

Leung, J. (2009) A quantitative online study exploring the factors associated with the experience and perceived importance of relational depth. Unpublished DPsych dissertation, University of Strathclyde, Glasgow.

Macleod, E. (2009) A qualitative exploration into therapists' perceptions of reaching relational depth when counselling people with learning disabilities. Unpublished MSc dissertation, University of Strathclyde, Glasgow.

McMillan, M. and McLeod, J. (2006) Letting go: The client's experiences of relational depth. *Person-Centered and Experiential Psychotherapies*, 5(4), 277–92.

May, R. (1958) Contributions of existential psychotherapy. In R. May, E. Angel and H.F. Ellenberger (eds) *Existence: A New Dimension in Psychiatry and Psychology* (pp. 37–91). New York: McGraw-Hill.

Mearns, D. (1996) Contact at relational depth. *Counselling*, 7, 306–11.

Mearns, D. (2007) Regarding Barbara Brodley's critique of Mearns and Cooper (2005). *Person-Centred Quarterly*, November, 23.

Mearns, D. and Cooper, M. (2005) *Working at Relational Depth in Counselling and Psychotherapy.* London: Sage.

Mearns, D. and Schmid, P.F. (2006) Being-with and being-counter: Relational depth: the challenge of fully meeting the client. *Person-Centered and Experiential Psychotherapies*, 5(3), 255–65.

Murphy, D., Cramer, D. and Joseph, S. (2012) Mutuality in person-centered therapy: A new agenda for research and practice. *Person-Centered & Experiential Psychotherapies*, 11, 109–23.

Omielan, R. (2009) The influence of relational depth on therapeutic relationships: a narrative inquiry into client experience. Unpublished MSc dissertation, University of Bristol, Bristol.

Rogers, C.R. ([1957]1990) The necessary and sufficient conditions of therapeutic personality change. In H. Kirschenbaum and V. Henderson (eds) *The Carl Rogers Reader* (pp. 219–35). London: Constable.

Rogers, C.R. (1959) A theory of therapy, personality, and interpersonal relationships, as developed in the client-centered framework. In S. Koch (ed.) *Psychology: A Study of Science*, vol. 3, *Formulations of the Person and the Social Context* (pp. 184–256). New York: McGraw-Hill.

Schmid, P.F. (2003) The characteristics of a person-centered approach to therapy and counseling: Criteria for identity and coherence. *Person-Centered and Experiential Psychotherapies*, 2, 104–20.

Schmid, P.F. and Mearns, D. (2006) Being-with and being-counter: Person-centered psychotherapy as an in-depth co-creative process of personalization. *Person-Centered and Experiential Psychotherapies*, 5, 174–90.

Stern, D.N. (2004) *The Present Moment in Psychotherapy and Everyday Life.* New York: W.W. Norton.

Wiggins, S. (2011) Development and validation of a measure of relational depth. Unpublished PhD dissertation, University of Strathclyde, Glasgow.

Wilders, S. (2007) Relational depth and the person-centred approach. *Person-Centred Quarterly*, February, 1–4.

Yalom, I. (2001) *The Gift of Therapy: Reflections of Being a Therapist.* London: Piatkus.

Part I

Experience and Evidence of Relational Depth

1

Meeting at relational depth in therapy: the lived encounter

Chris Brown, Anne Deacon, Jan Kerr and Kenny Ralph

For counsellors and psychotherapists, the experience of meeting a client at relational depth in therapy can be a profound and memorable experience, which has the potential to impact deeply on the therapeutic relationship and the client's psychological development. In this chapter, we explore the experiences and evidence of relational depth by presenting four therapists' accounts of meeting clients at this level of engagement. The aim is to bring the phenomenon of relational depth, as actually lived and experienced, to the fore, and to begin to develop an understanding of its nature and impact.

All accounts are written with the kind permission of the clients or, in the case of Tony, with his family. Clients' names are pseudonyms. Each of the therapists identify as person-centred practitioners, with substantial experience of working with a range of clients.

Grace (by Anne Deacon)

Grace was physically and mentally abused from a young child to her leaving home at 16 years old. She was beaten on a regular basis for anything and everything. Her meal would be put on the table at the same time as those of her mother, father and sister but she wouldn't be allowed to eat it until they had finished and had left the table; consequently, her food was always cold, and sometimes so inedible that she would want to be sick and she would be flung out of the back door, whatever the weather, to be sick in the drain.

Her mother taught her to spell her name wrong so she would be humiliated at school. Christmas was a terrible time for her, she never received a present but had to sit and watch her sister opening hers. Grace learned early in her life to keep her feelings under control and never show any emotion. Every waking moment was fearful for her as she never knew what might provoke another attack.

She came to me for counselling when she was 39 years old. She said that she wanted to find a way to have a better life. I counselled Grace for over two years. Grace struggled to understand what feelings felt like because she had never had the luxury of experiencing any. Even fear had been replaced by a void of nothingness. We worked for many months trying to recognize feelings and giving them the appropriate names.

There were many times when Grace's only means of understanding how unacceptable events in her life had been was through my deep empathy. Many times I would physically feel her pain and anguish and my expression and body language reflected this, and thus through my congruence during these situations, Grace was able to draw from me the enormity of what she had endured.

Then came the day when she was telling me of yet another beating and as my eyes filled with tears as I listened, she suddenly stopped mid-sentence and said to me: 'those tears should be mine, shouldn't they?' I nodded, Grace continued to look at me and then I saw her eyes begin to fill with tears as well. (This was the first time in 18 months that she had shown emotion.) She continued to look at me as if she needed to be connected to my tears to allow hers to flow. Time seemed to stand still, quietness had seemed to descend on the room, there was nothing happening, yet there was so much happening, Grace continued to look at me and the enormity of her pain was tangible. Then her tears came, slowly at first, as she blinked hard as if to force them out of her eyes. Then she was sobbing, her body shaking with the force. She looked at me now with panic in her eyes as she experienced for the first time what it felt like to cry for herself. I leaned closer, her tears were now falling onto her arms and clothes and the noises she made came from deep within her very soul.

I asked softly if she wanted me to sit next to her, she nodded, so I moved slowly across to the settee and sat down half-facing her (touch was something she was afraid of, so I needed to be extremely sensitive) and then made my hand available to her. It seemed a while before she very slowly moved her hand towards mine. I made no movement and gradually she touched my finger with hers. All the while her sobbing continued. Suddenly I was aware she was carefully and gently starting to hold my finger.

When I felt her finger touching mine, I was careful not to make much movement as I was aware of the courage it was taking for her to touch me. The way she was touching me was so tentative and uncertain that instinctively I didn't respond straightaway, but waited until she was holding my finger more securely. Then, very slowly, I held her back and we sat like that for what seemed an eternity. The contrast between her fragile touch and her racking sobs seemed a chasm apart.

I didn't feel any sense of a need to comfort her in any way, I felt a deep empathy for her and in that moment I was willing to just sit alongside her in that dreadfully painful and terrifying place she now found herself in. (In the past, to cry would have resulted in a beating.) She was not only crying for the first time but she was touching another human being, and to me, in that moment, she was saying: 'I trust you with my tears and with my touch.'

My chest cavity was full to the brim with emotion and it felt difficult to breath. I no longer felt any desire to cry for her pain. But the effort of just staying close was intense.

Eventually, her crying subsided. Just as gently and slowly as she had first held my finger, she now began to release it and, as if in slow motion, we took up our original positions facing each other. She looked into my eyes again and in that moment we both knew that something truly wondrous had just taken place.

Tony (by Kenny Ralph)

I started working as a support worker about seven years ago. One month into the job I met Tony. Tony was in his mid-twenties and has cerebral palsy and profound learning difficulties; he communicates through hand and eye pointing and vocalizations that indicate either contentment or distress. Touch is also a form of communication for Tony. He likes to hold hands; if he is tense, or agitated, he may well twist the thumb of the hand he is holding.

As I got to know Tony, I became struck, and was surprised, by the level of intimacy and intensity that I often felt occurred during our interactions. Tony really enjoys his food and so meal-times provide a great opportunity for interaction. It was not at all uncommon for Tony to reach out after he finished eating to give me a hug. These hugs were quite special; it may sound strange but they felt so genuine, they felt like more than just hugs. I noticed other forms of expression that seemed more powerful when they came from Tony. If the two of us were playing with toys on the floor, our eyes might meet and Tony would really hold that eye contact; again, it felt like more than just eye contact. It felt like an exchange of information or data, like two mainframes swapping files. I can't put into precise words what 'information' was 'swapped', but, generally, I felt a shared sense of gratefulness and a genuine warmth, something very close to love, and a tangible bond.

I labelled these exchanges (because an exchange is what I experienced) as moments of 'pure communication', or what has also been called 'relational depth'. I remember one of these moments particularly well. One night I was woken by Tony's laughter. This in itself was not unusual; Tony sometimes got out of bed and may have found something to amuse himself with. I entered his room, expecting to find him on the floor, but to my surprise he was lying in his bed. I didn't know what he was laughing at. Usually, I would have turned, walked out of the room and gone back to bed but Tony had spotted me. He propped himself up on his elbow, still laughing, looked at me and held out his hand. This was Tony's way of calling me over. I took hold of his hand and knelt on the floor next to his bed. By now I was also laughing; it is very funny to be in someone's company when they are in hysterics. We stayed like that for several minutes, just laughing together. I wasn't his support worker at that moment; it didn't matter that we should both be sleeping or that we would pay for this the next morning. At some point, it became more than just laughing, it felt like sharing bits of our selves. Looking back, I get such a strong sense of his being alive, there was so much energy pouring from him, like sunlight through a crack in the curtains. Usually, if Tony was feeling particularly boisterous, he would try to initiate more interaction: for example, he might try to hug me or perhaps get out of bed. But this time he did none of these things, he was happy just to lie where he was, laughing and holding my hand. Somewhere along the line, I stopped laughing *at* how funny it was to see Tony in hysterics; now I was laughing *with* Tony, like he had made me see his point of view, and he was grateful that I had got it. After ten minutes or so our laughter tapered off and we held each other's stare and smiled. It was when we were looking at each other's eyes that I got the sense of pure communication. It was like our laughter had been part of a journey and when we stopped and looked up we realized that we'd reached an oasis. Everything was peaceful and still. At some point, Tony started to drift off and I left him and went back to bed.

When I look back and attempt to describe what happened for me during that exchange, I struggle. I know I felt a shared warmth and appreciation. I am not able to say what thoughts were going through my head and I think that is because these examples have happened when I am 'in the moment'. I am not consciously processing what is happening to me during these interactions and feel quite certain that if I did try to examine them on any level, as they happened, then that moment would come to an abrupt end.

It is important to point out that the majority of our interaction was not as powerful as the examples I have given. Sometimes Tony was not in the mood and sometimes I was not. Either way, we both had to be present for these exchanges to occur. Also, these exchanges were not always 'positive'. One time, Tony held my eyes as he cried and a feeling of sorrow came over me. We ended up crying together. Looking back, I would say it was a therapeutic experience.

Claire (by Jan Kerr)

A year after qualifying, I approached a local cancer support centre and asked whether they had a requirement for a counsellor; having volunteered for several years within a hospice, I felt drawn to working with this particular client group. I was fortunate that the manager was open to my suggestion and a few weeks later I began counselling with them.

My first experience of following a client's journey through her partner's illness, his death, and the ensuing months until she was ready to re-engage with life fully was also my first experience of connecting at relational depth with a client. We worked together for a total of 24 sessions over a period of 12 months, and during this time we often experienced specific moments of encounter within a relationship that held a particular quality from the very first session together.

Claire, an open and articulate woman in her mid-fifties, called into our drop-in centre. After a discussion with a support worker, she arranged to meet me, despite stating that she did not want to 'waste' my time. Claire's husband, Stephen, had been treated successfully for cancer nearly two years earlier. It had come as a total shock a few weeks ago when they discovered that the cancer had returned, with no hope of recovery. The deterioration in his health during these recent weeks had been very rapid and neither was prepared for the enormity of the situation. They shared a close family unit and their six children were leaning on Claire for support. Coping with daily hospital visits, family commitments and the responsibility of working full time was now becoming stressful for Claire.

During our first meeting, Claire shared her story with me and I was aware that I was feeling a deep sorrow and compassion for her. She believed she was coping well. She spoke of balancing work, hospital visits, the concern of family and friends, Stephen's imminent return home to die – all of this as if there was no effort involved. I was struck by a sense of this woman being weighed down by the enormity of her situation. She acknowledged that although it was difficult, she was 'managing fine – after all, it is not me who has cancer'. I felt deeply moved and said gently: 'I hear that you are coping and that you are also supporting everyone but I am wondering who looks after you?' She looked at me for a few moments saying nothing, then tears began to flow down her cheeks as she sobbed uncontrollably.

As she cried, I sat quietly with tears in my eyes, not moving in to change anything so that Claire's flow was not interrupted nor impeded by me. As Claire's sobs subsided, she smiled at me and said: 'You know, that's the first time I've cried. Thank you.' I smiled back and said 'I'm glad' and for the next few moments we sat in comfortable silence. This shared intimacy felt incredibly powerful and there seemed a sense of connectedness between us. After she left, I felt energized and elated, which, given Claire's circumstances, seemed inappropriate. As I thought about our shared silence, it occurred to me that this was perhaps a moment of relational depth. Afterwards, in supervision, I touched on my surprise that this was possible so early on in a counselling relationship, especially in the first meeting.

Over the following weeks, Claire often struggled with feelings that she believed were inappropriate – anger and frustration at her husband for being ill, dying and withdrawing from her in his pain, leaving her isolated and lost. As I welcomed all of her without judgement, staying with her in these painful places while trusting that she would find her own ways to move forward, she was able to touch into her innermost feelings, which enabled her to become grounded and more accepting of who she was.

In our seventh session, Claire broke the news that Stephen had died a few days earlier. This was a huge shock, as the previous week he seemed to be responding well to treatment and they had been hopeful of having a few more months together. As Claire described Stephen's last hours, I was so engrossed that it felt as if I were listening with all of my being. There was a sense that the interaction between us was slower than normal and everything appeared heightened. By reaching out towards Claire psychologically and emotionally with all of myself, I met her at relational depth. I shared with her my deep sorrow and shock and she thanked me for listening. She stated that although she had a house full of relatives and friends, she had ached to be in this room just to have space for herself without having to pretend she was fine. She said: 'I know I can be real with you.' I felt moved and acknowledged this with her. I was aware that she seemed exhausted and on checking this with her, she agreed and asked whether we could sit quietly together for the remaining ten minutes. Silence can occur for various reasons within a session and can sometimes feel uncomfortable. However, as often happened with Claire, within this silence there was a shared intimacy and, for me, a privilege in being allowed to share these moments. Claire's comment about being real resonates with what meeting at relational depth means to me.

I believe that it is when there is no pretence, no façade and both of us touch something within each other that there is a deep understanding which needs no explanation, no words. It is at moments like these that I am struck by the healing potential of this work.

Claire discussed her feelings as she struggled to find ways to re-engage in life while working through her grief. At first she kept herself very busy, both at work and socially, in order to avoid the enormity of her loss. However, she soon became exhausted, gave in to the intensity of her feelings and withdrew from the outside world, leaving phone and door unanswered. Throughout this time, she maintained contact and attended our weekly sessions. She acknowledged that, during this time, this was the only place where she felt safe and could be who she really was. Despite our deep connections – or because of them – it was often a challenge to stay with Claire in her pain and despair as I empathically connected with her need to get it right. However, I trusted that offering her this space where she had the freedom to be truly herself without either judgement or pressure to change, while consistently offering her the core conditions (see Introduction, this volume), would enable her to find her own ways to recover and move forward.

This belief in the principles of the person-centred approach was reinforced for me when Claire discussed the family's plans to scatter Stephen's ashes. As

Claire shared her resentment and frustrations around the disagreements, she was extremely agitated, and I felt able to share my empathic response – of holding a sense of sadness. This reflection encouraged her to go into the reasons behind this ritual. The funeral had gone past in a daze and this ceremony was to be their personal and private farewell. She acknowledged that it had been difficult to hold onto this while she also had to consider the children's needs. Involving them had felt like an intrusion but having admitted this now, she was able to let go of her resentment. Claire then sat quietly in her thoughts and there was an air of calm around her.

The level of intimacy seemed very powerful and I felt privileged to sit alongside her in the silence. After a few moments, Claire spoke quietly and said it felt as if something spiritual had happened for her and she felt really close to Stephen at that moment. She noticed a sense of peace and not wanting to spoil this, asked whether we could sit together for the rest of our time. I agreed willingly. When Claire rose to leave, she asked if we could hug. She then thanked me for giving her this 'special time'. She left smiling and I felt energized for the rest of the day. This was a special session that allowed me to touch into the magic of this work. At times like these, I feel in awe of what can happen in a therapeutic process and know I am privileged to be a part of my clients' journeys.

Leon (by Chris Brown)

Leon and I began working together about three years ago; he was acutely despondent and had been medically diagnosed as depressed. From the onset of our alliance, I experienced him as intense and profoundly haunted by a rigid set of expectations he placed on himself. He had strict ideals on how he should behave towards and even think about others if he was ever to become a 'good person'; ideals Leon repeatedly made clear that he fell a long way short of. During our initial session, Leon disclosed he felt edgy and nervous as he explained that he expected to find it hard to discuss all he wanted to explore with me because he was not normally open with people, did not fully engage with them, or really know how to do so. I often experienced varying degrees of nervousness and strain as I waited for him to arrive; feelings which I found would slowly disperse as his session progressed.

Leon found it difficult to be punctual. However, I found myself respecting his tenacity and drive to recover and I liked him for what I experienced as his innate kindness and honesty, although the latter was most often clouded by his self-negativity and harsh self-judgement. On the few occasions when it appeared appropriate to disclose to Leon my positive experience of him, such interventions always seemed to waft over him without my sense of Leon being able to embody my sense of him in any way whatsoever.

My varying sensations of nervousness and strain in relation to Leon's arrival persisted for two years until a brief moment of what I recognize as relational depth transpired between us. I had just told Leon that I experienced him as extremely thoughtful, caring and kind, when, for the first time in our relationship, I felt a barrier in front of him fall away as a sense of uninhibited, free-flowing space seemed to gently open up between us. As I experienced this perceptible shift, I can remember thinking 'ah ... at last we are to truly meet', as, for the first time, Leon appeared to accept my truth about him (as I experienced him to be). He turned fully towards me as, also for the first time, he looked directly and profoundly into my eyes. I was very aware of organically letting all tension in me disperse, aware of allowing myself to become open and without veneer, to simply be myself as I was in the moment; to naturally allow Leon to look into the transparent me so that I might truthfully meet his willingness to accept himself (reflected in me) as I experienced him to be.

We held each other's deep defenceless gaze for a few silent, perfectly still moments as within these briefly shared seconds of close encounter a sense of tender fearlessness manifested – a tender fearlessness that seemed to permit us to see each other and to be seen wholly by the other without reservation; we were not client and therapist in these moments but two human souls willing to be definitely viewed and accepted, each by the other.

In this moment I knew Leon had experienced an instant of intimate connectedness with me without intentionally holding back any part of himself and without dread, and I with him. I was filled with a knowing that this experience would change both the dynamics of our psychotherapeutic relationship and Leon's relationship with himself in significant ways. I also knew that Leon would start arriving punctually for his sessions in future.

I cannot remember any further detail about the contents of this session, even the client log I keep in relation to my work with Leon contains no commentary other than the notes I made on the happening narrated above. Everything else that transpired was, and remains, obscured by the sense of power, intertwined with the feeling of serene humility I experienced within this specific phenomenological event. However, sure enough, Leon suddenly began to turn up on time, his general eye contact with me noticeably increased and he appeared to be considering himself with far less negative self-judgement.

While his journey remains punctuated with despondent or low moods at times, Leon is tentatively expressing his needs more openly to others and beginning to take risks in relating to those he already knows and with the new people he meets. Leon now always touches me when he leaves a session, by softly reaching out to securely shake my hand or occasionally with an appropriate and respectful hug – something he would have found discourteous, brazen and impossible to do a year ago.

At the time of writing this vignette, Leon and I are still working together and I remain privileged to be in therapeutic alliance with this emotionally courageous man.

2

Relational depth from the client's perspective

Rosanne Knox

> Do you know the ... is it, Michelangelo painting on the Sistine Chapel, where you have the two fingers? It's kind of that and there comes a point 'ch-ch-ch' and the contact is there ... like the film where one starts to communicate ... *Close Encounters*, you know the bit where one gives a bit and then the other gives a bit, and suddenly, it's there, and it's a bit like that really. I'm giving, I'm opening, I'm going to speak from the heart. It was there ... immediately, it was there, the communication was there, the language was the same, and everything's the same. It's being together. And then just like *Close Encounters*, it slows down, and it separates again. (client, from Knox, 2011)

The aim of this chapter is to provide an opportunity for the client's voice to be heard in our exploration of relational depth. Using research evidence from an extended series of qualitative interviews, I hope to demonstrate that:

1. Clients are able to identify specific moments of relational depth with their therapist.
2. They see those moments as highly significant, with a lasting positive effect both on the therapeutic process and on their lives, long after the therapy has ended.
3. Clients themselves both contribute to the emergence of, and then make use of, an experience of relational depth.

A process of a meeting at relational depth is proposed, with a series of moment-by-moment reactions, interactions and experiencing identified, as described by participants.

The study

Overall, the study included 26 participants who had all been clients of individual, face-to-face therapy; 15 were also therapists or trainee therapists, and 11 were clients whose only experience of therapy was as a client. I am indebted to all my participants for their openness and honesty in sharing with me their very personal experiences.

The study took the form of a series of qualitative interviews, with participants being asked in a very open-ended way to talk about the following three areas:

1. An experience of a specific moment of relational depth.
2. The perceived therapeutic value of the experience of a moment of relational depth.
3. What factors might have facilitated the moment of relational depth.

In order to focus participants on specific moments as opposed to the relationship as whole, prior to the interview they were given an abbreviated version of Mearns and Cooper's (2005, p. xii) definition of relational depth (see Introduction, this volume).

The interviews were recorded, transcribed and analysed using a grounded theory approach (Strauss and Corbin, 1968). Findings were divided into core themes (such as 'experience of self in the moment', 'experience of therapist in the moment' and 'experience of the relationship in the moment'), and then information from each transcript was listed under different categories (for example 'feeling understood in the moment') as they emerged from the data.

When I began these explorations, I only had a vague idea of what I expected to find. I am a person-centred therapist working with a wide range of clients, and both as a therapist and as a client, I had experienced moments of what I would describe as relational depth. As a therapist, it seemed that when such moments arose, the impact on the client was noticeable, with an apparently positive effect on the therapeutic process. Expectations at the start of the first study also reflected my own experience as a client when moments of relational depth were experienced as being highly supportive of the therapeutic process. I wondered whether other clients have similar experiences.

I was nervous, however, as I approached the research; what if none of the people I interviewed could identify a moment of relational depth? So it was with trepidation that I embarked upon what would turn out to be a long, exciting, frustrating, passionate, emotional and, ultimately, rewarding journey; and fortunately for me, the answer at the end of that journey was, yes, some clients do experience moments of relational depth with their therapist. However, it is worth noting that while most participants of the research were able to identify at least one moment they felt could be described as a moment of relational depth, many also spoke of having experienced several therapeutic relationships in which they felt there had been no moments of relational depth. While the reasons for the lack of relational depth were most commonly attributed to a cold, distant, overly formal manner or insufficiently caring or understanding therapist, some participants acknowledged that this might, to some extent, have been due to where they were in their own journey. A few mused that it might have been a level of connection that they were either not ready for themselves, or did not need or want at those times. They got what they needed and wanted at the time, and that did not include an experience of relational depth. However, there is no doubt that, for some clients, their therapist was doing, or not doing, something that not only prevented them (the client) from meeting at a level of relational depth when they wanted it, but also resulted in them keeping their distance, closing down, and ultimately left them feeling lonely, angry or upset. So while this research suggests that clients certainly can and do experience moments of relational depth, it also indicates that not only are they rare occurrences, but that there may be many missed opportunities.

When moments of relational depth were identified, participants typically struggled to find the precise words that would do them justice, or accurately reflect their experienced qualities. The experiences seemed elusive and fluid, and it was difficult to give them form; yet they were described as powerful, meaningful and very real. As one participant expressed it: 'We talked about the experience of the feelings and that was really … powerful. Really, really, powerful. I still feel it now actually (grabs chest).' As I progressed through the interviews, I soon came to see the moments being described to me as very spectacular events, life changing, and unique or rarely experienced in a person's life; as one participant said: 'That was a one off – I'm not expecting that to happen again!' Often during the interviews, I had a sense of being handed a delicate, precious flower to hold in my hand, and was acutely aware of the gentle handling that was needed in order not to damage it in any way, or even to bend it out of shape. Each individual petal was an important part of the whole, and could not be ignored, or held too tightly lest it be changed or destroyed. Each time, as I handed the flower back, I became aware not only of its delicacy, but also of its strength and power, and I knew that it had changed me in some way.

How clients describe an experience of relational depth

As they approached the moment of relational depth, most participants experienced a heightened sense of vulnerability, suddenly feeling afraid of their own emotions, or of feeling transparent to the therapist. As one participant said: 'It was as if I was speaking to that part of me, but outwardly instead of inwardly … I couldn't hide any more.' However, this also seemed to go hand in hand with, or was closely followed by, the feeling that it was alright to be vulnerable; as soon as the feeling of vulnerability arose, it was to some extent negated by the safety that the participant felt, and the ability to stay in the discomfort they were experiencing. As one put it: 'It kind of made it okay to be broken, um, because until then, brokenness was a sign of weakness, and um, I wasn't going to be weak.' In that sense, it might be said that they actually felt *less* vulnerable. However, this does highlight the need for therapists to tread gently, lest a client's anxieties about relating at depth outweigh their wish to do so.

Most participants also described feeling real or honest in the moment described, as one said: 'It was almost like the real [own name] stood forward after that. And I experienced the real counsellor.' Most associated the feeling of being real with a feeling of being whole, or a joining together of their own self, and a sense of connection that was both psychological and in the bodily sense. Many spoke of connecting with previously hidden parts of themselves: 'And the corners, to actually look in the corners … what's in the corners as well, and not feel judged, at that time.' These hidden parts were often experienced as painful, angry or simply disliked parts. As participants went on to describe their deeper intrapersonal explorations, they also attributed their ability to delve down in this way to the sense that their therapist was holding or 'grounding' them in some way: 'It's that gravity that enables you to go out in an orbit, but not to go flying off into space.' Several also described their therapist as providing an emotional 'safety net', so that while they accompanied them on their journey, they were also 'ready to nip round in front of me if I was going to fall'. This would seem to be an aspect that, while highly valued by clients, the therapists of Cooper's (2005) study into therapists' experiences of relational depth were unaware of providing. Indeed person-centred literature has tended to focus on the therapist letting go of their own foothold during such moments (Mearns and Cooper, 2005). However, this research suggests that from the client's perspective, at a moment of relational depth the therapist is experienced by the client as remaining grounded, acting as a kind of anchor for the client's explorations into the unknown.

An interesting aspect that was emphasized by nearly all the participants was that not only did they feel wholly understood and accepted in the moment, they also felt that their therapist knew and understood them in the general sense of their lives as a whole person, not just in the room at that moment. The sense of safety this engendered was highlighted by one client when she said: 'I was confident that she knew me well enough, not only what I was feeling, but also how much it was hurting, to actually hold those feelings.' Momentary empathy then, although important, may not be enough. In order to engage at a level of relational depth, clients, it would seem, may need to know that the therapist understands their everyday life – knows their stories, their hopes and fears, their aims and regrets, their dreams and losses, and their way of looking at life. Only then can they feel safe enough to put their trust in the therapist.

The aspect mentioned most frequently and passionately was that of the acceptance they felt from their therapist in the moment, along with the absence of any sense of judgement. The following quotation is a typical example:

> If I tell somebody my deepest secrets – I think they'll judge me ... that's what I feared, but actually I didn't sense it from her ... Well, yeah, such a simple thing really [acceptance]. Yeah. I suppose, quite difficult for me to accept myself. And I suppose she accepted me ... myself.

While it was clearly crucial that the clients felt understood, accepted and acknowledged in the moment, it also seemed to be equally important that their therapist was providing a precisely measured reaction to them at that point, which, for some, might be no reaction at all. As one participant put it: 'Any judgement, any criticism, or even a raised eyebrow ... would switch it off completely.' Here one begins to get a sense of the potential fragility of a moment of relational depth – let your client know that you understand and accept them, but even the tiniest reaction could 'switch it off'. This is just one of the many juxtapositions of the descriptions of a moment of relational depth:

- the client feeling vulnerable, but at the same time courageous
- the moment bringing with it a sense of power and strength, yet at the same time it is delicate and easily broken
- the therapist diving with the client into unknown waters, but the client is relying on the therapist to pull them out if they fear they will drown.

Seemingly, it is no easy task to engage at a level of relational depth – for the client *or* for the therapist.

An unexpected and interesting finding, and one not mentioned by therapists in Cooper's (2005) study, was that virtually all the clients said that their therapist was offering them something 'over and above' what they would expect from someone in a professional role. This had the effect of making the client feel that they mattered to their therapist, and had in some ways impacted upon them:

> It's actually, I'm a person in her life, I'm a person in her working life, who has some ... not importance, that sounds conceited, but has a place, and is considered and is thought about. My stuff means something to her ... everybody else's probably does, but I'm not just dismissed, when I've gone through the door. And I think that's important too.

Most spoke of a sense of genuine care from the therapist, with a human, personal element being emphasized. Some participants went so far as to say that they felt they were being offered something over and above Rogers' (1957) core conditions of empathy, congruence and unconditional positive regard (see Introduction, this volume). One said:

> I guess I was thinking unconditional positive regard there ... it's sort of ... It's more than that ... because he genuinely, genuinely ... there really is a genuineness ... so even if it is just a job, it doesn't come across as that.

These findings would seem to lend weight to Thorne's (1991, p. 76) proposition that when tenderness is present between two people, 'something qualitatively different will occur'. The notion of the therapist's genuine personal care for their client has been given little emphasis in psychotherapy literature over the years, possibly not being seen as part of the professional's toolkit, whereas it would seem from this research that the clients want to feel that the therapist has a genuine, personal interest in their wellbeing or recovery. Describing a relationship in which there had been no feeling of relational depth, one participant said of her therapist: 'And I felt almost that if he'd read in the paper during the week that I'd been killed, he probably wouldn't think too much about it.' This contrasted with her impression of the therapist with whom she did experience relational depth:

> I knew she really cared about me ... yeah, she felt really, really caring, and really attentive. I just felt like, you know, if I'd got run over she'd have been deeply distressed and gone to the funeral. I really felt she cared.

There is a valuable message for therapists here; clients can tell the difference between 'genuine' and 'professional' care. It raises some interesting questions that are worth thinking about. How much do you genuinely care for, and about, your clients? How much *should* you care about your clients? Is caring the same thing as providing the core conditions of empathy, congruence and unconditional regard as described by Rogers (1957), or something more than that, something extra, something more akin to what Thorne (1991) has described as 'tenderness'?

Another somewhat surprising aspect described by clients was the feeling of being real, in the sense of solid and tangible, or even more human; as one put it, 'more like a person'. Some related this to the validation they received from their therapist: 'As if to say, there *is* a me inside here, I'm really real, not just something I've created. It's real.' Participants almost seemed to be describing a sense of bringing themselves, and their feelings, into being, giving them substance and form, 'because they're not just wisps and clouds within me'.

This sense of self-validity then seemed to generate an experience of aliveness, with feelings of expansion, excitement and even euphoria being described. Ultimately, participants described being left with a sense of calm, peacefulness and wellbeing. Looking back at the diary she was keeping at the time, and also bringing in a spiritual element, one participant said: 'Almost like a hippy feeling about life, love all plants and people and just feel at one with everything. I've just used that on the heightened spiritual moments.'

It would seem, then, that an experience of relational depth can involve a roller coaster of emotions for the client – and for the therapist. Later in this chapter, I will return to this myriad of emotions in an attempt to draw together a more cohesive picture of the whole experience. But what of the relationship itself? How do clients see the relationship during an experience of relational depth?

Clients' descriptions of the relationship during a moment of relational depth

It is perhaps not surprising that clients saw the relationship as one of intimacy and depth during the described moments, with an emotional connection facilitating a deep understanding and knowing without words. One participant expressed it:

> I knew what she was going to say, she knew what I was going to say. Things didn't need to be said. Each knew what was going on for the other person. I understood where she was coming from and she understood where I was coming from.

Mearns and Cooper (2005) have described a moment of relational depth as one of 'mutuality'. Moreover, Murphy (see Chapter 14, this volume) has argued that mutuality is the basis for relational depth. But does this description represent an experience of mutuality? If mutuality is understood in terms of each person being fully real with the other, with the client acknowledging the therapist's empathy, congruence and unconditional regard, and both understanding each other in a reciprocal dance of 'I know that you know that I know', then undoubtedly that was an experience of these clients, whether or not they saw it in terms of mutuality. Certainly, some participants spoke of feeling warmth, compassion and even concern for their therapist, and needed to feel that they were giving something back.

The descriptions of a moment of profound engagement and connectedness being one where each person remains aware of their own separateness (for example Buber, 1970; Mearns and Cooper, 2005) are to some extent borne out by the finding of this research, with most participants describing a union rather than a fusion at the moment described. However, participants' descriptions varied as to the extent that they remained aware of their own separateness; some described blurred boundaries, and a couple went on to talk of a sense of merging or oneness. The fluidity of the connection was beautifully described by one participant:

> A bit like, er, I don't know ... one colour fading into another I suppose. But there was a ... I think the line was quite, the line between the two colours, if you look at it in terms of colours, the line was quite blurred in places, as to who was what,

> and what was what, although still distinct in parts, not wholly distinct, from, um, from me if you like.

This study suggests, therefore, that while it is certainly a feature of a moment of relational depth that each person remains aware of their own separateness, this can easily move into a state of merging. It also indicates that clients may see such a state of merging, oneness, or even sameness as potentially healing and facilitative.

The moment itself

There was an element of participants' descriptions that seemed to indicate something greater than, or perhaps outside, the relationship, and it occurred to me that the moment of relational depth was being described almost as a 'thing' in itself, something almost tangible, like a third force, and yet also very difficult to describe. This was also a finding of Wiggins who has referred to this aspect as 'atmosphere' (see Chapter 4, this volume). As participants grappled with words that adequately reflected their experiencing, the themes that emerged floated around a sense of another dimension, something deeper, both powerful and meaningful, and which stayed strongly in the memory for some time afterwards; some felt it was their own creation, others that it was something they had entered into – some larger space that was already there but normally out of reach. Several participants described the sense of being in a bubble. One described the feeling of depth and power:

> That for me that really felt we were getting beyond the cerebral, getting beyond the cognitive, we were absolutely communicating at such a primal level, and that felt incredibly powerful.

There was also a sense of participants wanting to do the memory justice, and not wanting to distort it in any way by bringing it up to a level of language, lest its essence, or any part of it, be lost in the process.

When conceptualizing a moment of relational depth, Mearns (1996) pointed to the rarity of such an experience in everyday life, which indeed seemed to be the perception of the participants in this study. Most participants described the experience as a rare or even unique event; some initially found it confusing, and even wondered if it was something that was not meant to happen.

The moments were frequently described as exciting and wonderful, and for many it was seen as something mystical or spiritual, supporting the descriptions of Rogers ([1986]1990), and Thorne (1991). It also lends weight to Rowan's (2005) assertion that psychotherapy can be seen as a bridge between psychology and spirituality, describing what he calls 'Ah' moments in therapy as spiritual experiences (see Chapter 16, this volume).

Therapeutic value

Moments of relational depth were perceived by most clients as healing, facilitating and enabling, often accompanied by a sudden insight or new way of looking at things. The moments were seen by many as a catalyst leading to change, with no turning back, and with an immediate lessening of painful and difficult feelings described:

> A light came on and illuminated my life, my existence, my whole being. Everything jumped into sharp focus ... It was as though prior to the session, I'd been walking around in darkness and suddenly, the counsellor had switched on runway lights, which highlighted a potentially new path that I could choose.

A major impact was on the therapeutic relationship itself, and in turn the therapeutic process, both because it took the ongoing relationship to a another level where greater authenticity was possible, and also because, as one put it: 'it's unlocked the door. And I can open it or close it as I want to or need to.' So having taken the risk to meet their therapist at a level of relational depth once, it remained easier to do so again.

Even more significantly, perhaps, participants described a variety of enduring effects of the described moments, which were seen as having a positive impact on their lives. Descriptions given included feeling more connected to self and others, being able to be 'the real me', feeling more positive, with a new self-confidence, and more able to tackle things and move on in their lives. Moreover, some described feeling reconnected to life, as if the moment of connection had, as Rogers ([1986]1990) suggested, alleviated their aloneness and, more than that, had almost given them a reason to live, as in the following example:

> But I've come away feeling slightly better and able to stand in the garden again and be in the world, and know that I'm not alone and I don't know what makes me know I'm not alone ... but that empathy that I felt, and that connection that I felt, it gives me nourishment.

There were no instances where an experience of relational depth was found to be detrimental or unhelpful to the client. No participant described becoming overinvolved in the relationship as a result of an experience of a moment of relational depth. One participant described reaching a point of being too afraid to go any further, but felt able to back off when she needed to. It is the case, however, that all participants actively volunteered to participate in the research; it is possible that they were, to some extent, motivated to do so by an experience that they perceived as positive. It was certainly the case that none showed any signs of regret that it had happened; on the contrary, most described it with great fondness for the memory and with such delicacy, so as not to distort it in any way, either in the recalling or in the recounting.

How might a moment of relational depth emerge?

Having now gained some sense of how moments of relational depth might be experienced by clients, and of any correspondence to outcome, I also wanted to find out how clients feel such moments arise. Do they occur spontaneously, or are they initiated or facilitated by the therapist, or by the client, or by both? Does it depend on the content of a particular session, or the quality of the relationship as a whole?

The therapist's role

Perhaps unsurprisingly, the overall findings of the study strongly suggest that specific moments of relational depth are more likely to occur in therapeutic relationships that are perceived by the client as having an enduring depth and closeness. The facilitating qualities of the therapist were felt to be their genuineness, warmth, empathy, gentleness and positive attitude. Also highlighted were straightforward courtesy, simple things that made all the difference; for example, 'she always seemed pleased to see me', and 'she always greeted me with a smile'. Perhaps more surprisingly, it was important to clients that their therapist was in some way similar to themselves, for example in age, social background, sexuality, religious or political beliefs and so on. If not similar, then at least the therapist had to be the right person for them, or a good match for their personality. This raises an interesting question around how possible it is for any therapist to connect with any client, no matter how different they are. However realistic that is, this finding certainly points to the compatibility of client and therapist being an element that can improve the likelihood of a moment of relational depth arising.

There are, of course, practice implications to be drawn from this, coupled with the finding that when talking about the relationship in which they experienced relational depth, many of the clients described having made a selective choice of therapist. Should clients simply be allocated clients then, or might there be a value in allowing clients to have a say in who their therapist will be?

Another important aspect for clients was the sense that the therapist was psychologically sound themselves, giving a security to the client in bringing their difficult material without risk to the therapist, and, in turn, without further risk to themselves. The clients had to be sure that, as one said: 'the counsellor has kind of passed the test ... They've kind of proved that they can handle it.'

In terms of what the therapist was actually doing during the relationship in which a moment of relational depth emerged, participants described them as creating a welcoming atmosphere, acting reliably and professionally, and being both patient and containing. Therapists were seen as being real, human and willing to show their own vulnerability and lack of perfection. From the client's point of view, then, perfection is not necessary, but a real, human, personal approach is much appreciated.

In the moments leading up to the experience of relational depth, most also saw their therapist as making an invitation to meet, sometimes in the form of a challenge being made. However, the precision and timing of the challenge was crucial. Some highlighted the importance of the forward-looking nature of the challenge: 'She said: "you still could have a good life" ... and I'm treading on a wire here, a high wire, and I could let it all go, or I can work for the future.' This was an aspect that seemed to be of such importance to many participants, some of whom spoke of coming to therapy in a very delicate state, and feeling unable to hold hope for the future themselves.

Perhaps the most unexpected finding of all was that before engaging at a level of relational depth, some clients said they were reassured by the sense that their therapist was 'on their side'. One expressed it:

> And to me, that was unbelievably powerful, because I was upset ... and she turned round and said: 'No, you are not being unreasonable, you are in your right, it's perfectly acceptable, for you to expect that.' And I think that was the beginning when I felt, this woman is really, really on my side.

This is undoubtedly a somewhat controversial finding, as it implies something other than either empathy or unconditional positive regard. Rather, it would seem to indicate a form of conditional positive regard, with the therapist affirming the client's point of view. Yet some participants seemed to have such a low sense of self-worth that they appeared to need the therapist's positive affirmation and encouragement in order to redress the balance. It was only when they felt sure that the therapist was genuinely on their side that they felt able to open up fully and relate at depth. While this might not sit comfortably with, well, probably most therapeutic approaches, it might be better understood as a form of pre-therapy – bringing the client to a point where they are able to benefit from a nondirective attitude, or even from being in receipt of unconditional positive regard. The concept of affirmation from others being a universal need, and a natural part of being human, is discussed by Cooper in Chapter 11.

The client's role

It has been suggested that working at relational depth involves something other than the classic person-centred approach, in that it would seem to imply working in a way that is directed by the therapist (for example Brodley, 2006; Wilders, 2007, Chapter 15, this volume). Nevertheless, a major finding of this research was that, according to clients, it is the client, and not the therapist, who initiates a meeting a relational depth. Most participants emphasized their own proactive role throughout. For some, it was a journey that started when they made an initial decision to engage in the relationship and in the therapeutic process. What is surprising is the way in which some of them stuck with it, even in the face of their own cynicism, or where they felt their therapist was getting it wrong.

Most participants felt that the crucial factor was their own readiness to engage at depth. They had to be prepared, and have come to the point of being able to meet their therapists at relational depth, and they had realized their need or desire to do so. Being apparently ever vigilant, they had also observed a change in the therapist, or a change in their own perceptions of the therapist, and had felt that the relationship itself had reached a point where they could take it to a deeper level. While there might have been triggers for the emergence of the moment, for example the occurrence of an external traumatic event, the therapist admitting a mistake, or the client being in a state of heightened emotion, the decision to engage at depth was the client's. As one described it:

> I found myself where it was either, open the door, and let it ... show it ... or close the door completely, again ... When I felt ready and decided it's my ... I've got to look at this.

While therapists (see, for example, Cooper's 2005 study into therapists' experiences) have described moments of relational depth as occurring spontaneously, the clients in this research identified a process of making a decision, taking a risk or, as some described it, a 'leap of faith', and finally letting it happen. At that point, there was a sense of opening the gates and with no turning back. Another said:

> And it was as if ... as if it was flowing ... as there was a flow ... almost like a stream, a river, that, I'd opened ... I'd opened a gate that allowed the emotions to actually come out rather than me feel them inside.

Conceptualizing a moment of relational depth: a process of experiencing

As I moved through the interview process and reflected on the resulting data, I began to see an experience of relational depth as a process of experiencing rather than as a single moment. It seemed as if such an experience might better be viewed as an *event* or a series of related moments, possibly with an identifiable pattern and timeline, with the experience of vulnerability, for example, as with many of the other described aspects, being present in one part of the overall experience, but absent from other parts. The overall event was described as a single experience, but something like a river, with one experiential moment flowing into another, rather than a series of separate moments being experienced one after the other. All were interrelated and part of a whole, but each with their own characteristics.

In most cases, the 'river' or flow of experiencing, as shown in Figure 2.1, appeared to flow as follows: participants reported an initial slowing down, delving deeper, coming to the point of allowing themselves to be vulnerable. They then opened up to the therapist, and, feeling safe, ultimately opened up to themselves, with a sense of wholeness and self-connection. This was followed by a feeling of vibrancy and excitement, which was described almost as a relational *peak experience* within, and central to, the overall event. This led to feelings of self-acceptance and self-worth and, ultimately, a sense of relief, calm, wellbeing and peace.

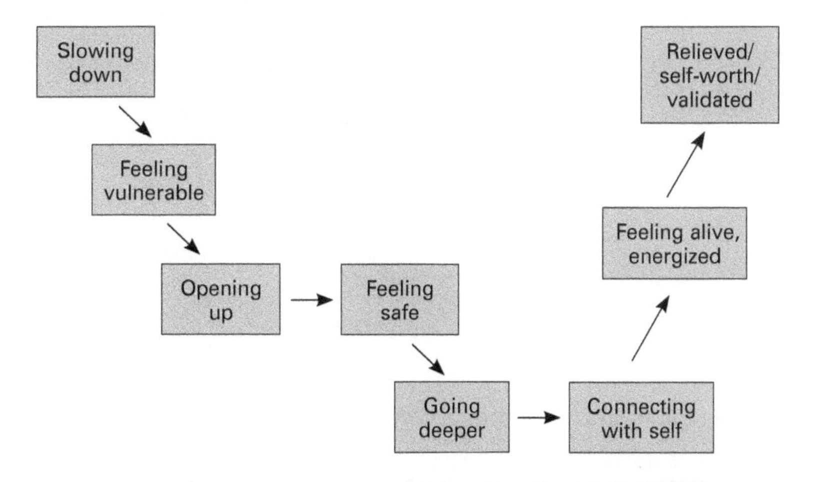

Figure 2.1 Client's moment-by-moment intrapersonal process

Throughout the overall experience, each step taken by the client also appeared to be dependent on what the therapist was offering at each particular moment, as shown in Figure 2.2. Feeling that the opportunity had been created, the client initially slowed down; sensing a gentle invitation from the therapist they then became acutely aware of their own vulnerability. This appears to have been the crucial moment in which the client's willingness to open up rested on the therapist's own openness and genuine care for the client. As the client opened up, they also needed to feel the therapist's support, and to feel held or grounded so that they would feel safe enough to stay with it. On feeling that the therapist was coming with them, accompanying them on their journey, they would go deeper. Here, the therapist's understanding was needed for the client to feel that they could fully connect with their own self, and, having done so, the therapist's acknowledgement and acceptance seemed to bring the whole experience to a peak moment of aliveness and exhilaration. Finally, the therapist's affirmation facilitated the relief, calm and self-validation that the client was left with. At this point, the therapist could gently step back and the depth of relating would gradually return to a more usual level.

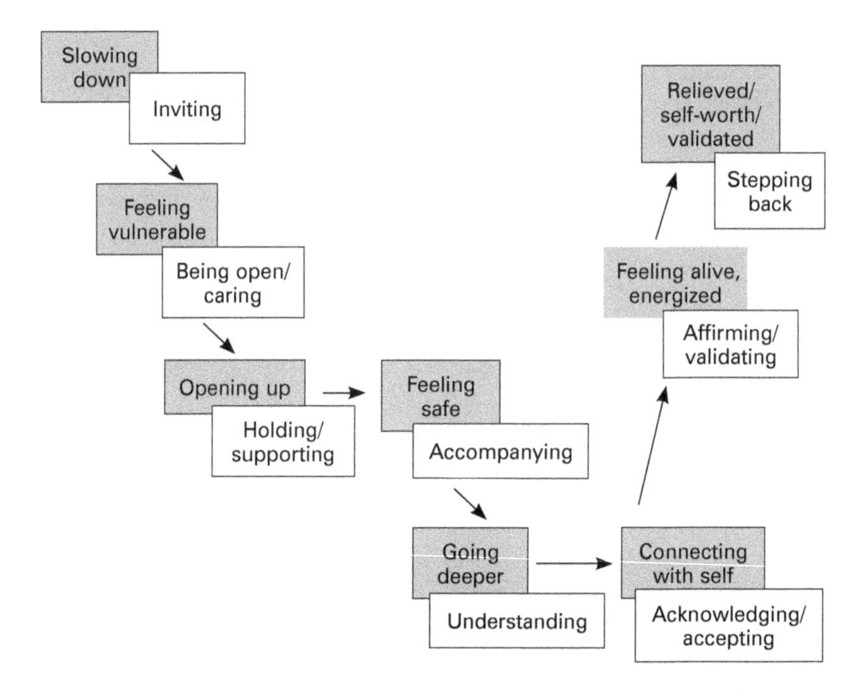

Figure 2.2 Client and therapist interactional moment-by-moment process

Note: Tinted rectangles denote clients and white rectangles denote therapists.

This moment-by-moment process of action, reaction and interaction may go some way to explaining the variety of descriptions of an experience of relational depth that have arisen. It is not proposed as a suggestion for what 'should' be happening in therapy; it is simply an account of what appeared to be the process of an experience of relational depth as perceived by clients. Hopefully, it might prove useful for practitioners and trainees, perhaps as a reminder of the delicate dance of therapy, and of the potential impact on the client of every small thought, feeling and action. Perhaps it can be used as an encouragement to bring one's own self to the relationship, to allow oneself to care in a very genuine and personal way, and to be open and willing to meet at relational depth if that is what the client wants.

Conclusion

This research provides initial evidence of the possible benefits to the client of an experience of a moment of relational depth. On the one hand, there was the effect of the insight and self-connection that the experience facilitated. On the other, there was the impact of the connection itself, resulting in a loss of aloneness and isolation, facilitating the client's reconnection to themselves, others, the world and life itself.

For practitioners, therefore, it would seem important to be open to such a moment when it arises. While this research suggests that a moment of relational depth is not something that usually is, or should be, initiated by the therapist, their responses and engagement with the client at such moments would seem to be crucial in allowing the client to take the decision to let go and engage at depth. At such moments, the therapist's every move would seem to be under scrutiny by the client, with any indication that the therapist is reacting unhelpfully, not understanding, or not accepting of the client or their material being enough to stop the client in their tracks. The primary implication for practitioners, then, is to be aware of the client's efforts to meet them at a level of relational depth, to be open to such a meeting, and to maintain a warm, human and inviting attitude, in line with the assertion by Schmid and Mearns (2006) that therapists should invite, not obligate, their clients to relate at depth.

References

Brodley, B. (2006) Regarding Baker, Johnston and Wenner 'Relational depth: How do we assess it?' *Person-Centred Quarterly*, November, 13–14.

Buber, M. (1970) *I and Thou*. New York: Scribner's Sons.

Cooper, M. (2005) Therapists' experiences of relational depth: A qualitative interview study. *Counselling and Psychotherapy Research*, 5(2), 87–95.

Knox, R. (2011) Clients' experiences of relational depth. Unpublished PhD dissertation, University of Strathclyde, Glasgow.

Mearns, D. (1996) Contact at relational depth. *Counselling*, 7, 306–11.

Mearns, D. and Cooper, M. (2005) *Working at Relational Depth in Counselling and Psychotherapy*. London: Sage.

Rogers, C.R. (1957) The necessary and sufficient conditions of therapeutic personality change. *Journal of Consulting Psychology*, 21(2), 95–103.

Rogers, C.R. ([1986]1990) A client-centered/person-centered approach to therapy. In H. Kirschenbaum and V. Henderson (eds) *The Carl Rogers Reader* (pp. 135–52). London: Constable.

Rowan, J. (2005) *The Transpersonal: Spirituality in Psychotherapy and Counselling* (2nd edn). London: Routledge.

Schmid, P. and Mearns, D. (2006) Being-with and being-counter: Person-centered psychotherapy as an in-depth co-creative process of personalization. *Person-Centered and Experiential Psychotherapies*, 5(3), 174–90.

Strauss, A. and Corbin, J. (1998) *Basics of Qualitative Research: Techniques and Procedures for Developing Grounded Theory* (2nd edn). Thousand Oaks, CA: Sage.

Thorne, B. (1991) *Person-centred Counselling: Therapeutic and Spiritual Dimensions*. London: Whurr.

Wilders, S. (2007) Relational depth and the person-centred approach. *Person-Centred Quarterly*, February, 1–4.

3

Therapists' experiences of relational depth with clients with learning disabilities

Eleanor Macleod

> There are moments which are almost like the defining points in the therapy, and it might not be anything that's being said, it might not be anything that's recordable in any way apart from a sensation or a sense of connectedness. (therapist, from Macleod, 2009)

In recent years, there have been a number of studies on relational depth (see Chapter 5, this volume), but few have focused on client groups that society views as 'different', like those from the learning disabled population. The above quote would suggest that connectedness in therapy may be a defining point in the therapeutic process. Therefore, studies like these are important to see whether the concept of relational depth is generalizable to a wider population. More importantly, perhaps, it is also sometimes assumed that clients with learning disabilities are not able to benefit from relational practices like counselling because of cognitive impairment (see, for example, Hodges, 2003). Hence, if therapists do experience relational depth with clients with learning disabilities, it would suggest a legitimacy in more relational therapies for this client group, and would call into question the practice of behavioural approaches that have been the preferred method of working with people with learning disabilities.

I am a person-centred counsellor and although I have not been formally trained in counselling people with learning disabilities, I have an interest in this area due to my professional and personal experiences. I believe that a deep connection and profound engagement with an individual is not dependent on their level of cognitive ability but more to do with the person's ability to access their emotions and share them with another human being. In my experience, being prepared to be flexible, adaptive and creative (in ways that you may not have been initially trained to do) is paramount in working with people with learning disabilities. In addition, in my experience, words are not the only medium in which to engage with clients, particularly for those who have difficulties in understanding and processing information, as well as verbally communicating. One therapist who took part in my research commented in their interview how 'we are all so bloody word fixated'.

One therapist whom I interviewed shared with me their experience of relational depth with a client with learning disabilities. The recounting of the experience by the therapist had a lasting impression on me and touched me not only as a counsellor, but as a human being. The following edited extract is, I feel, a good example of relational depth that gives a real sense of the challenges that can be presented to therapists when they counsel people with learning disabilities:

> I worked with a man with learning disabilities who could not do time, the maximum amount of time we ever did was 20 minutes, more often it was 10. He was referred to me because he was not talking at all and was being very self-abusive; he would punch himself and sit and rock. His dad had died about a year before and he had become totally withdrawn. He didn't want to come into the counselling room and eventually over a period of time he came into the room, eventually he started talking. I knew that he could bite, but I would just sit there and be with him sitting quietly and I'd say 'we're sitting' – Prouty stuff you know. [Garry Prouty was founder of the pre-therapy approach for working with people with severe contact difficulties; see Prouty et al., 2002.] One day I said to him: 'Oh, I'm just wondering about *Eastenders*' (as I knew that lots of people in the day centre watch a lot of TV). He sort of sparked up and got into something very deep about his dad, which moved me to tears. I think I said: 'Who did you watch it with?' and he replied 'dad' and then he started to look really sad. He suddenly lunged across at me and I thought, you know, just momentarily, I'm going to be bitten. As he lunged across he put his hand – and he's a big guy, a really big guy – he put his hand behind my neck and it looked like it was coming in this great big, sort of, gesture that was likely to, you know, lunge and bite, but he didn't – he came in this great big gesture and then his hand very, very, very tenderly touched the back of my neck and he leaned forward and he went 'I like you' and left the room. We had a few sessions after that – very short sessions: he'd talk about the television, he'd talk about dad and I would feedback where he was. The last time I worked with him he came to the room, he sat down and again he did the same great big lunge and then he kissed me on the cheek and he brushed my cheek with the other hand with such tenderness. I was so touched; he had tears in his eyes; I had tears in mine and he left and that was it – he didn't ever want to come again.

Learning disability

Learning disability is a term used to describe a variety of different developmental conditions; one of the most well known is Down syndrome. Understanding and processing information, as well as being able to communicate with others, can be difficult, although this varies according to the severity of the individual's learning disability.

Definitions for learning disability can be found in the World Health Organization's *International Statistical Classification of Diseases and Related Health Problems* (WHO, 1992) and the *Diagnostic and Statistical Manual of Mental Disorders* (DSM-IV-TR) (APA, 2000). For my research, the working definition that I gave to therapists was taken from the Scottish Executive (2000) report, *The Same as You?*, which describes people with learning disabilities as having

> a significant, lifelong condition that started before adulthood, that affected their development and which means they need help to understand information, learn skills and cope independently. (p. 3)

Historically, there has been a perception that people with learning disabilities could not benefit from counselling and that it was not appropriate for them (Hodges, 2003). This is thought to be based on the belief that a person's decreased cognitive functioning prevents them from taking part in this type of therapy (Strauser et al., 2004). Prout and Strohmer (1995) consider that this perception may be due to clinical biases, whereby people with learning disabilities have been labelled due to their condition, and that their actual cognitive functioning has not been taken into account. Traditionally, for people with learning disabilities who have psychological problems, treatments 'have tended towards behavioural management, skills training and medication' (Royal College of Psychiatrists, 2004, p. 6) due to the efficacy and evidence base for these type of treatments. Arthur (2003, p. 25) writes about people with learning disabilities' 'emotional lives' being an area that has been neglected due to institutionalization, where people were 'out of sight and out of mind'; however, this is gradually changing (Sinason, 1992; McWilliams and Prouty, 1998; Hawkins, 2002; Danby and Howlett, 2006).

The study

In this research, ten counsellors and psychotherapists (consisting of eight females and two males) were interviewed, all of whom had counselled at least one person with a learning disability. Five described their theoretical training/approach as person-centred, three as psychoanalytic/psychodynamic, and two as Gestalt.

Therapists were asked to recall the counselling work they had done with any client who had a learning disability and whether they had reached relational depth (as defined in the Introduction) with such a client. If therapists thought they had experienced relational depth, they were further asked about the reasons for this.

Nine of the ten therapists said that they had experienced relational depth when counselling clients with learning disabilities, with one saying they were not sure. However, during the course of their interview, this participant described the experience of meeting a client in a similar way to the other nine. As with the clients in the studies of Knox (Chapter 2, this volume) and others, therapists talked about their experience of reaching relational depth for themselves as therapists, for the client (as observed by them as therapists), in the relationship, and in the moment itself. As will be seen, descriptions of the experience of relational depth were very similar to descriptions of this experience with clients without learning disabilities (see Chapter 5, this volume); although a consideration of facilitating and inhibiting factors raised a number of important practice implications that may be unique to this group.

Therapists' own experience of relational depth

By far the most recurring theme in therapists' own experience of relational depth when working with clients with learning disabilities involved their 'understanding and/or being in touch' with their clients. Most of the therapists referred to themselves as being in touch, almost in tune, with their clients and having a real understanding of what it was like for them. One therapist said: 'What it is, what it feels like, is me really knowing what it feels like inside for him.' While this finding is similar to those of Cooper (2005), Knox, (2008) and Wiggins et al. (2012), it is worth remembering that several of these therapists' clients had limited verbal communication, highlighting the potential value of a shared understanding that is beyond words.

Four of the therapists said they felt privileged to have been able to work with the clients at this depth. One said they felt 'extremely privileged to be in that position where someone is sharing the depths of their life'. Four also expressed an emotional and physical reaction within themselves when working at relational depth with clients – similar to the experience of being impacted upon (see Chapter 5, this volume). Describing this as 'emotionally moving', therapists felt 'deeply moved' and experienced 'physical sensations' within themselves.

Three of the therapists spoke about a feeling of connection with their clients, as one said: 'There is a level of connection and you just feel this stuff, just my word I mean the depth of the, em, pain and sadness and isolation and you know and sometimes bewilderment.'

Therapists' observations of clients

As with Knox's (2008) study, most of the therapists observed their clients' willingness to be vulnerable, revealing even the parts viewed as unacceptable for people with learning disabilities in society. Again this highlights the subtle difference between being vulnerable and feeling able to show vulnerability. One therapist said that their client at this time was 'not keeping up a façade of what's expected and speaking … from the heart'.

Six of the therapists identified clients' increased insight/awareness where they felt their clients had had some kind of a breakthrough within themselves. The clients appeared to have a different insight and deeper awareness than they had prior to relational depth being reached. One therapist described this as 'a deep relational sort of moment in the work where somebody becomes aware of a different way of behaving or a different way of being or a different way of experiencing a problem' and stated that they had 'witnessed that on numerous occasions'. Again, similar to studies involving general client samples, this study does suggest that at these times it's as if clients have had a light bulb moment when relational depth has been reached, which has given them more clarity and a greater understanding of themselves.

Five of the therapists reported observing and experiencing emotional and physical changes within their clients. Examples included how clients physically held and presented themselves, their eye contact, relating in a different way and in their whole demeanour. In recounting this experience, one therapist said that at this time their client's 'whole posture changes, his "yes's" are much clearer, he's much more intent in looking at you, so he can really look at you full on'. This comment reflects my own experiences when I have witnessed a profound effect in a client's confidence and self-belief that was not apparent before relational depth was reached.

A finding particularly relevant to this client group was that four of the therapists noticed an increase in communication from their clients when relational depth had been reached. They spoke of their clients becoming more vocal, taking less time to think, and being more immediate with their responses. In describing what this was like, one therapist said 'that it tends towards, um, more – yes, more – more stuff getting said or getting communicated because it's not always said in words'. In my own experience, I have found that what is often lacking in society in general is the willingness of others to hear what people with learning disabilities have to say, and they often struggle to be heard. Reaching relational depth appeared to provide a catalyst for communication, enabling these clients to act on their need to be heard.

The relationship

Half of the therapists interviewed mentioned a sense of deepening trust in the relationship when working at relational depth. They saw this as reciprocal;

that the client trusts them as a therapist and that the therapist also trusts the client. Therapists spoke about actively working to build trust in the relationship to show that they were different from other people the client with learning disabilities may have encountered in their life, which then deepened relating. One therapist talked about building the relationship 'brick by brick', feeling that they had given the client what they needed to 'trust the process'.

Four identified connection within the relationship with their clients when working at relational depth. One therapist described this as 'times when, within the context of the fifty minute session, there'll be a lot of, um, face stuff, a lot of putting on whatever act is being put on em, but then within that there'd be points when there would be a real connection'. Connection within the relationship during these moments was seen as 'being really close and alongside' the client where therapist and client were linked in some way, which allowed the client to go deeper. Furthermore, four also identified a sense of equality and partnership within the relationship. The therapist and client were described as being on a par with each other, being equal and in it together, with no power differential during these moments. In my own experience, I have found that people with learning disabilities rarely have equality in many relationships that they have, and therefore in reaching relational depth, the impact of the power balance shifting from being one-sided to two-way with therapists was, for them, potentially highly significant.

The moment itself

As with previous studies, participants in this study also seemed to be describing the moment itself as having a particular quality and nature. Six of the therapists identified a sense of connection, like a flow, whereby therapist and client were linked in some way by an energy, running through both of them. One therapist said it was

> Like electricity flowing one from the other, it's almost like we're in the same flow of electricity. It's like two magnets that kind of join together and in that moment, and it might only be a moment, it's like this real connection.

Similar to the finding of Knox's (2008) study, five felt that the connection moved into what was seen as a blending of therapist and client, where a coming together and merging of both took place during moments of relational depth. During these moments, the therapist and client were 'standing on the same spot', and although they were two separate individuals, it was almost like they were one. One therapist said: 'You know: Is this me? Is this you? Is this something we've kind of, like, co-created?' Here again one can catch a glimpse of the fine line between the therapist and client meeting, with each remaining aware of their own separateness, and merging, where the boundaries between them become blurred.

Three of the therapists identified environmental changes when relational depth had been reached. These included noticeable changes within the room and the atmosphere, as well as a sense of 'stillness' during these moments. One therapist described how 'the environment in the room changes, it's either warmer or it just feels softer or lighter somehow, it's just like real'. Four of the therapists also identified a spiritual aspect/different dimension at these moments of relational depth. Therapists described this as almost like having their own world where they were at a very different level, a deeper soulful level. In describing this phenomenon, one therapist said:

> It's as if there are times, and this will sound weird in our current climate, it's as if there are moments when our souls are touching, and the way I know it is that with people who can speak you know it because they're feeding it back to you, they're maybe telling you, you can feel it too. When someone can't talk, all you've got left is what you're feeling and what they're feeling when you kind of tune in at that level. I suppose ways one might be able to measure it is our eyes will both fill with tears at the same time, we might both sigh at the same time, and there's a sense in which that client has transcended their whole difficulty. In people who've got quite contorted grimaces on their faces or quite jerky moments, or they're quite bouncy people because they can't quite sit still, in these moments they would be very still, their face will take on this very relaxed feel, and it is deeply moving, deeply moving and I know at those moments I have been in contact with their soul.

From this description one can see just how significant a moment of relational depth might be to a client with learning disabilities.

Three of the therapists identified moments of relational depth as being one where it had been done together and that it was a joint or shared journey, not just the client's alone. To describe this, one therapist said that 'there's very much a sense that, yes, there are two people in the room and she's not in the room on her own'. From my own experiences of relational depth, it has felt like I have been very much in it with the client and that they have not been alone in this.

Two described the moment as powerful, not only from the point of view that it was moving for them as therapists, but also that it was a strong sensation, almost overwhelming. One therapist said:

> and just in that moment – and that depth is something to maintain, that depth for that kind of time is very unusual for anybody actually, um, people who can talk will often talk it away, but somebody who can't – but it's powerful.

Factors that contribute to, or impede, relational depth

Therapists also identified additional factors, some which they felt facilitated reaching relational depth (contributory factors) and some which they felt impeded this when working with clients with learning disabilities.

Facilitative factors: therapists

Half the therapists identified how important it is to be prepared to learn and work on understanding what the client is communicating, to find a way to actually hear and understand gestures and expressions, as well as appropriately communicating with the client in a way that they can understand. My own experience of working with this client group has shown me that it is of paramount importance that any communication medium (verbal or otherwise) used with a client with learning disabilities needs to be clear, gauged at a level that is meaningful to the individual and one that they can comprehend. This does not mean that there is not some trial and error with communication, and as I have found, one often learns from the client. However, I believe that the willingness of a therapist to try different ways of communicating is what helps many clients to go beyond superficial relating.

Half also talked about being creative and resourceful, for example by using objects (such as pens, paper, balls, stones, shells), stories, dance, movement and drawing, as well as engaging in games and singing songs to work with clients at this depth. It is interesting to note, however, that most of those who worked in this way had not been trained in creative arts/therapy, but chose to adapt their ways of working, which enhanced the therapeutic process, their relationship with their client and led to reaching relational depth. Certainly, my own experiences have taught me that conventional ways of engaging with clients do not always work with those who have learning disabilities and that other forms of communication need to be tried in order to meet the client where they are. I view the expansion of my own creative repertoire and the development of my ability to think on my feet (or should I say seat) as a natural progression in my own journey as a counsellor, which I feel is necessary for working with this client group.

Three of the therapists viewed flexibility not only as a prerequisite for counselling people with learning disabilities, but also as facilitative of relational depth. In describing the necessity for flexibility, one therapist said that

> rigidity would rule out people with learning disabilities. If you're going to go down a rigid road, you know, go down it on your own, because you're not, you're not going to be able to go down their squiggly roads and circular ones.

In my own practice, being flexible is something that has been a necessity in order to counsel people with learning disabilities. While boundaries are important, rigidity does not allow a therapist to meet, follow and work with clients at any depth. If you are looking for, as one therapist said, a 'neat fifty minute session', then perhaps working with clients with learning disabilities is not for you. However, if you are prepared to expect the unexpected and to be challenged in a variety of different ways, which ultimately will enhance your work with clients without learning disabilities, then perhaps working with this client group is something you may want to consider.

Three of the therapists described actively showing their clients that they valued and accepted them for who they are. For many people with learning disabilities, their life experiences lead them to feel that they are neither accepted nor worthwhile; it was perhaps even more significant for this client group that their therapist was treating them differently, making a meeting at relational depth more possible. The efforts the therapists were making in order to understand their client's world were also different from their everyday life experiences where little or no effort was made by others to understand them. By therapists demonstrating that they wanted to know what life was really like for their clients, and showing them that they were interested in what was being communicated, it helped to deepen the level of relating.

Two therapists talked about following the client's lead and using whatever worked for them. This included therapists not having needs of their own, listening to the client and 'giving the client autonomy to plan the sessions to meet their needs'. In order to facilitate relational depth, one therapist said that this involved 'being prepared to follow where the client goes'. This certainly seems to reinforce my own experience and I would further add that as a therapist working with clients with learning disabilities, you need to have trust in the process, as the journey you are taken on may be unlike anything you have experienced before in work with other clients.

Facilitative factors: clients

Most of the therapists spoke about clients' ability to relate at an emotional level as being important, as well as clients' past emotional experiences contributing to this ability and their capacity for accessing that emotional part of themselves. One therapist said:

> It's not the kind of an intellectual ability that makes counselling therapy kind of work, it's much more of an emotional ability, and so someone's ability to be able to access their feelings, and for them to open up their thoughts and feelings for examination for consideration in therapy is the kind of decisive factor.

Therapists in my research made no mention of a person with a learning disability's intellectual ability as being a factor in reaching relational depth, and it appears that it is an emotional ability (not an intellectual one) that is important in relating to another at a level of relational depth. However, four of the therapists did consider that the client's capacity to relate to another person was a relevant factor. Some talked about conditions such as autism where relating to other people is difficult. Reaching relational depth with these clients was viewed as being dependent on where the individual clients fell on the spectrum, the severity of their condition, and their capacity to relate emotionally with another person – one rule did not fit all.

Four of the therapists spoke about the importance of the client having power in the relationship, with the freedom to lead at their own pace the nature and level of relating. Of particular importance was listening to the client and giving them the 'space and pace' to make their own decisions regarding how they would engage within the relationship. This aspect would seem to be crucial for this client group, as many of their life experiences have been so far removed from the type of relationship one might find in a therapeutic setting. If you were to imagine a life where you had very little power, did not have a voice and things happened *to* you, not *with* you – what would that feel like?

Facilitative factors: staff and family

Interestingly, a contributory factor in reaching relational depth with clients with learning disabilities was what was described by therapists as a positive, supportive attitude of the clients' families and staff. This included surprisingly basic elements such as bringing the client to the sessions, and believing in the value of the person attending counselling. Positive reinforcement by these important people in the individual's support network was felt to impact significantly on the level, quality and depth of a client's engagement with their therapist.

Impeding factors

The therapists identified the following impeding factors when working with clients with learning disabilities.

Staff and family's negative/unsupportive attitudes

Over and above the benefits of supportive family and staff was the detrimental impact on the therapeutic process where their attitude was distinctly negative and unsupportive. Such attitudes included a lack of understanding, not seeing counselling as important, and actively sabotaging the person's counselling by criticizing or even making fun of it, all of which had a noticeably negative effect on the level, quality and depth of the client's engagement with their therapist.

Environmental distractions

Some therapists identified distractions both inside and outside the counselling room as impeding their client's abilities or efforts to meet at a level of relational depth. Therapists talked about providing counselling in venues not always conducive to the building of a therapeutic relationship. Some of the most inappropriate settings were rooms within centres for people with learning disabilities. However, as attempts to make changes would often lead to the person being prevented from attending the sessions at all, the therapist simply made the best of the situation and found a way of working with it.

Therapists' inflexibility

Two of the therapists identified the inflexibility of therapists as an impeding factor in reaching relational depth with clients with learning disabilities. If therapists worked rigidly within their own therapeutic model and were not prepared to try something different, they felt this would inevitably impede reaching relational depth.

Clients' having to please persona

Two of the therapists identified clients' 'having to please' persona as an impeding factor in reaching relational depth. Therapists talked about society's expectation that people with learning disabilities should please and be compliant. In order to be able to work at relational depth with clients with learning disabilities, one therapist said that it was about 'needing to get through the needing to please' before depth could be reached. Another therapist said that this could be 'a real barrier', which can undermine the work because 'what you are having to fight with is the outside world wanting people to be like that'. Certainly, my own experiences have taught me that just because a person with learning disabilities smiles all of the time does not mean that they are smiling inside. I have learned that, as a counsellor, it is important to help such clients to express their range of emotions, not just the ones that society dictates are acceptable.

Conclusion

As in work with other clients (Cooper, 2005), therapists working with clients with learning disabilities can experience moments of deep connection. The 'emotional/physical reactions' that therapists experienced confirm these similarities with other therapeutic work and relate to Cooper's (2005, p. 90) study, whereby therapists were 'impacted upon' by clients. The consistencies with other studies imply that, regardless of a client's intellectual ability, therapists can still make a real connection and work at depth with clients with learning disabilities.

The aspect of 'openness/showing vulnerabilty/allowing the therapist in' in this research also supports Mearns and Cooper's proposition (2005, p. 60) of engaging 'the client at a level that is closer to the client's experience of what is critical to their existence, as well as the presentational level of their expressing'.

Therapists in this research experienced clients as willing to show who they were, as well as observing clients as 'speaking from the heart', revealing 'a real part of themselves' that they kept hidden in the outside world for fear of not being accepted. Again, this implies that regardless of a client's intellectual ability, clients with learning disabilities make choices, just as other clients do, about whether to reveal their inner world to therapists and let them in.

Compared to other client groups, research into counselling people with learning disabilities is a small but developing field. There is much scope for further work into how clients with learning disabilities experience relational depth, and indeed how they experience the counselling relationship. However, this would necessitate information being devised in a meaningful, accessible format that clients with learning disabilities can relate to and understand. In addition, there is the issue of consent and how this is obtained.

In concluding this chapter, I would like to express my gratitude to the therapists who so generously volunteered their time to share with me their experiences of counselling people with learning disabilities.

References

APA (American Psychiatric Association) (2000) *Diagnostic and Statistical Manual of Mental Disorders, Fourth Edition, Text Revision, DSM-IV-TR*. Washington, DC: APA.

Arthur, A.R. (2003) The emotional lives of people with learning disability. *British Journal of Learning Disabilities*, 31, 25–30.

Cooper, M. (2005) Therapists' experiences of relational depth: A qualitative interview study. *Counselling and Psychotherapy Research*, 5(2), 87–95.

Danby, J. and Howlett, S. (2006) *Learning Disability and Sexual Abuse: The Use of a Women-only Counselling Service by Women with a Learning Disability*. Newcastle: Newcastle City Council.

Hawkins, J. (2002) *Voices of the Voiceless: Person-centred Approaches and People with Learning Disabilities*. Ross-on-Wye: PCCS Books.

Hodges, S. (2003) *Counselling Adults with Learning Disabilities*. Basingstoke: Palgrave Macmillan.

Knox, R. (2008) Clients' experience of relational depth in person-centred counselling. *Counselling and Psychotherapy Research*, 8(3), 182–8.

Macleod, E. (2009) A qualitative exploration into therapists' perceptions of reaching relational depth when counselling people with learning disabilities. Unpublished MSc dissertation, University of Strathclyde, Glasgow.

Mearns, D. and Cooper, M. (2005) *Working at Relational Depth in Counselling and Psychotherapy*. London: Sage.

McWilliams, K. and Prouty, G. (1998) Life enrichment of a profoundly retarded woman: An application of pre-therapy. *Person-Centered Journal*, 5(1), 29–35.

Prout, H.T. and Strohmer, D.C. (1995) Counseling persons with mental retardation: Issues and considerations. *Journal of Applied Rehabilitation Counseling*, 26, 49–54.

Prouty, G., Van Werde, D. and Pörtner, M. (2002) *Pre-Therapy Reaching Contact-impaired Clients*. Ross-on-Wye: PCCS Books.

Royal College of Psychiatrists (2004) *Psychotherapy and Learning Disability*, Council Report CR116. London: Royal College of Psychiatrists.

Scottish Executive (2000) *The Scottish Executive Report: The Same as You?* Edinburgh: Scottish Executive.

Sinason, V. (1992) *Mental Handicap and the Human Condition: New Approaches from the Tavistock.* London: Free Association Books.

Strauser, D.R., Lustig D.C. and Donnell, C. (2004) The relationship between working alliance and therapeutic outcomes for individuals with mild mental retardation. *Rehabilitation Counselling Bulletin*, 47, 215–23.

Wiggins, S., Elliott, R. and Cooper, M. (2012) The prevalence and characteristics of relational depth events in psychotherapy. *Psychotherapy Research*, 22(2), 139–58.

WHO (World Health Organization) (1992) *International Statistical Classification of Diseases and Related Health Problems, 10th Revision*. Geneva: WHO.

4

Assessing relational depth: developing the Relational Depth Inventory

Sue Wiggins

It was when I first read *Working at Relational Depth in Counselling and Psychotherapy* (Mearns and Cooper, 2005) that I became inspired to create a relational depth inventory; I wanted to find a way to tap into those particular encounters that the authors describe as 'moments', 'times' or 'experiences' of relational depth. I knew this would be a considerable task because it required attempting to quantify a deep, meaningful and uniquely human experience, one which, until then, had only been researched qualitatively. This posed the question: How does one quantify such a deep and personal experience as relational depth? In this chapter, I seek to answer this question while documenting the process of how the Relational Depth Inventory (RDI) came into being.

Creating any psychological measure usually means rigorously investigating the subject in question, and creating the RDI was no exception; the research methods served to look in detail at what it is that makes up a moment of relational depth as experienced in therapy.

In order to create any measure, one has to be as sure as possible that all items on it are valid, that is, that they accurately assess the intended elements of the construct in question. In the case of the RDI, I needed to be confident that the wording and phrasing of items adequately tapped into the experience of relational depth, experience that may or not be explicit in any definition. However, Mearns and Cooper's (2005) definition of relational depth as 'profound contact and engagement between two people' (see Introduction, this volume) provided a useful start to the creation of questionnaire items, along with the six Rogerian conditions for therapeutic personality change that are implicit within it (see Introduction, this volume).

Raw data

I now had a working definition of relational depth along with an outline of its theoretical underpinnings. However, I did not want to create items based on only one researcher's experience and interpretation of the above definition. It felt important to have a consensus of opinion. Fortunately, therapist and trainee therapist descriptions of moments of relational depth had been collected during training workshops. Also, Rosanne Knox (Chapter 2, this volume) had collected raw data from clients who had described their experiences of moments of relational depth in a qualitative interview study. Item creation began by subjecting these descriptions and phrases of relational depth to a grounded theory analysis, a method of research used to organize large numbers of qualitative data, with resulting categories that could guide questionnaire items.

Results of the grounded theory analysis

The qualitative data in this case were the numerous descriptions of relational depth. I used an open coding method that continually compares each particular word or phrase to develop categories and subcategories. As a result, the grounded theory analysis eventually identified patterns and trends across the various descriptions of moments of relational depth. Unlike some methods, which attempt to manipulate data into fitting a particular model or theory, this type of analysis attempts to facilitate the creation of a model or theory from the data. As a consequence, throughout this process I tried to harbour no preconceived ideas but simply to see myself as a facilitator in the research process. Eventually, domains, categories and subcategories emerged from the analysis.

Questionnaire items were created from the resulting subcategories. Below are the results, showing four domains, each with categories and subcategories. The particular questionnaire item that each subcategory became is also shown.

1. *Experience of relationship*
   a. Connected
      i. Both of us connected in some way – item 24
      ii. We had things in common – item 2
      iii. Love – item 11
      iv. A meeting of minds – item 12
      v. Intimacy – item 46
   b. Mutuality
      i. There was give and take – item 4
      ii. Mutuality – item 41
      iii. At one with the other – item 43
      iv. Equality – item 50

c. Security
   i. A sense of privacy in the relationship – item 14
   ii. Trusting the relationship – item 18
   iii. Safe item – 19

2. *Experience of self*
   a. Heightened self
      i. Liberated – item 1
      ii. Flow – item 2
      iii. Spiritual – item 10
      iv. In an altered state – item 20
      v. Magical – item 23
      vi. Expansive – item 36
      vii. Happy – item 38
      viii. I was transcendent – item 40
      ix. Spontaneous – item 48
      x. Open – item 53
      xi. Enlightened – item 64
   b. Invigorated self
      i. Intense feelings – item 5
      ii. Energized – item 16
      iii. Courageous – item 17
      iv. Revitalized – item 21
      v. Scared – item 22
      vi. Angry – item 26
      vii. Sexual – item 32
      viii. Exhilarated – item 56
      ix. Excited – item 58
      x. Empowered – item 59
   c. Immersed self
      i. Opposing feelings – item 13
      ii. Weird feelings – item 25
      iii. Paradoxical – item 27
      iv. Immersed – item 45
      v. Soulful – item 62
   d. True self
      i. A sense of being in the moment – item 8
      ii. Centred on the present – item 15
      iii. Self-value – item 31
      iv. Vulnerable – item 34
      v. In touch with self – item 47
      vi. I was being real – item 54
      vii. Aware of experience – item 63

3. *Experience of/towards other*
   a. Respect
      i. Other person respected me – item 6
      ii. Other person valued me – item 9
      iii. Value of other – item 49
      iv. Respect of other – item 52
   b. Trust
      i. Other person trusted me – item 28
      ii. Trust of other – item 57
   c. Being available
      i. I was there for other – item 44
      ii. Other was available to me – item 61
   d. Empathy
      i. Empathy for other person – item 35
      ii. Other was empathic towards me – item 37
   e. Other being real – item 42

4. *Experience of atmosphere*
   a. Dynamic
      i. Transformative atmosphere – item 60
   b. Peace
      i. Silent atmosphere – item 30
      ii. Still atmosphere – item 39
      iii. Timeless atmosphere – item 51
   c. Significance
      i. Meaningful atmosphere – item 7
      ii. Inexplicable atmosphere – item 29
      iii. Awesome atmosphere – item 33
      iv. Unique atmosphere – item 55
      v. Paradoxical – item 27
      vi. Immersed – item 45
      vii. Soulful – item 62
   d. True self
      i. A sense of being in the moment – item 8
      ii. Centred on the present – item 15
      iii. Self-value – item 31
      iv. Vulnerable – item 34
      v. In touch with self – item 47
      vi. I was being real – item 54
      vii. Aware of experience – item 63

It came as a surprise to find that some of the subcategories above include some rather unusual and perhaps unexpected descriptions. For example, in domain 2, 'Experience of self', under the category of 'Invigorated self', you will see the subcategories 'angry', 'scared', 'excited' and 'sexual', to name but a few. These words are included in this analysis, not because I had created them, or because I think they represent relational depth, but because they existed in the original raw data. To remain faithful to these data, these and other level 3 subcategories were formed into questionnaire items to create a preliminary questionnaire.

Preliminary questionnaire

When the subcategories were formed into questionnaire items, they were presented in such a way that a respondent could be first asked to describe an important event in therapy. After the important event description question, a further question was added, which intended to ask the respondent to what extent they encountered various experiences during this event. These experiences comprised the 64 items created from the categories above, and were presented using a 5-point Likert scale (a Likert scale is a multiple choice style of question used widely in questionnaires). The intention was that respondents would utilize the 64 items and rate how accurately each one described their experience of the important event. To help readers understand how the questionnaire was presented, the box below provides an excerpt from the preliminary RDI.

Excerpt from 64-item (preliminary) RDI

Please take a minute to think back over your relationship so far with this therapist or client. Of the events which have occurred so far, select one that stands out in your mind as particularly important. This event or experience can be positive, negative or neither, as long as it felt important to you. Please briefly describe this event below in not more than about three sentences.

Now, with this particular event in mind, please rate how accurately each of the items below fits your experience of this event

	not at all	slightly	somewhat	very much	completely
1. Liberated	☐	☐	☐	☐	☐
2. We had shared things in common	☐	☐	☐	☐	☐

I did not ask participants to describe a moment of relational depth. Had I done so, it would have been rather a circular exercise; the items themselves were intended to assess relational depth and were based on its experiences. I wanted descriptions of all kinds of events, whether or not relational depth was present, in order to give a variety of descriptions to analyse.

Over 350 participants completed the online questionnaire, which asked them to describe an important event in therapy and then rate that event using the 64 items. It is important to note that the link to the online questionnaire was sent to many counselling and psychotherapy organizations. As a consequence, while both therapists and clients participated, it is likely that many of the client participants were also therapists in their own right, who were simply describing their experiences as a client at some stage. The resultant data from this would be analysed using various quantitative methods, which would hopefully uncover which experiences were most associated with relational depth.

Results from preliminary questionnaire

Participants' important event descriptions were assigned scores (on a scale of 0 to 3) by pairs of raters, as to how strongly or clearly relational depth was seen to be present in the event. A score of

- 0 meant that the description was *clearly not* relational depth
- 1 meant it *probably was not*
- 2 meant it *probably was*
- 3 meant it was *clearly or strongly relational depth*.

Raters did not automatically assume that there were different levels of relational depth. They were, however, looking for the degree of clarity or strength of relational depth present in the events described. This has great significance because at the time of writing, there was no evidence to suggest whether presence of relational depth, in a particular moment, is on a continuum or is an 'all-or-nothing' experience. To give the reader an illustration of the descriptions given, I have included some examples of each of the four levels below.

Therapist examples:
- Level 3: 'We felt a deep connection in the silence.'
- Level 2: 'For what felt the first time in a long time the client saw themselves differently, heard themselves affirming their own values.'
- Level 1: 'I expressed how I long to reach out to the person behind the laughter and jokiness, but have difficulty with this.'
- Level 0: 'I did not feel I was connecting with this client at all.'

Client examples:
- Level 3: 'A level of understanding was assumed and we became closer.'
- Level 2: 'A session where I was able to be myself as a small child and to gain the ability to comfort myself without feeling embarrassed by the process and where I felt emotionally held by the therapist.'

- Level 1: 'Remembering a traumatic event in my childhood.'
- Level 0: 'The therapist used a word that I felt pathologized me and I felt shocked and offended.'

It is the researchers' ratings of these descriptions and the participants' own ratings of their important events (using the 64 items) that have helped shape the current version of the RDI. The next section describes how I came to create the shorter (24-item) RDI from these results.

Creating a revised 24-item RDI

Using participants' responses from the 64-item RDI, redundant items were omitted. For this exercise, I used quantitative analyses (largely correlation, which look at associations between items). By redundant items I mean those which are not needed; the following example might illustrate. The two items 'other person valued me' and 'other person respected me' were so closely correlated as to render it unnecessary to include both. In total, 10 items were deleted, leaving a balance of 54 items. I then needed to establish whether these remaining items had enough similarity to be assessing the same thing; consequently, a test for internal consistency (Cronbach's alpha) was conducted. The test suggested that seven further items should be omitted, including 'opposing feelings', 'paradoxical', 'vulnerable', 'scared', 'weird feelings', 'angry' and 'sexual'. This makes conceptual sense, as it is questionable as to whether these items have anything to do with relational depth. However, there is the argument that 'scared' and 'vulnerable' may be an independent aspect of relational depth. This would parallel the identification of a roughness/distress dimension of therapy process alongside depth/value/effectiveness in research by Orlinsky and Howard (1977, 1986) and Stiles and Snow (1984). At the time of writing, however, there is no clear evidence that this was the case.

Forty-seven items remained but I still wanted a much shorter questionnaire. To achieve this, I needed to create a profile of those significant events that were rated as having a presence of relational depth. Consequently, questionnaire item scores were checked to assess the degree to which they were associated with relational depth presence (as rated by raters from the important events, above). A total of 30 items were found to be associated with relational depth. These are listed in Table 4.1 in order of strength of association.

These 30 items became the basis for the 24-item questionnaire. The reason why the 30 items became 24 is that some items were omitted (for example 'flow', 'soulful') after some participants during a pilot reported an inability to understand the wording. Many thought the wording was 'therapist jargon'. This was not identified earlier as the preliminary questionnaire had been completed by a sample of participants, a large proportion of whom were most probably therapists who would have understood the terminology more readily.

Table 4.1 RDI items most associated with relational depth presence

Item	*PC*	*Item*	*PC*
24. Both of us connected	.47	62. Soulful	.35
11. Love	.46	55. Unique atmosphere	.34
52. Respect for other	.40	50. Equality	.33
46. Intimacy	.40	3. Flow	.33
6. Other respected me	.40	31. Self-value	.33
41. Mutuality	.39	33. Awesome atmosphere	.32
61. Other was available to me	.39	48. Spontaneous	.32
43. At one with the other	.38	54. I was being real	.31
8. Being in the moment	.37	45. Immersed	.31
12. Meeting of minds	.37	10. Spiritual	.31
39. A still atmosphere	.37	4. Give and take	.30
28. Other trusted me	.36	21. Revitalized	.29
60. Transformative atmosphere	.36	1. Liberated	.29
51. Timeless atmosphere	.36	40. Transcendent	.29
23. Magical	.35	37. Other empathic towards me	.29

Note: PC refers to Pearson correlation, a measure of the strength of the association between two variables.

Additionally, some other items were reworded in such a way that they incorporated two items. To illustrate, the item 'love' (item 11 on the 64-item version) was changed to 'warm personal bond ... as fellow human beings' (item 24, new version). It seemed to me that this new item not only tapped into the experience of love (warm personal bond) but also tapped into the experience of mutuality (fellow human beings). Similarly, the rest of the items were reworded.

Using the 24-item version

The RDI-Revised (RDI-R), the revised 24-item version of the RDI, was used in two studies; one was a validity study and the other a process outcome study. Both studies were carried out simultaneously and both used data collected from 42 participants of the Strathclyde Research Clinic. Here, clients attended therapy sessions and completed the RDI-R at every tenth session as well as completing various outcome measures (explained in more detail later). For the validity study, a further 120 clients were recruited online via a website that presented the 24-item RDI-R.

Validity and reliability

There was good evidence that the RDI-R is unidimensional, in that it largely assesses one underlying dimension: relational depth. In addition, some of the most difficult-to-endorse items were those assessing spiritual experiences ('I felt in touch with my spiritual side') (this was later changed to 'I felt a spiritual experience' in a second revised client-only version, the RDI-R2, a copy of which is in the Appendix) and client empathy ('I felt I understood what it was like for my therapist'). This would imply that these two items assess very rare or strong presence of relational depth. Items that had moderate difficulty were items assessing a deep connection ('warm personal bond ... as fellow human beings' and 'I felt my therapist and I were connected in some way') (this was from a client-only version of the RDI-R2), indicating that these experiences are more typical characteristics of relational depth.

Perhaps the most important finding is that there was a small but significant number of people who were not targeted well by the RDI-R. Such people typically had quite high scores on all items, meaning that there were not enough items that had sufficient difficulty for such people. It would be easy to think that these respondents are scoring highly on all items simply because they are showing the strongest form of relational depth in existence. However, this thinking makes the bold assumption that the RDI-R, as it stands, is measuring the strongest relational depth in existence. This might not be the case and we cannot make that assumption. The evidence is contrary to this; that for some people all items are easy to endorse. In plain English, this implies that to target persons who experience unusually strong relational depth, more items needed to be added to the inventory, and that such items needed to be more difficult to endorse than its existing items. Consequently, any added items need to be able to assess very strong presence of relational depth as well as address experiences that may be beyond words. Therefore, items 25 ('I felt a profound connection between my therapist and me') and 26 ('I felt the experience with my therapist was beyond words') were added (see Appendix). In addition, another two items were reworded slightly: item 6 was reworded from 'I felt in touch with my spiritual side' to 'I felt a spiritual experience' and item 15 from 'I felt I was going beyond my ordinary limits' to 'I felt I experienced something beyond the ordinary.' Item 15 was changed in this way because some respondents felt that the item could have been misinterpreted as going beyond professional boundaries. Please see the Appendix at the end of the chapter for the RDI-R2 client version.

Process outcome study

Over 40 clients completed the RDI along with various outcome measures, such as the Clinical Outcome Routine Evaluation (CORE), the Strathclyde

Inventory (SI) and the Personal Questionnaire (PQ). The CORE is a widely used outcome measure, which consists of questions asking the client how they have felt during the past week. It was intended that clients complete the same questionnaire before and after therapy, and at regular intervals in between, so as to monitor any possible improvement. The SI is similar, with the exception that it was designed to be a more person-centred form of outcome measure. The PQ is completely different, in that it asks clients to create their own items and to state what they want to address in therapy. The clients then rate their own items before, during and after therapy. Such measures were, in the normal way, completed by clients both before and after therapy (or after around ten sessions) in order to check for therapeutic change. The Working Alliance Inventory (WAI) was also completed by participants at regular intervals. This is a questionnaire that essentially assesses the working alliance between client and therapist, as experienced by the client.

The results demonstrated that, having controlled for pre-therapy scores on all outcome measures as well as controlling for working alliance (WAI), the RDI scores are shown to be a significant predictor of post-therapy outcome scores. This suggests that the experience of a moment of relational depth is a significant predictor of overall outcome when taking into consideration working alliance and the client's pre-therapy state. This implies that one experience, moment, event or time spent engaging at relational depth can significantly contribute to overall therapeutic outcome. This is a rather unexpected finding, as one would expect the more enduring and continued working alliance to contribute more to outcome. This seems to suggest that the profundity of one relational depth experience resonates with and continues to benefit the client long after the event has passed – that the one experience has an enduring effect. This is very much consistent with Knox (2008, Chapter 2, this volume), who, in a qualitative study, found that clients considered a moment of relational depth to be a moment of change or a catalyst that had enduring effects.

Conclusion

I would encourage and invite therapists and researchers to use and test the RDI. It is a fairly simple measure to use and can be presented to clients at any point during therapy, although it is probably better *not* to present it at the very first session. Those using the RDI (during practice or for research) are free to change the wording that asks the client to describe a 'moment or event'. In other words, one is free to change the type of moment depending on what is being researched. For example, one may wish to research the presence of relational depth during times when the client feels moments of despair. In this case, they would ask clients to describe a moment or event when they felt despair rather than the 'particularly helpful moment' that is currently on the RDI-R2. Therefore, this part of the RDI-R2 can be flexible according to what kind of moment or event the researcher or therapist wishes to research. Of course, they would have to keep this consistent for all respondents in their study and not change or remove any of the items.

I hope the research I have documented here helps to show exactly how the RDI-R2 came into being and helps us develop a deeper understanding of the meaning of relational depth. I also hope that the research findings above can help us all in our meetings with clients and enable us to understand how one important relationally deep moment may help pave the way towards a client experiencing a positive therapeutic outcome.

Appendix Relational Depth Inventory (RDI-R2)

RDI-R2 Client version

Client ID ________ Session ___
Interviewer ____ Date _______

Below you are asked about a **particularly helpful moment or event** which you might have had during a therapy session. Please take a minute to think back over your relationship so far with this therapist. Of the events which have occurred so far, select a specific moment or event that stands out in your mind as particularly helpful. Please briefly describe this helpful moment or event below in a few sentences, and indicate about how long ago or in roughly what session it occurred.

Now, with this specific moment or event in mind, please rate how accurately each of the items below fits your experience. Please tick the appropriate box to indicate your answer.

During this specific moment or event...	*Not at all*	*A little*	*Moderately*	*Very much*	*Completely*
1. I felt a sense of freedom	☐	☐	☐	☐	☐
2. There was give and take between my therapist and myself	☐	☐	☐	☐	☐
3. I felt my therapist respected me	☐	☐	☐	☐	☐
4. I felt I was 'living in the moment'	☐	☐	☐	☐	☐
5. I felt my therapist understood what it was like for me	☐	☐	☐	☐	☐
6. I felt a spiritual experience	☐	☐	☐	☐	☐
7. My therapist and I both knew what was in each other's mind	☐	☐	☐	☐	☐
8. I felt more alive	☐	☐	☐	☐	☐
9. I felt a kind of magic happened	☐	☐	☐	☐	☐
10. I felt my therapist and I were both connected in some way	☐	☐	☐	☐	☐

▶

During this specific moment or event...	*Not at all*	*A little*	*Moderately*	*Very much*	*Completely*
11. I felt my therapist trusted me	☐	☐	☐	☐	☐
12. I felt my therapist was being genuine with me	☐	☐	☐	☐	☐
13. I felt the atmosphere was kind of awesome	☐	☐	☐	☐	☐
14. I felt I understood what it was like for my therapist	☐	☐	☐	☐	☐
15. I felt I experienced something beyond the ordinary	☐	☐	☐	☐	☐
16. My therapist and I felt close to each other	☐	☐	☐	☐	☐
17. I felt my therapist and I were equal	☐	☐	☐	☐	☐
18. I felt I had lost all sense of time	☐	☐	☐	☐	☐
19. I felt respect for my therapist	☐	☐	☐	☐	☐
20. I felt I was being genuine with my therapist	☐	☐	☐	☐	☐
21. I felt a sense of having my own power	☐	☐	☐	☐	☐
22. I felt my therapist was there for me	☐	☐	☐	☐	☐
23. I felt I had a better understanding of myself and/or others	☐	☐	☐	☐	☐
24. I felt a warm personal bond between myself and my therapist as fellow human beings	☐	☐	☐	☐	☐
25. I felt a profound connection between my therapist and me	☐	☐	☐	☐	☐
26. I felt the experience with my therapist was beyond words	☐	☐	☐	☐	☐

References

Knox, R. (2008) Clients' experiences of relational depth in person-centred counselling. *Counselling and Psychotherapy Research*, 8(3), 182–8.

Mearns, D. and Cooper, M. (2005) *Working at Relational Depth in Counselling and Psychotherapy*. London: Sage.

Orlinsky, D.E. and Howard, K.I. (1977) The therapist's experience of psychotherapy. In A.S. Gurman and A.M. Razin (eds) *Effective Psychotherapy: A Handbook of Research* (pp. 586–9). New York: Pergamon.

Orlinsky, D.E. and Howard, K.I. (1986). The psychological interior of psychotherapy: Explorations with the Therapy Session Report Questionnaires. In L.S. Greenberg and W.M. Pinsof (eds) *The Psychotherapeutic Process: A Research Handbook* (pp. 477–501). New York: Guilford Press.

Stiles, W.B. and Snow, J.S. (1984) Dimensions of psychotherapy session impact across sessions and across clients. *British Journal of Clinical Psychology*, 23(1), 59–63.

5

Experiencing relational depth in therapy: what we know so far

Mick Cooper

The aim of this chapter is to draw together findings from recent studies on the experience of relational depth, including those described earlier in this book, to give a state-of-the-art review of what the research currently tells us about moments of deep connection: its prevalence, nature, consequences and antecedents.

Before reviewing this literature, however, there is an important preliminary question to ask: Can research, and particularly quantitative, number-based inquiry, ever tell us anything meaningful about relational depth? Surely, it could be argued, relational depth is such a subtle, holistic and complex phenomenon – something that individuals find so 'hard to put into words' – that to try and analyse and present it in empirical terms would be to undermine the very essence of what it is. This viewpoint is captured by a humanistic trainee interviewed by Connelly (2009), who said:

> I'm quite happy for it [relational depth] to be elusive ... There's a fear of, you know – it's like kind of butterfly catching, isn't it? – there's a fear of catching something very beautiful and trying to define what it is. And then, and in that process, losing what it is.

Moreover, it could be argued that the very process of 'scientifically' measuring, quantifying and empirically examining phenomenon is antithetical to a worldview based around relational depth, with its emphasis on I-Thou relating (Buber, 1947), as opposed to I-It reductionism and objectification.

No doubt there is much validity to this argument. However, there are also ways in which an understanding of the world based around relational encounter can be seen as pointing towards the value of research inquiry. First, relational depth is about openness and fluidity – a willingness to move beyond fixed, sedimented assumptions – and research evidence can be a powerful means of challenging our own beliefs and expectations, and engaging more fully with what is actually 'out there' in the world (see Cooper, 2010a). As Carl Rogers (1986, cited in Cain, 2010, p. 42), for example, wrote in relation to person-centred practice:

> There is only one way in which a person-centred approach can avoid becoming narrow, dogmatic and restrictive. That is through studies – simultaneously hard-headed and tender-minded – which open new vistas, bring new insights, challenge our hypotheses, enrich our theory, expand our knowledge, and involve us more deeply in an understanding of the phenomena of human change.

Second, relational depth is about moving away from all-or-nothing thinking, to an appreciation of the intricacies and complexities of any person or phenomenon. So, although research evidence may not give us definitive answers to questions about relational depth, it can be one very valuable means of edging forward in our understanding: something that should no more be discounted than it should be revered as a 'royal road' to the 'truth'.

In the review that follows, I have focused only on research that explicitly examines the concept of 'relational depth', as developed by Mearns (1997, 2003) and Mearns and Cooper (2005), and as defined in the Introduction (this volume). As discussed in this Introduction, there are several closely related concepts but, as far as we are aware, little empirical research has been undertaken in these fields. As most of the contemporary research also focuses on relational depth as a *moment* of experiencing (see Introduction, this volume), this is the focus of the review.

Do therapists experience relational depth with their clients?

For relational depth to be a meaningful therapeutic construct, it must be something that is actually present, at least to some extent, within the therapeutic relationship. An important initial question, therefore, is: Do therapists actually experience relational depth with their clients and, if so, are there any particular kinds of therapists who are more likely to experience it than others?

Probably the best evidence in relation this question comes from an online survey conducted by Leung (2008). His respondents were 140 therapists from a variety of orientations (although primarily humanistic), and he found that almost 98 per cent reported at least one experience of relational depth with a client. Moments of relational depth in therapy could also be identified by eight out of eight experienced person-centred therapists in a qualitative interview study (Cooper, 2005), and nine out of ten primarily person-centred/

humanistic therapists who worked with clients with learning disabilities (see Chapter 5, this volume).

In terms of prevalence, therapists in the Leung survey were asked to rate on a 7-point scale how frequently they had experienced moments of relational depth with their clients (1 = not at all, 7 = all the time). The average rating was around the midpoint of the scale, 4.06.

These data suggest that a large majority of therapists have experienced moments of profound connection with a client, and at a moderate level of frequency. However, there are three reasons why the actual percentage of therapists who have experienced relational depth may be somewhat lower than this suggests:

1. Respondents to these studies were self-selecting, such that therapists with a greater interest in the therapeutic relationship – and potentially more likely to experience relational depth – may have been more likely to take part.
2. Participants may have wanted to present themselves, particularly in the interview studies, in a positive light, hence overstating the extent to which they had experienced moments of deep encounter.
3. The majority of participants in these studies were of a person-centred or humanistic orientation – therapeutic approaches that place strong emphasis on the relationship – such that it is not clear whether these figures would generalize out to less relationally oriented therapies.

With respect to the last of these points, however, Leung (2008) found no significant differences in the extent to which humanistic, psychodynamic and other (mainly cognitive behavioural therapy) practitioners reported experiencing relational depth. Nevertheless, with respect to differences across professional groups, Morris (2009) did find that psychologists (clinical and counselling) working in the NHS were less likely to recognize such experiences of encounter in their work, with just three out of six interviewees (50 per cent) identifying moments of relational depth.

In terms of other individual variables, Leung (2008) found no significant differences between male and female therapists. However, therapists with more years of practice did report a greater frequency of relationally deep encounters.

In summary, then, research suggests that a large proportion of therapists, perhaps most, have experienced moments of profound contact with their clients. Evidence is strongest for practitioners of a person-centred or humanistic orientation, and with some indications that more experienced practitioners are most likely to experience relational depth.

Do clients experience relational depth with their therapists?

Early literature and research on relational depth (for example Cooper, 2005;

Mearns and Cooper, 2005), as above, tended to focus on relational depth as experienced by therapists. Perhaps this was on the assumption that, as a mutual, bidirectional experience, if therapists were experiencing relational depth, clients would be too. But this assumption is by no means a given. Indeed, from much of the psychotherapy research, it is evident just how different clients' and therapists' experiences of the same relational encounters can be (see, for example, Cooper, 2008, p. 2). And given that, for relational depth to be healing, it must be actually *experienced* by the client, a critical question to ask is whether clients, as well as therapists, do also experience moments of profound connection in therapy.

Again, some of the best evidence for this comes from Leung's (2008) online survey. Of 119 participants who responded as clients, Leung found that 78.2 per cent could identify a moment of relational depth. This is significantly less than the proportion of therapists identifying moments of profound encounter with their clients, but still a substantial proportion of respondents. Knox, as discussed in Chapter 2 (this volume), also found a relatively high proportion of clients identifying moments of relational depth with their therapists; and all three of the clients interviewed by Omielan (2009) in his series of narrative case studies also described moments of profound connection.

In terms of frequency of experiencing moments of relational depth, clients in the Leung (2008) survey gave a mean rating of 3.87 on the 7-point scale (1 = not at all, 7 = all the time): again towards the midpoint of the scale and not significantly different from therapists.

McMillan and McLeod (2006), however, obtained a somewhat different picture from their qualitative study of ten clients' experiences of the therapeutic relationship. Here, specific moments of intense closeness were found to be 'relatively rare'. In attempting to reconcile these findings with those of Leung (2008) and Knox (2011), it is important to note that the latter studies asked participants directly about their experiences of relational depth, while McMillan and McLeod (2006) inquired more broadly about the therapeutic relationship. Hence, with McMillan and McLeod (2006), some experiences of relational depth may have been overlooked; while in the former studies, participants may have felt under some pressure to identify specific moments.

In each of these studies, there are also the problems, again, of self-selected participants, impression management concerns, and many of the clients also being therapists, meaning that the actual percentage of clients who have experienced moments of profound connection may be considerably less than the 78.2 per cent identified by Leung. At the same time, however, the fact that clients were significantly less likely to have experienced relational depth than therapists may be attributable to the fact that, while clients may only have worked with one or two therapists, therapists may have worked with tens or even hundreds of clients – hence having much more opportunity to experience relational depth. In this respect, it is by no means clear whether therapists or clients, over an equivalent number of relationships and/or period of time, would be most likely to experience a profound depth of connection.

In terms of which kinds of clients may be most likely to experience relational depth, Leung (2008) found just one significant difference: clients of humanistic therapists were significantly more likely to report this experience than clients of psychodynamic therapists.

In summary, there is evidence that at least *some* clients have experienced moments of profound connection with their therapists, although it is unclear how common this experience is across a typical client population.

Do clients and therapists experience relational depth at the same time?

There is evidence to suggest, then, that both therapist and client in a therapeutic relationship may experience moments of profound connection to the other. But will they experience it at the same time, that is, 'synchronously'? In other words, if a therapist is feeling deeply connected to their client, can they assume that their client is also experiencing a profound sense of connection at that moment, or could it be that the client is experiencing something altogether different?

In an attempt to answer this question, an 'analogue' study was set up, that is, a study not using bona fide clients, in which pairs of practising or trainee counsellors were asked to conduct 'counselling' sessions of 20 minutes in length (Cooper, 2010b, 2012). 'Clients' were asked to speak about anything of concern, and therapists were asked to respond as they normally would do to their clients. The one difference was that, at each minute, participants were asked to rate how deeply connected they felt to their partner using a zero to ten scale (0 = not at all connected, 10 = deeply connected). This, then, gave an opportunity to see how closely therapists' and clients' ratings of connection to the other would match over time.

Results of this study suggested that the degree of synchrony between therapists' and clients' perceptions of connection is actually relatively high, with an average correlation of around 0.76 across 80 pairs (a correlation of 0 means no matching at all, a correlation of 1 means exact matching). This translates into an average overlap in perceptions of around 45 per cent. Figure 5.1 illustrates ratings from one therapist–client pair of about this magnitude. As can be seen here, while there are some moments in which some disparity exists (for example minute 6, in which the client experiences a reduction in depth of connection but not the therapist), in general, the degree of matching is fairly marked – even above and beyond a general deepening of connection as the session progresses; for instance minute 15, in which both participants experience a reduction in depth of connection, and then a return to greater engagement at minute 17.

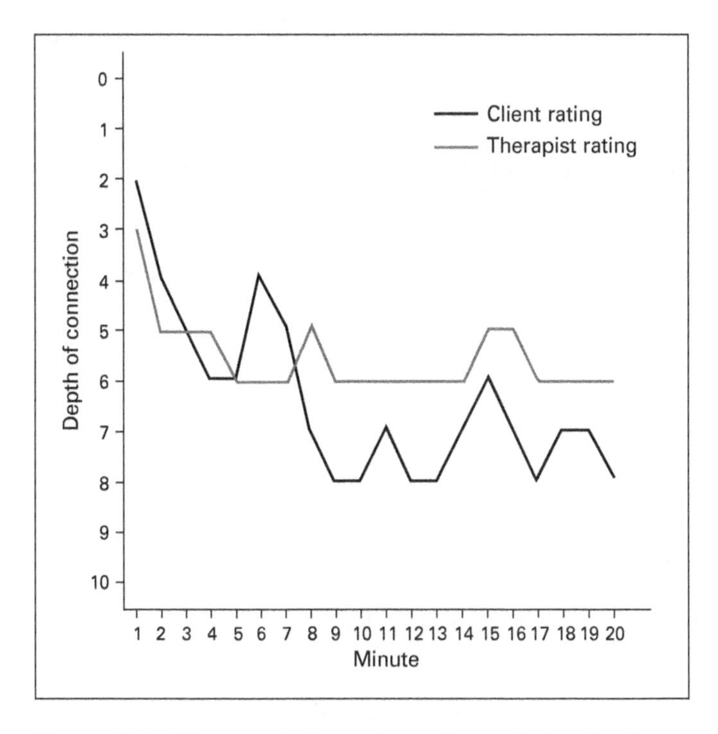

Figure 5.1 Client and therapist ratings of depth of connection
Note: Lower scores indicate greater depth of connection.

This research has several limitations. First, participants were all trainee and practising therapists, such that the 'clients' may have been much more able to tune in to their therapists than most everyday users of therapy. The sessions were also artificial, relatively short, and there was no build-up of a long-term therapeutic relationship. In this respect, the study was much more about feelings of connection than profound moments of relational depth. Of course, asking a person to rate their degree of connection to another person in an actual session is also likely to have made it more difficult for them to relate, although a single case study that invited participants to rate their levels of connection *after* the session also indicated moderate levels of synchrony (Frzina, 2012). Finally, it is quite possible that the relatively high correlation between the two sets of ratings was due to both client and therapist experiencing a general deepening of relating over time, rather than any specific synchrony in experiencing. Nevertheless, two people's ratings of how connected they feel to each other do seem to show some similarity, suggesting that the experience of relational depth may, at least for some of the time, be a genuinely two-person, mutually experienced phenomenon. This also means that therapists can be relatively assured that, if they are feeling deeply connected to their client, there is a good chance (but not a certainty) that the client will be experiencing this as well.

What is it like to experience relational depth?

How does it feel to encounter another at a level of profound depth? More importantly, perhaps, is there some shared, specific experience that a wide range of individuals can recognize, or is relational depth a much more diffuse phenomenon, varying markedly from individual to individual? This was one of the first empirical questions to be asked (Cooper, 2005), and my initial study of person-centred therapists' experiences of relational depth has been followed by interview studies of psychologists' experiences (Morris, 2009), clients' experiences (Knox, 2008, 2011, Chapter 2, this volume; McMillan and McLeod, 2006), trainee therapists' experiences (Connelly, 2009), and the experiences of therapists working with clients with learning disabilities (Macleod, 2009, Chapter 3, this volume). There has also been a 'mixed methods' study, that is, combining quantitative and qualitative inquiry, of clients' and therapists' experiences of relational depth, which included an online survey (Wiggins, 2007, Chapter 4, this volume).

In my initial study (Cooper, 2005), the experience of relational depth was understood in terms of three overarching domains: 'self-experiences', 'experiences of the other' and 'experiences of the relationship'. Knox (2008, 2011) and Wiggins (2007, Chapter 4, this volume) adopted this structure but added a fourth domain, 'experience of the moment itself' or 'atmosphere'; and this four-domain structure was subsequently used by Macleod (2009, Chapter 3, this volume). Connelly (2009) developed a different set of four domains: 'physical', 'emotional', 'spiritual' and 'silence'; as did Morris (2009) with her three domains of 'empathic attunement', 'relational connectedness' and 'use of self'; but these two structures can be relatively easily subsumed into the four-domain structure established by Knox and Wiggins.

Self-experiences

Self-experiences, the first of these four domains, are those things that participants reported experiencing 'in' themselves at times of relational depth. Across the studies (Connelly, 2009; Cooper, 2005; Knox, 2008, 2011; Macleod, 2009; Morris, 2009; Wiggins, 2007; Chapters 2–4, this volume), one of the most common features here was a sense of aliveness: a feeling of energy, exhilaration, empowerment and revitalization, often with a heightened awareness and a greater perceptual clarity. Participants also described feeling spontaneous, free and in-the-moment, with a sense of being very authentic, real, congruent and open at these times – a wholeness or fullness of being.

Frequently, participants described very physical sensations during moments of relational depth; for example electrifying or tingly feelings, and a level of emotional intensity. Paradoxically, however, participants also described feelings of slowing down at moments of relational depth – a sense of calm, peacefulness, relaxation, safety and stillness. They also talked about being immersed in the moment, absorbed, and free from distractions, with some participants likening it to an altered state of consciousness.

Moments of deep connection were generally associated with feelings of satisfaction, happiness, wellbeing and warmth, with a sense of self-worth, self-acceptance and specialness.

Experiences of other

At these times of relational depth, others were experienced as very genuine: real, human and present – coming from the 'core' of their being (Connelly, 2009; Cooper, 2005; Knox, 2008, 2011; Macleod, 2009; McMillan and McLeod, 2006; Morris, 2009; Wiggins, 2007; Chapters 2–4, this volume).

Experiences of the relationship

Participants described powerful feelings of connection, closeness and intimacy with the other at these moments of deep connection (Connelly, 2009; Cooper, 2005; Knox, 2008, 2011; Macleod, 2009; Morris, 2009; Wiggins, 2007; Chapters 2–4, this volume) – a 'heart-to-heart' meeting – often taking place without words. A deep sense of trust was experienced, with some participants also describing feelings of love. At these times of connection, high levels of mutuality were also often felt (see Chapter 14, this volume): a sense of equality, partnership, or of being on a journey together, with a co-acceptance, co-openness and co-reflectiveness. Some participants also described experiencing a bidirectional flow: 'like electricity flowing one from the other' (Macleod, 2009, p. 42); and others described a mutually enhancing reciprocity: not just that they knew the other, but that they knew the other knew that they knew. In a few instances, participants also described feelings of union, fusing or blending: an interlinking or blurring of boundaries.

Experiences of the moment itself

In some of the studies (Connelly, 2009; Cooper, 2005; Knox, 2008, 2011; Macleod, 2009; Wiggins, 2007; Chapters 2–4, this volume), participants described aspects of the experience of relational depth that were less to do with specific intra- or interpersonal experience and more to do with the moment itself, or with the particular atmosphere surrounding the moment. For instance, participants described experiencing these moments of relational depth as unique, rare or strange: something that was surprising, unexpected and difficult to put into words. They also described them as meaningful or significant. Another common feeling during these moments was of being on a different dimension or level, or a strong spiritual or mystical connection. Changes in the perception of time were also commonly described – that it was standing still or being distorted in some way.

Unidimensionality

Although this four-domain structure is a useful means of conceptualizing relational depth, research suggests that the experience of relational depth is a relatively holistic, integrated phenomenon. Indeed, a statistical analysis conducted by Wiggins (2007) suggests that many elements of each of these domains overlap with elements of other domains. In a subsequent analysis, Wiggins found that her Relational Depth Inventory (RDI, a measure designed to assess the depth of particular moments in therapy; see Chapter 4, this volume) was 'pretty much one-dimensional' (personal communication, 2011), suggesting that the principal features associated with an experiencing of relational depth do seem to exist concurrently.

Variations across experiences

In general, a remarkable degree of consistency existed in participants' descriptions of the experiences of relational depth – both across participants in the same study and across studies (Connelly, 2009; Cooper, 2005; Knox, 2008, 2011; Macleod, 2009; Wiggins, 2007; Chapters 2–4, this volume).

However, some significant differences have emerged in how clients and therapists described their experiences of relational depth, consistent with their specific roles. For instance, in terms of self-experiences, therapists were particularly likely to describe feelings of respect and empathy for others (Wiggins et al., 2012), heightened empathy and focus, with an enhanced acceptance of the other, and a feeling of being privileged to engage with their clients at this level of depth (Cooper, 2005; Macleod, 2009; Morris, 2009). By contrast, at times of relational depth, clients were more likely to describe feelings of being known, understood, cared for and accepted; as well as feeling vulnerable (Knox, 2008, 2011; Wiggins et al., 2012) and scared (Wiggins et al., 2012) and delving deeply into themselves (Knox, 2008, 2011, Chapter 2, this volume). Consistent with this, therapists were more likely to perceive their clients as vulnerable and opening up at these times (Cooper, 2005; Macleod, 2009; Morris, 2009); while clients were more likely to perceive their therapists as empathic, warm, inviting and creating opportunities, with a sense of reliability, trustworthiness or solidity; and offering something 'over and above' the core conditions (see below) (Knox, 2008, 2011, Chapter 2, this volume).

These differences between therapists' and clients' experiences of relational depth raise the question of whether it is, indeed, a mutual experience – with bidirectional feelings of empathy, understanding and openness – or whether, as McMillan and McLeod (2006, p. 289) argue, this is primarily the therapists' perception. What evidence there is so far suggests that the answer is probably somewhere in between. On the one hand, as discussed above, therapists are much more likely to experience feelings of empathy and understanding *towards* the other at times of relational depth than clients; and, indeed, items on 'understanding the therapist' and 'knowing the other's mind' were among the least endorsed by clients on the RDI (Wiggins, 2011a). On the other hand, and contrary to McMillan and McLeod's findings, clients *have* specifically described feelings of mutuality with their therapists at times of relational depth (Knox, 2008, 2011, Chapter 2, this volume) and, perhaps surprisingly, this is most marked in non-therapist clients. One client stated, for instance:

> There are times when we two, very open ... damaged individuals. She [the therapist] opens up her damage to me and I open my damage to her ... And when we do connect, and when [name of therapist] affirms me, what I need that, I am actually contributing to her life, and I know she's contributing to mine. (Knox, 2011, p. 210)

Summary

Research into the experience of relational depth paints a vivid picture of what it is like to meet another human being at this level of profound connectedness. It is, to summarize:

> A sense of connectedness and flow with another person that is so powerful that it can feel quite magical. At these times, the person feels alive, immersed in the encounter, and truly themselves; while experiencing the other as open, genuine and valuing of who they are. (Cooper, 2009)

The striking commonalities in how this experience is described – both across participants within the same study and across studies – suggest that the phenomenon of relational depth 'is a real and distinctive occurrence' (Cooper, 2005, p. 93). At the same time, however, the evidence does suggest that there are certain asymmetries in how moments of relational depth are experienced by therapists and clients, with the former more likely to experience feelings of empathy and acceptance towards the other, and the latter more likely to experience feelings of vulnerability and self-inquiry. Whether this is a fundamental challenge to the assumption of mutuality in relational depth, however, or simply a difference of focus and content, remains to be seen.

What is the relationship between relational depth and therapeutic outcomes?

A key assumption behind the concept of relational depth (see, for example, Mearns and Cooper, 2005), indeed, its very raison d'être, is that deeper levels of relating lead to 'better' outcomes in counselling and psychotherapy. But is there actually any evidence that this is the case?

Some of the strongest evidence to support this hypothesis comes from a recent study by Wiggins (2011b, Chapter 4, this volume). Using her RDI, Wiggins invited clients to identify a particular helpful moment or event in therapy, and then to rate how accurately 24 items associated with relational depth fitted with this experience. Wiggins then looked at whether relational depth was predictive of positive therapeutic outcome, and found that it was, with depth of relating accounting for a striking 10–30 per cent of the overall outcomes. In other words, the more that clients experienced relational depth at a particular helpful moment in therapy, the more they improved.

In addition, research by Murphy (2010, Chapter 14, this volume) suggests that the association between clients' rating of the therapist core conditions and outcome is enhanced when mutuality exists in therapists' and clients' perceptions of the therapeutic relationship.

More subjective evidence come from Leung (2008), who asked participants to rate, on a 7-point scale, how important they thought moments of relational depth were for personal change and for the outcomes of therapy (1 = not at all, 7 = extremely). On average, therapists gave it a rating of 5.69 and clients gave it a rating of 5.78, indicating that these moments were seen as being very important for therapeutic change, with no significant difference between therapists' and clients' ratings. Participants were also asked to rate, using a similar 7-point scale, the extent to which they thought these moments of relational depth had an enduring impact. Both therapists and clients gave this a mean rating of 5.87, again suggesting that moments of relational depth were seen as being strongly therapeutic. A majority of clients in Knox's (2008, 2011, Chapter 2, this volume) interview studies also felt that moments of relational depth had had a significant positive impact, both immediately and in the longer term; as did clients interviewed by Omielan (2009).

In terms of the specific effects that a meeting at relational depth might have, participants in Knox's (2008, 2011, Chapter 2, this volume) research identified two immediate impacts: a general experience of the moments as facilitative, healing and changing; and a positive effect on the therapeutic process itself. Participants in these studies also described the long-term effects of these moments: an increased sense of connection to their own selves, feeling more powerful, feeling better, and improved relationships with others.

In summary, new research by Wiggins (2011b) and Murphy (2010) suggests that the depth of relating and mutuality between therapists and clients at particular moments in therapy is strongly predictive of positive therapeutic outcomes. However, these studies are in need of replication, and it is important to emphasize that they do not necessarily establish causality: it may be, for instance, that a third factor, such as clients' levels of motivation, determines both the depth of relating and outcomes. More qualitative evidence, however, does support the view that moments of in-depth relating have a direct positive effect.

What facilitates a meeting at relational depth?

A meeting at relational depth, as Mearns and Cooper (2005) argue, is not something that therapists can *make* happen. But are there ways in which the likelihood of such a depth of encounter can be enhanced? Given, as indicated above, that such meetings may have important therapeutic benefits, this may be a key question to ask. Research on facilitative factors, as well as inhibiting ones, is still in its infancy (Knox, 2011; Knox and Cooper, 2010, 2011; Macleod, 2009; see Chapters 2 and 3, this volume), yet, already, some of the most fascinating findings in the field are beginning to emerge here.

Therapist factors

In looking at the therapist factors that were associated with the emergence of moments of relational depth, Knox (2011, Chapter 2, this volume; Knox and Cooper, 2010) identified two main domains: who therapists were, and what therapists did. In terms of the first of these categories, 'therapists' personal characteristics', clients described the therapists who they had related at depth with as warmth, empathic and courteous. In addition, they had experienced these therapists as *psychologically sound*: strong, comfortable with their own selves, and willing to relate at depth. Perhaps most interestingly, though, clients also felt that these moments of relational depth had taken place with therapists who were, in some way, similar or matching to themselves, for example with similar beliefs or perceived lifestyles. The clients also described these therapists as the 'right' sort of person, with some, particularly the non-therapists, likening them to the mother or father they had never had. This last finding is consistent with research by McMillan and MacLeod (2006, p. 285), who found that many participants described their therapist in deeply facilitative relationship as 'like a good or ideal mother'.

In terms of what a therapist who they had related at depth with had *done*, Knox (2011, Chapter 2, this volume; Knox and Cooper, 2010) found that clients emphasized their patience, their ability to create a welcoming and safe atmosphere, and to act in a way that was trustworthy, reliable and professional. Being accepting, open and understanding were also important features of these therapists. However, two further, particularly interesting factors also emerged. First, clients talked about the way these therapists had been *really* real and human: just genuine, themselves and not faking things or putting themselves on a professional pedestal. Second, and very much in line with findings from McMillan and MacLeod (2006, p. 285), they describe these therapists as offering something 'over and above' what they would expect from a professional relationship: a genuine, very real commitment and care. This experience of feeling deeply cared for and nurtured in relationships in which relational depth was experienced was also identified by Omielan (2009). Interestingly, too, the clients emphasized how the therapists who they had met at depth felt really on their side: not just a neutral, nonjudgemental presence, but someone who actively prized them, and saw things in their way. They also talked about the therapist's encouragement and pride in them, and holding the hope for their future.

Client factors

Perhaps the most interesting finding to emerge from Knox's (2011, Chapter 2, this volume; Knox and Cooper, 2010, 2011) interview studies with clients, however, is that the key precursors of a meeting at relational depth may be less to do with therapists, and more to do with the clients themselves. Clients, in these studies, did describe how challenges from the therapist, or changes in how they experienced the therapist or the relationship, preceded moments of relational depth. But they also talked extensively about the importance of their own readiness and desire to engage at depth, and how that had been an essential precursor to the depth of meeting. In addition, while clients talked about heightened levels of emotion prior to the moment of relational depth, they also described it as something they had proactively entered into: a deliberate choice to take the risk and open up.

Summary

While therapists cannot make moments of relational depth happen, the research suggests that they may be able to facilitate their emergence through communicating a genuine care and a commitment to clients, as well as creating a safe, professional and warm therapeutic environment. Ultimately, however, it may be that clients, rather than therapists, are the principal factor in determining whether or not meetings at depth will take place, and more evidence is needed on what it is that clients do to make this happen.

What factors inhibit a meeting at relational depth?

Unsurprisingly perhaps, clients' perceptions of the qualities of therapeutic relationships in which relational depth was *not* experienced was the near reverse of those in which it was (Knox, 2011, Chapter 2, this volume; Knox and Cooper, 2010). Therapists were experienced as cold and distant, uncaring, and failing to understand the client or invite them into deeper levels of relating. In some cases, they were also experienced as too different from the client, and using a therapeutic style that the client did not feel suited them. In addition, they tended to perceive these therapists as inexperienced and unprofessional and, in some instances, manipulative or misusing power.

Research from Connelly (2009) with trainee therapists also found that fear and anxiety were experienced as inhibiting an openness to relational depth, as were personal defences. Participants also spoke of the risk of being shamed.

Conclusion

To summarize what the research tells us so far: a majority of therapists, particularly of a person-centred and humanistic orientation, seem to have experienced moments of relational depth with their clients. At least some clients seem to have experienced these moments too, and there is some evidence to suggest that this experiencing is relatively synchronous. The experience itself can be described as a feeling of deep immersion in a connection with another human being who is experienced as very genuine and real. There is a growing body of evidence to suggest that the experiencing of moments of relational depth is associated with positive therapeutic outcomes, and it seems that therapists can facilitate the likelihood that these moments will emerge by expressing their genuine care and commitment in the therapeutic relationship. Ultimately, however, it may be that clients are the principal determinants of whether or not an encounter at relational depth takes place.

Relational depth is not something that we can, or would ever want to, pin down. It exists by virtue of its mystery, its ability to surprise and take hold of us and transform our lives in ways that we cannot predict or control. And yet, by discovering more about it, we can help to keep it central to our lives and our work: a never-ending inquiry into the heart of therapeutic relating, where the journey, and not the destination, is the ultimate goal.

References

Buber, M. (1947) *Between Man and Man* (trans. R.G. Smith). London: Fontana.

Cain, D.J. (2010) *Person-centered Psychotherapies*. Washington, DC: APA.

Connelly, A.E. (2009) Trainee therapists and relational depth. Unpublished MSc dissertation, Sherwood Psychotherapy Training Institute, Nottingham.

Cooper, M. (2005) Therapists' experiences of relational depth: A qualitative interview study. *Counselling and Psychotherapy Research*, 5(2), 87–95.

Cooper, M. (2008) *Essential Research Findings in Counselling and Psychotherapy: The Facts are Friendly*. London: Sage.

Cooper, M. (2009) Relational depth: Where we are now. Paper presented at the 2nd Relational Depth Research Conference, University of Nottingham.

Cooper, M. (2010a) The challenge of counselling and psychotherapy research. *Counselling and Psychotherapy Research*, 10(3), 183–91.

Cooper, M. (2010b) Synchrony in clients' and therapists' experiences of relational depth: An analogue study. Paper presented at the COSCA 7th Counselling Research Dialogue, Sterling.

Cooper, M. (2012) Clients' and therapists' perceptions of intrasessional connection: An analogue study of change over time, predictor variables, and level of consensus. *Psychotherapy Research*, 22(3), 274–87.

Frzina, J. (2012) A case study exploring experience of relational depth between therapist and client in a single session recorded during a skills practice. *Counselling Psychology Review*, 27(2), 52–62.

Hatcher, R.L. and Gillaspy, J.A. (2006) Development and validation of a revised short version of the Working Alliance Inventory. *Psychotherapy Research*, 16(1), 12–25.

Knox, R. (2008) Clients' experiences of relational depth in person-centred counselling. *Counselling and Psychotherapy Research*, 8(3), 118–24.

Knox, R. (2011) Clients' experiences of relational depth. Unpublished PhD dissertation, University of Strathclyde, Glasgow.

Knox, R. and Cooper, M. (2010) Relationship qualities that are associated with moments of relational depth: The client's perspective. *Person-Centered and Experiential Psychotherapies*, 9(3), 236–56.

Knox, R. and Cooper, M. (2011) A state of readiness: An exploration of the client's role in meeting at relational depth. *Journal of Humanistic Psychology*, 51(1), 61–81.

Leung, J. (2008) A quantitative online study exploring the factors associated with the experience and perception of relational depth. Unpublished DPsych dissertation, University of Strathclyde, Glasgow.

Macleod, E. (2009) A qualitative exploration into therapists' perceptions of reaching relational depth when counselling people with learning disabilities. Unpublished MSc dissertation, University of Strathclyde, Glasgow.

McMillan, M. and McLeod, J. (2006) Letting go: The client's experience of relational depth. *Person-Centered and Experiential Psychotherapies*, 5(4), 277–92.

Mearns, D. (1997) *Person-Centred Counselling Training*. London: Sage.

Mearns, D. (2003) *Developing Person-Centred Counselling* (2nd edn). London: Sage.

Mearns, D. and Cooper, M. (2005) *Working at Relational Depth in Counselling and Psychotherapy*. London: Sage.

Morris, G. (2009) Psychologists' experiences of relational depth: A qualitative interview study. Unpublished DPsych thesis, University of Strathclyde, Glasgow.

Murphy, D. (2010) Psychotherapy as mutual encounter: A study of therapeutic conditions. Unpublished PhD dissertation, Loughborough University, Loughborough.

Omielan, R. (2009) The influence of relational depth on therapeutic relationships: A narrative inquiry into client experience. Unpublished MSc dissertation, University of Bristol, Bristol.

Wiggins, S. (2007) Developing an inventory designed to assess relational depth. Unpublished MSc dissertation, University of Strathclyde, Glasgow.

Wiggins, S. (2011a) Development and validation of a measure of relational depth. Unpublished PhD dissertation, University of Strathclyde, Glasgow.

Wiggins, S. (2011b) Relational depth and therapeutic outcome. Paper presented at the 17th Annual BACP Research Conference, Edinburgh.

Wiggins, S., Elliott, R. and Cooper, M. (2012) The prevalence and characteristics of relational depth events in psychotherapy. *Psychotherapy Research*, 22(2), 139–58.

PART II

Relational Depth in Context

6

Working at relational depth with children and young people

Sue Hawkins

This chapter explores the concept of relational depth in therapeutic relationships with children and young people. I will explore theoretical perspectives through my practice as a psychologist working with young offenders.

Most of us can remember the relationships with adults we had as children that changed us for the better. Perhaps it was a family member, a teacher or youth worker or a friend who listened, gave us time, understanding, or who trusted or believed in us. Rogers ([1980]1990) described the actualizing tendency, the innate human potential for growth, and the capacity for it to be activated by a positive relationship experience.

In a longitudinal study in Minnesota of the childhood attachments of 180 people from birth to adulthood, Sroufe et al. (2005) found that children needed only one secure attachment figure in order to thrive and that this could be a professional, such as a teacher or social worker, a carer or family member. This research reinforces the notion that for children and young people who have experienced poor early attachments, a good therapeutic relationship can serve as a 'corrective relational experience' (Jordan, 1991).

My therapeutic work is with young people who have been convicted of offences, mostly violent. My clients are generally male, working class and aged between 13 and 18. Nearly all have a background of abuse, neglect, trauma, bereavement or loss and economic disadvantage. Many have either suffered or witnessed domestic abuse; physical, emotional and sexual. Most have grown up in families where boundaries are lacking or frequently transgressed. Many have taken on a caring role in relation to their parents or siblings. Most have had an unsatisfactory experience of education, including school nonattendance or exclusion. Nearly all of them are frightened, traumatized, hurt and angry and can manifest these feelings through violence to others and harm to themselves. Although each client's history is unique, most have experienced difficulties in their formative attachments. They seem to share a sense of disconnection from their 'inner world' of thoughts and feelings, their inherent worth, their families, friends and society.

Working at relational depth with this client group can feel challenging. There are constraints in terms of the physical environment. For example, interview rooms in youth offending team buildings and young offenders institutions have security cameras and doors with windows. However, I believe it is possible for two people to create their own climate within the therapy room and transcend these limitations.

As Mearns and Cooper (2005) suggest, relational depth cannot be forced, nor does it relate only to verbal communication. For example, I recently worked with a nine-year-old boy who presented as withdrawn and 'frozen' after witnessing the traumatic death of his brother, two years before. For four months, I worked with him weekly at his school, primarily using sand trays and miniatures. For the first four sessions, he mostly played in silence. In the fifth session, he invited me into his world of play, suggesting I build a house for the character, SpongeBob SquarePants, and from then on, we played together, me following his lead. We never talked about his brother's death, although death was frequently a theme in his play, but it felt that there was a 'knowingness' between us that we were exploring this issue and that it was only safe for him to express it metaphorically. After a session in which, through play, he narrated the story of SpongeBob SquarePants being visited at night by the ghost of his friend (represented by a toy skeleton), he looked me directly in the eye and asked if he could take the skeleton home. In this moment of connection, I sensed there was a mutual understanding of the significance of this but felt it would be painful and unnecessary for him to verbalize it and so I simply agreed he could keep the skeleton.

Gradually, this boy seemed, almost miraculously, to 'thaw out'; he began to interact more with others in school and display positive feelings and an 'aliveness' that previously had been absent. During this time, I would periodically want to question and analyse what was happening – after all, I wasn't really 'doing' anything. However, my sense was of inhabiting the world of the 'right brain', where language wasn't necessary, but there was also a powerful connection between us, a way of being together that would ultimately be healing.

Relational depth: connecting to the felt sense

For many children, language as a means of expression does not come naturally. This can be due to their age, cognitive ability, personality or individual preference for mode of expression. Many of the young people I work with seem highly attuned to the unspoken aspects of communication. In the therapeutic relationship, this ability allows young people to sense very subtle communications between two people; communications that seem to operate outside conscious awareness.

Even for articulate young people with access to expressive language, like all of us, much of what they know has never been consciously thought or verbalized. 'Felt sense' is the term Gendlin (1981) used to refer to the unclear preverbal sense of 'something', as in something is experienced in the body. This is closely linked to the term 'embodied empathy' (Cooper, 2001). The felt sense is not the same as an emotion. This bodily felt something may be of a situation, or of something that is 'coming', like an idea or the line of a poem. It is not necessarily something that will be expressed in words, for example it might be the right line to complete a drawing or the next note in composing music. In fact, Gendlin argues that we can never capture the felt sense in words without distorting it. It is always more than its expression.

I believe that the child development process in Western societies involves the shutting down of the felt sense and the prioritizing of the intellectual faculties, so that by the teenage years, 'heart awareness' is largely lost. Many of my young clients have built robust walls around their 'hearts', mainly to protect themselves against hurts. While walls provide a boundary and protection, they also exclude people and make intimacy ('into-me-see') difficult.

Many young people I have worked with can present cognitive justifications for even the most violent crimes. I have noticed that as my clients start to get in touch with their heart awareness or felt sense, they appear to have less desire to hurt themselves or others. When I am in touch with my own heart-centredness and respond to a client from this place, my work becomes more creative and I find myself responding spontaneously without consciously thinking about what I am saying or doing. I trust my moment-by-moment sensing without analysing it. Gendlin (1981) compares this process to the golfer whose body just knows how to move. Knowing when to swing is a felt sense for the golfer, not a mental process.

Presence and relational depth

My interest in relational depth developed out of an interest in 'presence'. This did not come from my training as a person-centred therapist, but through an experience I had in Thailand seven years ago, when I attended a meditation class in a temple in Bangkok with a friend. The monk led us through a meditation and told us about his life. As we left, both my friend and I sobbed – it had been a brief but deeply moving experience that seemed to transcend words. It was only later that I could pinpoint the monk's powerful presence as the transformative factor. He had seemed so peaceful and completely in tune with everything and everyone around him. He radiated love and compassion.

Geller and Greenberg (2002) describe three aspects of therapist's presence:

- *inwardly attending:* how the experience of the client resonates in the therapist's body
- *receptivity:* taking in and accepting the fullness of the client's experience
- *extending and contact:* being transparent and accessible to the client.

I often notice subtle shifts in my body when I am with clients, frequently located around the heart area. Sometimes I can describe the sensation but often it is purely physical. When I can inwardly attend and communicate from it, clients seem to make leaps in healing, maybe because they are able to get in touch with their own heart-centredness.

Ellingham (2007) suggests that such an experience of relational depth is like that of mystics who describe experiencing oneness with a greater reality while still retaining a sense of self. Ellingham (2009) suggests that the transcendent aspect of relational depth links with the Buddhist concept of 'mindfulness'. This fits with my experience. After my experience in Bangkok, I began a daily meditation practice, through which I gained a sense of openness, stillness and emptiness that enables me to be more available and connect more fully and at a deeper level with my clients.

These moments arise unexpectedly and are usually fleeting. In such moments, I feel a sense of being in complete alignment or congruence within myself, with my client and with the universe. It feels as though we are both 'plugged into' something greater. I sometimes experience this timelessness as an absence of thought, as my sensing is centred in the stillness of the present. These moments of deep connectedness can be even more powerful when working with children and young people than with adults. I remember a session with a traumatized 10-year-old boy, whose feelings often manifested as rage. We had been very still, connected and 'in the moment', making a farm together out of art materials. Out of the stillness, he asked me: 'Sue, God still loves me even when I'm angry, doesn't he?' I confirmed that I believed this was indeed the case.

Thorne (1991, p. 76) spoke of the quality of tenderness, which he described as 'a quality which irradiates the total person'. Through the quality of tenderness, the notion that 'suffering and healing are interwoven' is communicated (Thorne, 1991, p. 76), which is pertinent to my work. My most successful work has been with clients who, consciously or unconsciously, have decided that they have experienced enough suffering and want it to stop. The point at which this happens is different for each individual. For some it might be when they enter the youth justice system and for others it might be when they are released from custody.

The challenges of working at relational depth with children and young people

Thorne (1991, p. 76) also describes tenderness as 'a quality which transcends male and female but is nevertheless nourished by the attraction of one for the other in the quest for wholeness'. With young people who are stuck in rage, aggression or violence, it is important not to dismiss those feelings or urges, as they frequently stem from the 'masculine' drive to try to protect others. However, it is useful to work to balance them with the more 'feminine' qualities of tenderness, empathy, kindness and compassion. For most of my clients, these qualities have been largely absent in their families.

Furthermore, Thorne (1991, p. 76) describes tenderness as 'without shame because it is experienced as the joyful embracing of the desire to love and is therefore a law unto itself'. Although I fully relate to Thorne's description of feeling love for a client, I can equally relate to his

> deep and almost pathological distrust of something which brings such joy and such clarity. It is as if *joy and knowledge are forbidden fruits* and the experience of them must therefore be evidence of dubious motives and unhealthy desires or of insanity. (Thorne, 1991, p. 77)

The motives of therapists who work with children and adolescents are even more likely to be questioned than those of workers with adults. Sadly, we live in a culture where love for a child or young person outside one's own family or social network is often eyed with suspicion. Therapy with children and young people seldom takes place in a private, confidential place and workers are trained to be vigilant against potential allegations of abuse, despite the fact that statistically children and young people are far more likely to be abused within their own homes.

In our material world, love can be contaminated and distorted and associated with control, dependency, possession, lust, rejection, jealousy, hurt, abandonment and abuse. This has been the past experience of 'love' for many of my young clients. Thus, to provide a different model of love is, in itself, therapeutic and healing. I would describe the process of working with a young person as aligning with the qualities of love and compassion, communicating with my client from that place so that my positive feelings towards them can become internalized, and trusting that if I am successful, the client's desire to harm themselves or others will fall away without any deliberate attempt to try to make it happen. This goes against the conventional perspectives within youth offending that focus directly on the offending behaviour. But as Rogers (1951, p. 491) states in proposition 5 of his 19 propositions: 'Behaviour is basically the goal-directed attempt of the organism to satisfy its needs, as experienced in the field as perceived.' In other words, behaviour is the symptom of distress, not the cause.

Working with Tom

I will attempt to illustrate some of the qualities of working at relational depth through my work with Tom, a client who kindly agreed to be interviewed for this chapter.

Tom spent nine months in custody, convicted of a violent sexual offence. He initially only agreed to work with me because it was part of his release conditions that he see a psychologist. We both felt uncomfortable about this but decided we would have three sessions, after which he could stop if he wished. Our third session had come to an end. Tom was agitated as he had no money for the weekend and wanted to get to the bank before it closed. The words that I spontaneously uttered were: 'Come on, I'll give you a lift.' I hadn't consciously thought why it felt right to do this. If I had, I may not have acted on my intuition. In that moment I didn't know, in a cognitive sense, why I made the offer. I was 'out of my mind', in the sense that I was being guided by a sense beyond thoughts of 'right' and 'wrong' therapist behaviour.

Tom got into my car and, as I didn't know the area, I asked him to navigate. He directed me through a council housing estate. We chatted about cars, but in between the chitchat, he suddenly said: 'See that house over there? I was held hostage at gunpoint in that house.' My response was: 'That sounds terrifying', then, 'I know that happened – I read it in your file, but I didn't know that was the house.' Tom said: 'Turn left here and drop me on the corner.'

It felt that this was a significant moment of relational depth in which Tom trusted me enough to tell me about the most terrifying event of his life. The disclosure was merely factual and 'bookmarked' to return to later. I couldn't have pursued it more at that time, partly because I was driving but also because I felt Tom had reached his intimacy threshold and I needed to *empathically match* the depth of relating that felt comfortable for him.

I later wondered whether I had been foolish in allowing Tom into my car in an unfamiliar area but realized that was only significant if I believed in 'the story of Tom', as told by other people, over my own sensing. I also questioned my boundaries as I never usually have contact with young people outside the therapy room but this felt like an exceptional situation. In the next few sessions, Tom told me about his early experiences of domestic violence and abuse and linked these with his own offences. It seemed my trust in him was reciprocated.

Our sessions continued and every week something dramatic happened in Tom's family, which prevented us from focusing on the past. A can of worms had been opened as family members began to tell each other of abuse they had experienced, narratives spanning generations. Part of me felt scared and unsure where we were going; hurtling along to an unknown destination. I felt my trust in the client's actualizing tendency and the healing quality of the relationship were being severely tested.

One week, Tom arrived for the session feeling enraged. His sister had disclosed being sexually abused by a family friend and he felt he could not ignore this. He knew where the perpetrator lived and said he was willing to go to prison for killing him.

Despite my fear that Tom might actually do this, I knew that, to be facilitative, I had to connect with and accept all of him without condition, including the potentially violent, even murderous part. Mearns and Thorne (2000) stress the importance of listening to the whole of the client and engaging with the many configurations of self. I am very careful in my work with young offenders not to focus on one aspect of self and ignore the aspects that I might find less palatable, as the client's own struggle is to accept and integrate these different parts.

Tom talked through his feelings, the potential consequences of his actions and I told him that, although I obviously could not stop him from seeking retribution, I felt he deserved better than a life in custody. This felt like a profound moment and Tom paused, took a deep breath and told me how much it meant to him to hear that. It felt like he was really absorbing my feelings towards him. The following week, Tom told me that during that week he had bought a staple gun and had planned to go round to the perpetrator's house and torture him by 'stapling his balls to the table' but that 'something' had stopped him. He seemed confused as to why he had not responded in the way he usually did.

In a later session, Tom told me that he had been out shopping and had bumped into the man who had taken him and his family hostage when he was eight years old. The shock was intense as Tom's mother had told him the man was dead. There was a verbal exchange in which Tom had been assertive rather than aggressive and I was impressed that in such a trying situation, he had not resorted to violence. Another week, he explained that he had similarly bumped into the man who had sexually abused his sister and again a verbal exchange ensued but no violence. I shared with Tom my shock at all these seeming 'coincidences', and he said that he felt 'someone up there' was testing him. It seemed true that had they happened any earlier, Tom might not have had the skills to respond in the way that he did. I experienced the sense of 'moving between worlds of the physical, the emotional, the cognitive and the mystical' that Thorne (1991, p. 76) describes.

During all these 'tests', I felt a corresponding test of my faith in my abilities as a therapist and in Tom's ability to learn and grow from the experiences rather than fall back on 'default' violent behaviour. Trusting one's intuitions can feel risky in this work because, if my intuitions are wrong, there are serious consequences to reoffending for both my clients and their potential victims. I felt like a tightrope walker, carefully walking the wire with Tom, the only difference between us being that, for him, there was no safety net.

Throughout this period, I wondered whether I could offer Tom enough for him to heal and whether I could hold my nerve. In my 15 years of working as a therapist, it was the greatest test of my faith in the healing power of love. I wondered whether Tom had experienced enough compassion and caring from me to care enough about himself to not risk breaching his licence conditions.

After six months of working together, however, Tom completed his licence period without reoffending. I feel confident that he will never return to custody. Although Tom's childhood offered a distorted view of love and relationships, towards the end of our work together he began a new relationship. He discusses his relationships in the interview:

Tom: I came out of a violent relationship and now I'm in a new one and nothing violent happens. It's all about communication. I grew up in an environment where no one could communicate. But when you learn how to communicate properly, you don't have to communicate with your body language – I used to hit walls as my way of saying, 'Please, stop having a go', but now I've learnt to communicate with my mouth and not my fist … I've come on in leaps and bounds – I'm now able to treat my girlfriend in a nice manner. We still have our arguments, don't get me wrong, but I don't hit out. We can relax together without all this trauma stuff … I have a safe place in my head that I can always go to and you've got to have a safe place.

Sue: That's such an achievement, Tom – you didn't have a safe place growing up as a child.

Tom: Never mind a safe place, Sue, sometimes I didn't even have a *place* – I lived on the streets and was in and out of care homes.

I was interested in Tom's comment about communication because I had only ever perceived Tom to be socially skilled and articulate. But being verbally skilled is not much use unless someone will listen:

Tom: You're constantly battling with yourself when you have no one to talk to … when you're living in that world on your own, you don't really understand your own feelings and you feel like a weirdo for having them.

This feeling of aloneness is commonly described by the young people with whom I work, which is why connection, to be 'felt' by another human being, is so important.

To survive, young people who grow up in households where there has been abuse or violence become experts at reading other people, gauging subtleties in their communication so they can quickly work out people's disposition and intentions – whether they care, are genuine, trustworthy and so on. This sense is often finely tuned and therefore they need to be met by a congruent and consistent adult. Many of my clients have been let down, rejected, criticized or abandoned by significant others, so I am sensitive to where this could be perceived to be happening in our relationship. Most tend to mistrust others, so it is important to be vigilant about issues of trust in the therapeutic relationship.

Being believed and trusted were very important for Tom. He discusses how these were significant factors in previous relationships and how he feels the need to bring me proof of things that happened. For example, he has brought his sister and girlfriend in as 'witnesses' to events for fear of not being believed. He related this to his experiences of early abuse and neglect when his mother told him that nobody would believe him if he reported it.

In my work, I want to share as much of myself as is necessary to build a relationship with a young person. This is different in every relationship. Tom discusses the importance of my self-disclosure for him:

Tom: When you tell me about some of your day-to-day activities, it makes a person feel more comfortable – you tell me little things about your life and before you know it, you've got a kind of friendship thing going on … If you don't know anything about a person, you're not gonna want to open up to them. That's a big thing – if you hadn't told me anything about your life, I'd be thinking, 'Why should I tell you anything about mine?'

Self-disclosure means sharing my thoughts and feelings about a young person, including my absolute and unconditional prizing of them as a human being, which is vital for trust to develop.

Offering unconditional prizing, compassion or love for a young person feels quite a radical position to hold at times in a youth offending culture and system, which increasingly focuses on the 'victim' and punishment of the 'perpetrator' and sees these as fixed roles. However, I cannot see how one can begin to feel compassion or empathy for another until one has received those qualities within a secure relationship. I sometimes feel I am at odds with some of my colleagues, in the sense that I fear my trust and belief in my clients might be judged as naive.

Towards the end of our work together, Tom began to develop a sense of the essential worthiness of all human beings, and through experiencing compassion and prizing in our relationship, he was able to feel it for others. In this way, a therapeutic relationship offers a 'corrective relational experience' (Jordan, 1991), in that it changes both the relationship with self and how the client relates to others. Tom felt so certain that I would judge him that in the first session, he immediately told me about his offence. In the interview, I remind Tom of this:

Sue: I felt that from the start you needed to get your offence out in the open, like, 'If you're gonna judge me, please just quickly get it over and done with.'

Tom: Sue, you are *not* wrong, you are *not* wrong.

Young people who have committed acts of violence can carry a lot of shame, which frequently echoes the shame they experienced in their families. Shame can be such a toxic emotion that it is a huge risk to open themselves to another with the possibility of being further shamed. While working with Tom, I oscillated between trusting the process and feeling fearful. However, I believe that when I was at my best, there was very little 'ego' present and at such times, the relationship seemed to have the capacity to heal what needed to be healed. I had to work hard on my fears to maintain this quality and there were times when my fears became obstacles to being fully present.

Conclusion

The ability to work at relational depth is not something that can be easily taught but it can be modelled and developed through practice. I believe that moments of profound connection have a spiritual and transcendent quality and are encouraged by a spiritual practice such as meditation.

I am sincerely grateful to Tom for being the special person that he is and for choosing to take this journey together. This relationship has provided an invaluable opportunity to develop my capacity to work with young people at relational depth and to learn to love unconditionally – what a gift. In my work with Tom, we have both inhabited the role of teacher and pupil, as we have been prepared to risk being fully human, to risk feeling shame and to trust that some mutual growth and learning would develop from our encounter.

References

Cooper, M. (2001) Embodied empathy. In S. Haugh and T. Merry (eds) *Rogers' Therapeutic Conditions: Evolution, Theory and Practice*, vol. 2, *Empathy* (pp. 218–19). Ross-on-Wye: PCCS Books.

Ellingham, I. (2007) Non-directivity and relational depth: Two forms of mysticism? *Person-Centred Quarterly*, May, 1–3.

Ellingham, I. (2009) Person-centred therapy and the mindful I/thou, mystical/spiritual dimension: The multi-level nature of relational depth and mental distress. *Person-Centred Quarterly*, November, 2–4.

Geller, S.M. and Greenberg, L.S. (2002) Therapeutic presence: Therapists' experiences of presence in the psychotherapy encounter. *Person-Centered and Experiential Psychotherapies*, 1, 71–86.

Gendlin, E.T. (1981) *Focusing* (2nd edn). New York: Bantam Books.

Jordan, J.V. (1991) Empathy, mutuality and therapeutic change: Clinical implications of a relational model. In J.V. Jordan, A.G. Kaplan, J. Baker Miller et al. (eds) *Women's Growth in Connection: Writings from the Stone Center* (pp. 283–90). New York: Guilford Press.

Mearns, D. (1996) Contact at relational depth. *Counselling*, 7, 306–11.

Mearns. D. and Cooper, M. (2005) *Working at Relational Depth in Counselling and Psychotherapy*. London: Sage.

Mearns, D. and Thorne, B. (2000) *Therapy Today: New Frontiers in Theory and Practice*. London: Sage.

Rogers, C.R. (1951) *Client-Centred Therapy*. London: Constable.

Rogers, C.R. ([1980]1990) Growing old: Or older and growing. In H. Kirschenbaum and V. Henderson (eds) *The Carl Rogers Reader* (pp. 37–56). London: Constable.

Sroufe, L.A., Egeland, B., Carlson, E. and Collins, W.A. (2005) *The Development of the Person: The Minnesota Study of Risk and Adaptation from Birth to Adulthood*. New York: Guilford Press.

Thorne, B. (1991) *Person-centred Counselling: Therapeutic and Spiritual Dimensions.* London: Whurr.

7

Facilitating posttraumatic growth through relational depth

David Murphy and Stephen Joseph

Working as psychologists specializing in psychotherapy at an NHS trauma service, we have seen first hand how traumatic life events can have a devastating effect on a person's psychological health. By the time people reach therapy, the traumatic event might not be the most apparent difficulty in their life and while the client may have problems of posttraumatic stress, they may also report feelings of depression or anxiety, difficulties functioning at home or at work, or substance misuse. People who have experienced trauma often come to therapy with multiple problems.

In instances when a person has been diagnosed with posttraumatic stress disorder, they will be referred for therapy in line with National Institute for Clinical Excellence (NICE, 2006) Clinical Guideline 26 for the treatment and management of posttraumatic stress disorder (Joseph et al., 2010). The guidelines indicate that the treatments of choice are trauma-focused cognitive behavioural therapy, eye movement desensitization and reprocessing, or pharmacotherapy. Despite provision of person-centred and experiential therapies for posttraumatic stress in UK specialist trauma services, there is a lack of randomized controlled trial evidence to support entry into the guideline (Murphy et al., 2012). However, relational approaches might be offered within the guidelines if the recommended approaches fail, or the client expresses their preference to receive nondirective therapy.

Many clients report relationally focused therapy to be helpful and person-centred and experiential approaches are currently gaining empirical support (Pavio and Nieuwenhuis, 2001). In addition, we also suggest that clients who have experienced neglect, abuse or domestic violence especially benefit from the genuine warmth and prizing of the social environment created in person-centred therapy (for a recent analysis of the nature of the person-centred relationship, see Zucconi, 2011). Often, people have unfulfilled needs for acceptance and to be valued. In the person-centred relationship, such needs can be satisfied. The satisfaction of these needs relate specifically to meeting both affective and cognitive processing needs.

The aim of this chapter is to demonstrate how relational depth in counselling and psychotherapy can be of therapeutic benefit for clients who have experienced trauma and may facilitate posttraumatic growth.

Posttraumatic growth

Posttraumatic growth is a useful term to describe the process of the struggle with affective-cognitive processing and adjustment following a traumatic event to find new meaning and purpose to life, develop closer relationships and revise the self-structure. Reviews of the literature suggest that posttraumatic growth is a common outcome, occurring in approximately 30–70 per cent of trauma survivors (Linley and Joseph, 2004), and that this is the case following a wide range of traumatic events (Joseph and Linley, 2008; Joseph and Butler, 2010). Posttraumatic growth encompasses a broad range of experiences; however, these can be grouped under three main areas: changes in relationships, finding a new purpose/meaning in life, and changes in perception of the self-concept.

It is a misconception, however, to think that posttraumatic growth excludes the possibility of posttraumatic stress. Posttraumatic growth and posttraumatic stress are interrelated and often exist simultaneously. It is thought that a curvilinear relationship exists between the two responses (Butler et al., 2005). So, when people experience very little by way of posttraumatic stress after an event, they are unlikely to experience much, if any, posttraumatic growth. However, as the level of posttraumatic stress increases, so too the likelihood of posttraumatic growth increases, although it appears this is only the case up to a certain point. As the intensity of posttraumatic stress becomes too overwhelming, the chances of growth become suppressed. Thus, too much posttraumatic stress might actually inhibit the chances of growth occurring at all.

Facilitating posttraumatic growth narratives within the relational (depth) perspective

An explanation for the finding that a moderate amount of posttraumatic stress fuels the development of posttraumatic growth is derived from social-cognitive processing theories of trauma. Through socialization processes, people develop a framework of assumptions by which they navigate new experiences and which help them maintain a sense of consistency and continuity of experience. A traumatic experience challenges existing assumptive frameworks about the world (Janoff-Bulman, 1985). In person-centred terms, this brings a disruption to available processing capacities and causes psychological distress, possibly leading to disorganization and a perceived total breakdown of the self structure (Joseph, 2004, 2005). It is posited that posttraumatic stress signifies the person's affective-cognitive need to rebuild their shattered assumptions about the world and that posttraumatic growth describes the changes that occur to the person's self-structure as a result of successful rebuilding (Joseph, 2011).

To understand the transformation of posttraumatic stress into posttraumatic growth when meeting at relational depth, two ideas are helpful. The first is the organismic valuing process theory, an affective needs-based system of motivation that directs the organism towards the integration of new trauma-related information into the self-concept. The second is facilitating the client in the affective-cognitive process of creating a coherent narrative following the trauma.

Organismic valuing theory

Building on cognitive processing theories, Joseph (2011) has developed a model of posttraumatic growth, based on Rogers' theory of the organismic valuing process (OVP), which incorporates and accounts for the phenomenology of both posttraumatic stress and posttraumatic growth.

Using Rogers' conception of the breakdown and disorganization of the self together with the defensive strategies of distortion and denial, the OVP theory of posttraumatic growth proposes that, following trauma, a person is intrinsically motivated towards *accommodation* of the new trauma-related information in such a way as to increase psychological wellbeing. Depending on the context, such changes can be seen as either positive or negative. An example of *positive accommodation* may be a new sense of mastery in which the person is able to take on new challenges in life. In contrast, an example of *negative accommodation* might be a case of a police officer who didn't wait for back-up support to arrive and was assaulted; he realized that even though he carried safety equipment, there is sometimes a very real risk of violence. Then, after generalizing this risk to all new situations, he decided that it was better to avoid all such risks and to leave the police service altogether. In this latter case, the officer's striving towards greater mastery of the environment has led to a more restricted outlook on life's challenges. While there is an intrinsic drive towards accommodation, people are cognitively conservative and inclined towards *assimilating* the new trauma-related information within the existing self-concept (Joseph and Linley, 2005; 2006).

Because the OVP model of growth is consistent with person-centred psychology, we suggest that relational depth, as a particular relational experience with its roots in person-centred therapy, can for some clients facilitate posttraumatic growth. In particular, the OVP theory of posttraumatic growth has been shown to account for posttraumatic stress and subsequent posttraumatic growth following severe childhood abuse (Murphy, 2009).

Creating a coherent narrative

The 'narrated self' can be a useful metaphor for showing how the stories that people tell themselves about their traumatic experiences can eventually lead either to growth or to getting trapped in more persistent and chronic processing difficulties, such as posttraumatic stress. Meichenbaum (2006) has identified several examples of prototypic personal narratives that are grounded in specific cognitive processes associated with posttraumatic growth. That is, each of the cognitive processes gives rise to a self-narrative that captures something of the essence of posttraumatic growth. Meichenbaum (2006, p. 355) suggests:

> that the nature of the self-narrative plays a critical role in determining whether individuals and groups manifest chronic persistent distress and posttraumatic stress disorder (PTSD) or whether they will evidence resilience and posttraumatic growth.

Meichenbaum's (2006) model makes a number of useful suggestions, among them are that the kinds of thinking and behaviours that lead towards posttraumatic growth include:

1. Seeking, finding, reminding and constructing benefits for oneself and others.
2. Establishing and maintaining a future orientation with altered priorities.
3. Constructing meaning, a coherent narrative, and engaging in special activities or 'missions' that transform loss so that something good that will come out of it.

Zucconi (2011, p. 6) considers that the meaning of adopting the values of a person-centred approach is to 'enter into and belong to a constructed world of values' and also 'to create clinical settings that actively promote different narratives'. As such, posttraumatic growth narratives can result from the mutual collaboration between client and 'experienced guide' working at relational depth. Mearns and Cooper (2005, pp. 98–112) provide a compelling account of therapy with a traumatized client called Rick, in which they indicate the difficulties faced when working with a client who is 'communicatively disconnected'. Elsewhere, Murphy (2009) published a case study with a traumatized client following severe childhood abuse. In this chapter, we will use some of the qualitative data that was collected in that study to highlight how meeting at relational depth is a key process in facilitating posttraumatic growth and a natural consequence of person-centred therapy when the therapeutic conditions are present to a high degree. In doing this, we will highlight the changes that occurred by making reference to changes in the self-narrative of the client.

Working with Mac

Mac was 50 years old and had been referred to therapy as a result of suffering years of childhood abuse. The early sessions are somewhat of a blur with regards to content, as Mac presented in a very confused state and talked virtually entirely about 'programmes running in his head' and that he was on the 'verge of a big idea'. This was always communicated through topics related to the environment and developing sources of power (in the sense of energy) and the communication often *appeared* to be very chaotic. I had never encountered a client experiencing such a level of distress following trauma and I had doubts about my ability to work with Mac. After serious consideration about this in supervision, further collaborative discussion with Mac and the clinical director of the referring agency, we agreed that we would work together for a year and see what progress could be made. What I didn't know at that time was that the therapy would last for almost five years.

To work at relational depth and facilitate posttraumatic growth, both client and therapist have to be willing to experience a mutual 'letting go' (MacMillan and McLeod, 2006). Letting go in the relationship with Mac was essential in several ways. There was no doubt that Mac experienced psychotic and dissociative episodes, but I had to 'let go' of having any specific aims of therapy and any inner desire towards 'looking good' and worrying about 'appearing' to be a competent therapist by *making* change happen. More importantly, perhaps, was letting go of the need to 'understand the content' of what Mac was saying, especially in the early sessions, and allow myself to be taken along in the journey. There were risks with this, as the world into which I was attempting to enter with Mac was one that had little relation to my own sense of reality. Maintaining the 'as if' quality to my empathic understanding was to prove critical in keeping a sense of my own self and not getting lost in his world of severe and prolonged abuse. The therapy moved slowly, and as Mac's attempts at communicating his experience were so confusing I often found myself being pulled in when trying to really understand him. To some extent, I was drawn in by the apparent depth of Mac's knowledge of environmental issues. However, later in the work, we collaboratively developed awareness that this apparent *delusional* belief was, in fact, a totally coherent, albeit elaborate, aspect of his dissociative process and protected him against the real experiences of trauma that were held within the organism. In reality, there were times when I literally didn't have a clue what was being spoken about, yet even during those occasions I was always striving to hold on to my unconditional positive regard for Mac and continue to communicate this through my empathic understanding. However, this was not easy when Mac was so severely distressed. I had to let go of knowing and engage in what Mearns and Cooper (2005) have described as a letting go of anticipations of what might happen in the therapy.

Through the process of letting go, I was engaged in really 'listening'. This kind of listening is deep and one in which the client is permitted as much space as they require. This is not listening with an agenda, that is, with the aim of listening to enable interpretation, but about listening to the whole of the client, their words, their emotions and the metaphors they express. It is about listening to the whole being of the person and attuning to their current and immediate expression of self. This kind of listening enables the development of a deep empathy for the client's traumatic experiencing.

In the examples of dialogue from the sessions highlighted below, it is apparent that at times I was reflecting back and giving recognition to the various configurations of self (Mearns and Thorne, 2000), or, as Mearns and Cooper (2005; 122) suggest, of the 'multidirectionality' of the actualizing tendency. In terms of trauma, this equates to the organism striving towards accommodation and driven by affective-cognitive processing of the new, unprocessed, trauma-related information. It also reflects the perceived need of the self-concept to assimilate the information, so as to avoid being overloaded with the demands of processing these experiences, where the self is perceived as being under threat. It is organismic striving that leads to the integration of configurations of self. Where Mearns and Thorne (2000) caution about the danger in 'zero sum responding', it is important in trauma therapy to recognize and acknowledge both the striving of the organism towards integrating the trauma-related information, and the wisdom of the organism in knowing when exposure has reached its existing current capacity for processing. This means allowing the client to process the trauma at their own pace and for processing those aspects of the traumatic event the client identifies as most significant.

An openness to being changed by the client is required of the person-centred therapist. A person-centred therapist who is closed off from being changed implicitly denies the full humanity of the client. In the therapy with Mac, I learned a great deal and was changed through the experience. I learned a very basic lesson, that in bearing witness to an intensely traumatic narrative, I cannot be responsible for making change happen. I learned that the more I *wanted* Mac not to have had to endure the past abuse, the less facilitative I could be and the less able partner I was for the therapeutic journey. I had to accept that I could not change these terrible events or his responses to them, and that to be of the greatest service, I needed to be fully present and available in the therapeutic relationship.

The first of the four exchanges is taken from session 18. Prior to this session, the issue of searching for understanding had been expressed several times, albeit with little obvious emotional expression, and the familiar pattern of talk about programmes running in Mac's head was a constant presence. Below, we try to show how the relationship was deepening as Mac began to process both the affective and cognitive aspects of experience. A change in the self-narrative occurred from being externally focused and containing the 'I don't know/understand' self-narrative to an internally focused and autobiographical self-narrative, accompanied by an emotional expression of anger towards the abuser. A narrative shift is marked by what has been referred to as the 'innovative moment' (White and Epston, 1990). In this exchange, the innovative moment is proposed to be the point at which Mac states: 'well I can but I can't'. This marks a change from the 'I don't know/understand' cognitive processing aspect of the self-narrative to one in which he knows, remembers and (re)experiences the anger felt towards his abuser, both now and at the time of the trauma, and thus connects the affective processing with the cognitive aspects of the self. A bridge is built from the affective experience of being abused and the reasoning and meaning he makes from the experience. Naturally 'well I can but I can't' conveys an ambivalence and uncertainty in fully acknowledging this experience. The anger that is then communicated helps re-create a new meaning in the present.

In the session, Mac is angry and questioning the motives of the abusers:

Mac: … what I can't get to is why, why they did it to us.

T: It just makes no sense to you, no matter what you do, there's just no sense to it.

Mac: I'm not like that, so why were they? Mrs 'X' who used to come into the school wasn't like that, so why did they do it?

T: Huhm, it doesn't make sense to you, why they did this to you yet some other people didn't.

Mac: I know, I'm just no good at recognizing who's bad and who's good, like there's something wrong with me that I just can't see it coming, well I can but I can't.

T: You find it hard to know what to expect from people, like who'll treat you good and who won't.

Mac: Yeah, like I … I avoid getting close, no matter where, even if someone in the pub put their arm around me, I hate it, I get all (pauses) … uncomfortable. You know … (long pause), I call it the stubble effect.

T: Stubble effect?

Mac: Yeah, you know, when a bloke's got stubble on his face … (pauses) ... It reminds me of being back in the school, when the dirty bastard's all over you and the stubble scrapes against ye skin.

In this passage, close listening and attentive empathic reflection enabled the relational connection to deepen. It is the confused 'I don't know/understand' self-narrative that is empathized with and that feels heard. Then, as attention becomes more internally focused so too does the narrative, the quality of interaction shifts to a deeper level. The story is told of the trauma trigger, and the simple *unknowing* empathic reflection 'stubble effect?' is made. The pause signifies the rise of the affective response and (re)experiencing of the actual traumatic event, whereas in the previous line, the trigger event is narrated. As the newly formed 'knowing' narrative is encountered, the level of contact between us moves to yet a deeper level and Mac congruently recalls the experience of being abused.

The second exchange highlighted is from session 26. The innovative moment is apparent when Mac states not having to 'be so much on guard against what's coming next'. This is considered to be an innovative moment, in that it marks a significant departure from his usual state of hyperarousal, in which he is hypervigilant, 'on guard' and unable to distinguish between the *unprocessed* affective-cognitive trauma information and that which is being presently experienced:

Mac: People actually like me, I mean, when I walk in the pub people say 'hello Mac' and smile, they really seem genuinely happy to see me. They don't want anything from me, there's no catch, or at least there doesn't seem to be, they just like me for me.

T: It seems like you feel okay around the people you've met in the pub, like you can accept their wanting to know you without having to think too much about what they may want from you.

Mac: That's right. For the first time, except for here, I can see that people really like me. They like what they see. I don't have to be, be so much on guard against what's coming next.

T: It's like for the first time in your life you're feeling as though you can relax when you're around others, not having to look out for the danger.

Mac: That's it but there's more than that. I mean, it's like I can really see that people like me, and that means so much. Like whatever they did to us in the school and how it made me grow into that twisted rose, it's like it's not like that anymore.

T: So it's like how you felt about being the twisted rose is somehow changed by people seeing something they like and respect.

Mac: That's it, its respect. People respect me and that's never been there. I've never had that, that respect. There's always been a catch.

The 'on-guard' self-narrative is one which Mac perceives a constant threat. The relief of being able to relax when around other people was palpable. Additionally, a further shift is highlighted in a further innovative moment where Mac states 'that's it but there's more than that', as he shifts from the existing self-narrative of 'the twisted rose' to one where he considers himself to be 'respectable'. Mac talked a lot about being the twisted rose as he considered his environment when growing up, considering himself to have been somehow emotionally deformed. As we explored the experience of being relaxed around other people, he could more accurately perceive others' views about him and came to view himself as someone worthy of respect. The moment where Mac realizes that there is 'no catch' to being respected is critical. He sees how he has enabled himself to be seen and to see others' responses to him as a result of the relational deep within the therapeutic relationship we had developed. He reflected back several times how he felt respected in our relationship and that he thought this had given him confidence to venture out into the world more and experience others. The metaphor of the twisted rose within this narrative is a powerful and ongoing point of reference throughout the therapy.

The next example becomes apparent by looking at change over a period of time and is highlighted through exchanges from sessions 68 and 93:

Session 68:

Mac: I mean you've got to realize how bad it was in there, I mean I hope you don't know, but it was so bad you got to realize what it did, what it does.

T: It's like you hope I don't know because you wouldn't want me to experience that, but you want me to know how it was for you?

Mac: I just can't get away from it, you gotta see that.

T: You mean, like ... you're not there now and yet you can't get away from it.

Mac: (leans forward and bangs fist on table) What they did was wrong, WHY? Why do that, to another human being? THAT BASTARD!

T: It was wrong what they did to you and you're angry about that.

Mac: There was just no one there ... alone you can't stand up to that. What could I do? Till then I'd resisted, but that was it, that was when I was done (cries heavily).

T: It just felt like you couldn't go on anymore, the fight was over.

The change in self-narrative is highlighted by the internally focused 'beaten me' in session 68, where Mac recounts one of many experiences of having been severely beaten by a carer. The self-narrative in session 93 states explicitly that 'I can take whatever happens', in reference to building a relationship with his son whom he hasn't seen for many years. The transformation from being the 'beaten me' to the emergence of a more resilient aspect of the self that 'can take whatever happens' is a significant sign of posttraumatic growth.

Session 93:

Mac: I spoke to X (son's name) yesterday. We talked on the phone. My son! (M clearly ecstatic, eyes wide and smiling broadly).

T: That sounds like a really special moment after all this time thinking and talking about the possibility of this happening one day.

Mac: We talked about what he's doing, he's going to college, he likes sport like me and he likes computer gaming like me, we talked for ages about all kinds of things. We didn't talk about the schools though, he doesn't need to know.

T: So you found you've a lot of things in common.

Mac: I just said, I needed to get away and that I'd tell him more someday. I said I was sorry and he said it was okay. He seemed to understand things have been hard for me. I think he liked me, I hope he did. I hope we can build a relationship, slowly at first I know.

T: You want to get to know him really well, and build a relationship, with all the risks that go with that (tears in eyes).

Mac: I've gotta risk it, I don't wanna lose him again, if I don't try now then I'll lose anyway. I can take whatever happens (tears in eyes).

The shared experience in Mac talking to his son is only a part of the story here. At the moment we both experienced tears welling up, it is the unspoken and intersubjective, 'inter-affective' knowing that is shared that marks the moment of depth. The *knowing* is that he feels ready to risk a relationship, other than the therapeutic relationship, that might be lost but is worth the risk – he states 'if I don't try now then I'll lose anyway. I can take whatever happens.' This statement of intent involves a *mutual recognition* of a significant shift in Mac's story and one that bolsters his decision to move into the relationship with his son. The shared moment is one of his knowing that he can take whatever happens and his *recognition* and *experiencing* of my knowing his knowing that he can take whatever happens. This is a moment of mutuality inherent in working at relational depth (see Chapter 14, this volume).

Conclusion

The concept of posttraumatic growth opens up new ways of thinking about trauma that resonate with person-centred and experiential therapies. Meeting at relational depth can be key to facilitating change following trauma. We have attempted to show that meeting at relational depth, letting go of assumptions, listening, being open to change and willing to move and follow the client in whatever direction they move can facilitate posttraumatic growth.

References

Butler, L.D., Blasey, C.M., Garlan, R.W. et al. (2005) Posttraumatic growth following the terrorist attacks of September 11th, 2001: Cognitive, coping and trauma symptom predictors in an internet convenience sample. *Traumatology*, 11, 247–67.

Janoff-Bulman, R. (1985) The aftermath of victimisation: rebuilding shattered assumptions. In C.R. Figley (ed.) *Trauma and its Wake*, vol. 1 (pp. 90–112). New York: Brunner/Mazel.

Joseph, S. (2004) Client centred therapy, post traumatic stress disorder and post traumatic growth: Theory and practice. *Psychology and Psychotherapy: Theory, Research and Practice*, 77, 101–20.

Joseph, S. (2005) Understanding posttraumatic stress from the person-centred perspective. In S. Joseph and R. Worsley (eds) *Person-centred Psychopathology* (pp. 190–201). Ross-on-Wye: PCCS Books.

Joseph, S. (2011) *What Doesn't Kill Us: The New Psychology of Posttraumatic Growth*. New York: Basic Books.

Joseph, S. and Butler, L.D. (2010) Positive changes following adversity. *PTSD Research Quarterly*, 21(3), 1–8.

Joseph, S. and Linley, A. (2005) Positive adjustment to threatening events: An organismic valuing theory of growth through adversity. *Review of General Psychology*, 9(3), 262–80.

Joseph, S. and Linley, P.A. (2006) *Positive Therapy: A Meta-theory for Positive Psychological Practice*. London: Routledge.

Joseph, S. and Linley, P.A. (2008) Psychological assessment of growth following adversity: A review. In S. Joseph, and P.A. Linley (eds) *Trauma, Recovery, and Growth: Positive Psychological Perspectives on Posttraumatic Stress* (pp. 21–38). Hoboken, NJ: John Wiley & Sons.

Joseph, S., Regel, S., Harris, B. and Murphy, D. (2010) *What to Expect When Being Counselled for Post-traumatic Stress*. Lutterworth: British Association for Counselling and Psychotherapy.

Linley, P.A. and Joseph, S. (2004) Positive change processes following trauma and adversity: A review of the empirical literature. *Journal of Traumatic Stress*, 17(1), 11–22.

McMillan, M. and McLeod, J. (2006) Letting go: The client's experiences of relational depth. *Person-Centered and Experiential Psychotherapies*, 5(4), 277–92.

Mearns, D. and Cooper, M. (2005) *Working at Relational Depth in Counselling and Psychotherapy*. London: Sage.

Mearns, D. and Thorne, B. (2000) *Person-centred Therapy Today: New Frontiers in Theory and Practice.* London: Sage.

Meichenbaum, D. (2006) Resilience and posttraumatic growth: A constructive narrative perspective. In L.G. Calhoun and R.G. Tedeschi (eds) *Handbook of Posttraumatic Growth: Research and Practice* (pp. 355–68). New York: Routledge.

Murphy, D. (2009) Client-centred therapy for severe childhood abuse: A case study. *Counselling and Psychotherapy Research*, 9(1), 3–10.

Murphy, D., Archard, P., Regel, S. and Joseph, S. (2012) A survey of specialised UK traumatic stress services. *Journal of Psychiatric and Mental Health Nursing*, DOI: 10.1111/j.1365-2850.2012.01938.x.

NICE (National Institute of Clinical Excellence) (2006) *Post-traumatic Stress Disorder: The Management of PTSD in Adults and Children in Primary and Secondary Care* (Clinical Guideline 26). London: NICE.

Paivio, S.C. and Nieuwenhuis, J.A. (2001) Efficacy of emotion focused therapy for adult survivors of child abuse: A preliminary study. *Journal of Traumatic Stress*, 14(1), 115–33.

White, M. and Epston, D. (1990) *Narrative Means to Therapeutic Ends*. New York: Norton.

Zucconi, A. (2011) The politics of the helping relationship: Carl Rogers' contributions. *Person-Centered & Experiential Psychotherapies*, 10(1), 2–10.

8

Group relational depth

Gill Wyatt

Throughout time, people have experienced meetings with others that have lifted their spirits, deepened their motivation and increased their effectiveness. Whether this is within a loving, vibrant family, an innovative training course, a collaborative team, a performance with audience, or a group of strangers united by facing adversity, the shared experience seems to weave a web of connectedness around and through the people involved, making the group energized, coherent and whole. In contrast, we probably can also recall less fulfilling experiences in groups where there was fragmentation and a misuse of power. Mistrust, passivity and alienation developed alongside excessive competition, scapegoating and bullying. The overall experience was, at least, uninspiring, uncomfortable and bruising and, at worst, shaming, abusive and scarring.

This chapter explores these differing experiences in groups through the lens of relational depth. Research findings are presented that help to clarify the nature of group relational depth, how it is facilitated, the outcomes achieved and their significance. The possible significance of group relational depth is also explored in relation to the complexity of the social, political, economic and ecological challenges facing us in the 21st century, and the realization that they cannot be resolved with the same consciousness that created them. It is suggested that group relational depth can play a part in clarifying the shift of consciousness that is needed and become part of this very process.

Setting the context

A group can be defined as three or more people who relate and interact together. They share a common identity or purpose that connects them to one another (Lago and MacMillan, 1999; Barnes et al., 1999). This common purpose or identity can arise from shared activities and interest based on learning, leisure or work. A group can be a family, a committee or a whole organization; with people we know or meet for the first time.

The nature of relating can be described in many ways through philosophy, using mathematical formulae and concepts such as a machine or an interconnected web. The meaning we give to relating depends on our worldview (Wyatt, 2010). Today, it has been argued that we face a 'cultural turning point' (Lipton and Bhaerman, 2009). The old Newtonian/Cartesian worldview has given us unimagined technological and material advances and, at the same time, untold difficulties and challenges. The pervasiveness of fragmentation prevents us seeing the complexity and connectedness of systems. Materialism and consumerism have been prioritized over human relationships and our connection with nature, which has led to fractured families and communities and the devastation of our natural world. Desmond Tutu (cited in Wheatley, 2002) has spoken evocatively of 'a radical brokenness in all of existence', and Sue Gerhardt (2010), a relational psychotherapist, has called our society 'selfish'. She clarifies: 'we are living in an impoverished emotional culture, the end product of decades of individualism and consumerism, which has eroded our social bonds' (p. 12).

This suggests that the evolutionary task facing us is to challenge this 'radical brokenness' and 'selfish individualism'. Thomas Berry (1999, p. 11), a cultural historian, describes this transformation as humans evolving from being a 'disruptive force on the planet Earth' to becoming 'present to the planet in a way that is mutually enhancing'. Groups all over the world are engaged in the evolutionary possibility that embraces a more qualitative, organic interconnectedness. Their work is inspired by the search for cooperative world-centric values, which address the needs of the individual *and* the needs of all (people and all nature).

Carl Rogers' work (1957, 1980), founded on the formative tendency and his therapeutic conditions, challenged the power base of the dominant worldview. The role of the actualizing tendency contested the role of the expert and gave rise to a more participatory way of relating. His six 'necessary and sufficient conditions' described each of the qualities necessary for relating to be growth enhancing. His emphasis was innovative and challenging, and Rogers (1978, p. xiii) referred to his work as 'the quiet revolution'.

Relational depth brings these conditions together and emphasizes the significance of the 'wholeness of the conditions'. Rogers (quoted in Baldwin, 1987, p. 45) himself perhaps started this process when he wrote about 'something around the edges of these conditions that is really the most important element of therapy'. The exploration of 'tenderness' by Brian Thorne (1991), 'presence' by Shari Geller (Chapter 13, this volume) and 'encounter' by Peter Schmid (Chapter 12, this volume) has continued this exploration of the Gestalt (wholeness) of the conditions.

Relational depth has two different aspects – 'moments of intense contact and connection' between and 'enduring experiences of connectedness' in ongoing relationships (Mearns and Cooper, 2005). The nature of relational depth is that realness, empathy and prizing are experienced 'at a high level'. In addition, what is particularly salient is that they are mutually experienced.

Both the client and the therapist are providing 'the conditions'. This is a striking reformulation of Rogers' theory. Mearns and Cooper illuminate the nature of this mutuality by describing the interpenetration of 'co-transparency', 'co-acceptance', 'co-understanding', 'co-receiving' and 'co-intentionality'. They are suggesting that Rogers' conditions are 'flowing backwards and forwards between therapist and client through the channel that connects them' (2005, p. 46). This mutually enhancing interconnection could be seen as creating a Gestalt, which involves a 'multiplier effect' – the whole being greater than the sum of the parts. Relational depth, then, can be seen both as the process of reaching this Gestalt and the 'whole' that emerges.

The nature of group relational depth

If the nature of relational depth is mutual, multidirectional and co-creative, imagine what can happen in a group with the complexity of connections between its members. Special moments of connection and cohesiveness are the 'stuff' that holds families, organizations and communities together, and rituals and celebrations have often existed to create this enlivening connectivity and linkage. Is group relational depth part of this 'stuff'?

Figure 8.1 demonstrates this complexity of groups. Each link between people will have its own relational quality and the web holds together all these different qualitative relatings, similar to Foulkes' 'group matrix' (Barnes et al., 1999). The matrix or web for any group is thus different. It is determined by the unique connectivity within the group and all the corresponding meanings and significances created and shared between the group members. Could group relational depth be when the nature of this connectivity is mutually enhancing and co-creative as a result of the group's culture being shaped by realness, prizing and understanding?

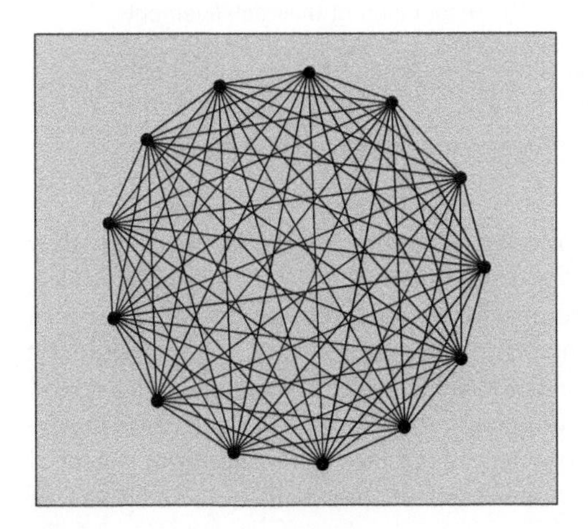

Figure 8.1 The interconnected web of a group

The qualitative 'feel' of group relational depth

The following two experiences of mine may help to clarify the differing 'qualitative feel' of the connectivity within a group. The second example could be considered as an example of group relational depth or, at least, of a group moving towards it.

Example 1. A disconnected family

The family, mother, father and three children, were getting ready for their summer holiday, a caravanning trip to the highlands of Scotland. Each efficiently completed their allotted tasks. Instead of a light-hearted banter of a family excited to be going on their summer holiday, there was a brittle tolerance of each other. The youngest, having finished what she was doing, asked her brother if she could help, but he sneered his refusal. Upset, she sought out her father who had her fill the radiator with water. Tasks were completed but with an attitude of minor hostility and aloofness. The father was distant, the mother anxiously busy. As the family got into the car, finally ready, the atmosphere was tense, cold and unpleasant.

Example 2. A cooperative counselling training group

The group was meeting for their self, peer and tutor assessments at the end of their first year of a Diploma in Counselling. The year had been challenging. The warmth and understanding experienced by most was as a result of much hard work exploring underlying perceptions and patterns when difficulties had emerged. During the day, each student assessed their learning over the year and then their peers and tutor gave their feedback; each person's different reflection adding to the thread that grew, connecting their contribution to the student's own assessment and each other's comments. This deepened the recognition of their achievements, and clarified future challenges ahead. Many voiced being in awe, or even transformed, by what they had achieved together and how it had culminated during the assessments.

The first group achieved its objective of 'setting off on holiday' but they related mechanically, with a lack of warmth and care for each other. An underlying mistrust and fear gave rise to a sense of isolation and disconnection. In contrast, the second group opened and learned to trust. They faced any conflict that developed and explored the underlying perceptual patterns and differences. A warm appreciative connection grew from their authentic immediacy as they learned how to collaborate and tap into both their own potential and the group's. This second group illustrates the 'mutually enhancing feel' of group relational depth.

Researching group relational depth

To discover more about the nature of group relational depth, I asked 17 practitioners, 10 person-centred and 7 non-person-centred, who included counsellors, facilitators, consultants and lecturers, three research questions that invited them to focus on the concept of relational depth or any other concept they might use in relation to their experiences of special moments of relating and ongoing connectedness in groups. They recounted experiences from workshops, counselling training, stakeholder/engagement work, musical performances, dialogue processes, ecopsychology and wilderness events, families, local community action and education initiatives, degree courses at universities, intentional communities and temporary community-building groups, flash mobs, personal development, therapy and encounter groups. A few people responded by sending me their previously published research, so this research combines previously unpublished and published data.

Experiences of group relational depth

The first question asked was: 'Have you had experiences that you might refer to as relational depth in a group? Please describe your experience, including what happened in the group.'

Many experiences recounted started with one person taking a risk, being vulnerable and authentically expressing something deeply felt and emotionally significant to others in the group. It was their presence and the immediacy filled with vulnerability and realness that reached out and touched others. This being touched was described as 'awe', and was expressed by one respondent as: 'The group was mute in its acknowledgment of her pain.' There was nothing to do, no words to speak. Others expressed an emotional and bodily felt empathy, an affinity or shared understanding. 'Resonance' captures this 'felt sense' and a 'flow' occurred between people. Alan Coulson (1999, p. 173), one of the research respondents, referred me to his earlier writings where he describes resonance as 'a feeling of connectedness through emotional affinity', which has a 'subconscious element', unlike cognitive-based empathic understanding. Harmony with others was also mentioned, along with feeling close, connected and a sense of belonging: 'Yes I know this, this connects us, this seems to be part of being human.'

After slowing down and silence, sometimes people then expressed heartfelt compassion and understanding that expanded the experience of emotional resonance. Or the heartfelt sharing by one triggered an 'Oh my God moment' as participants voiced their own similar experiences. It was as if there was a multiplier effect as the resonance grew from the depth of sharing through the connectivity of the group, expressed by 'being in tune with both "I am" and "they are"'.

Different accounts described shared events and activities with the whole group working together. There was 'engaged participation' with everybody involved and contributing. Work groups' decision making was surprisingly effective and agreements were made easily, which enlivened the group: 'A way forward would emerge that everybody recognized.' Others talked about differences being faced and facilitated so the group conversed together honestly and authentically. The processes described included how they had struggled, been frustrated, felt alienated and lost; how they had opened to learn how their patterns, their projections and other 'self-erected' barriers influenced and organized their experiences. From opening to these differences, conversation became more connected, like a thread of shared meaning being spun and there was a recognition that 'we can achieve more together'.

Other elements described from these experiences applied to each of the previous two groups – one person initiated experiences and whole group experiences. They spoke of feeling warmth, moving physically closer, of intimacy, of being received and accepted and of 'love'; also of being 'uplifted' and of 'higher energy', of the experience being transformational for all. Many spoke of feeling a sense of community, of feeling part of something bigger, of 'union', of being part of a whole: 'The experience deepened our sense of oneness and group mind.' For some, this was a spiritual experience, a connection with the universe, 'a tribal communalism'. People recounted knowing themselves better from feeling known, of having a clearer sense of self-identity at the same time as being part of the whole. Coulson (1999, p. 170) conveys the paradoxical nature of both attending to self and connecting to others: 'It is as if I am going simultaneously *inward*, joining more with myself, and going *outward*, joining more with others.' Less competition, less individual expression from the conditioned or 'ego-bound self' and a movement, an expansion to the 'larger or higher Self' were also mentioned.

The following working definition attempts to draw these themes together. Group relational depth occurs through sufficient trust developing from the presence of authenticity, prizing and understanding. The mutually enhancing connectedness and resonance, which arise from one person authentically sharing at depth or from the whole group working together, lead to cohesion and feeling part of a whole. Individuals feel more fully themselves, at the same time as being part of a whole. This connecting-up, shift, or multiplier effect is often experienced as a sense of 'communion' or even 'love', enlivening and profound, which is experienced as lifting the group into wiser, more effective and creative functioning.

Facilitating group relational depth

The second research question was: 'What do you consider are the factors that facilitated this experience?' This addressed why some groups achieve this connectedness and others don't.

Before the group starts

The importance of planning and organizational issues was recognized, because of their influence in shaping the group. Mhairi MacMillan (2004) clarified the significance by referring to 'conscious intention', a concept explored by John Wood (1999, p. 158): 'Intentions must be chosen and stated carefully so as to "aim" the workshop in a constructive direction from the start.' Factors that influence this 'conscious intention' include venue, ambience, timing, duration, catering, identifying potential participants, how to publicize the event and, most importantly, the purpose of the group. The staff need to honestly explore any differences about the focus of the group and their specific role, as undisclosed or unresolved issues among the staff were reported as having profoundly disruptive effects on the group by setting up conflicting expectations rather than a shared context that would facilitate a shared commitment.

An unfolding process

The next group of facilitative factors refer to an unfolding process and 'the mindfulness of all'. People were ready to listen as some had 'battled', and others had 'found their voice and been heard'. It was the 'right time', with a specific event sometimes acting as a catalyst. The development of trust and safety was seen as central; the phrase, 'deep trust began to expand when the most vulnerable aspects of our humanity became central to the process' captures this well. Other themes identified included:

- An individual's courage to take a risk, connect to deep experience and authentically express themselves.
- A group culture of empathic understanding, respectful acceptance and authenticity.
- A willingness to be unrehearsed, vulnerable, open, making space for the unknown and welcoming newness.
- The group being willing to face differences, explore any conflicts with the assumptions that created them. This is about 'suspending' certainty and the belief 'I'm right'.
- A movement into 'now', a slowing down and a letting go of the 'conditioned self', with less concern for how one is received.

Many of these themes are brought together within the concept of 'presence', and it was acknowledged by many how equally facilitative presence is whether from a participant or a facilitator. This immediacy, of being fully absorbed, was described by Peter Schmid 'as fully being-with and fully being-counter' (personal communication) and by Mhairi MacMillan (2004, p. 70) as the 'loss of conscious self-interest', so we speak from 'somewhere deeper within the organism'. Rogers' well-known quote on presence eloquently expresses the same sentiment (1980, p. 129):

> When I am at my best ... when I am closest to my inner, intuitive self, when I am somehow in touch with the unknown in me ... then whatever I do seems to be full of healing. Then simply my presence is releasing and helpful to the other.

Alan Coulson (personal communication) suggests:

> I suspect the key is self-forgetting, which permits us to move into the common ground of 'Self' rather than the isolated terrain of 'self', which enables interpersonal risk-taking of a degree normally too scary to engage in.

This is in strong contrast to more repetitive patterns of relating from the 'conditioned self', which can be experienced as rigid, superficial and inauthentic. Participants operating from a 'set formulae' or being in 'trained counsellor mode', even when 'making skilful empathic responses' (MacMillan, 2004, p. 73), will seldom lead to experiences of presence and relational depth, as when one participant acts as a counsellor to all who speak in a group or when many people take up a counsellor role in response to one person. Table 8.1 provides an example, taken from a workshop, of these facilitative factors.

Many of the factors that facilitate group relational depth apply equally to participants and facilitators. The research did provide specific comments about facilitators, which included being skilful and providing a range of inputs, being open to self and others, and whatever happened, that is, 'trusting the process', an ability to embody the person-centred attitudes and being non-defensive, 'being the best I can be', being able to hold and 'care for the energy of the group' and accompanying the group as it unfolds.

Outcomes and their significances

The third research question asked was: 'What were the outcomes and/or significance of what happened in the group?

At the personal level, these outcomes and their significance could be summarized as a 'centred and unfolding sense of self'. This included a fuller, richer participation in the group, where they trusted their experiences and took risks with new behaviour, which led to greater wisdom and resilience to meet challenges. Some spoke about being profoundly touched and healed from past traumas, even 'transformed', and others spoke about 'spiritual awakenings', making 'changes in life's direction', 'health bringing changes', having healthier relationships, feeling connected to nature and the world, 'having an open heart' and being inspired into social activism. One person acknowledged the personal upheaval and the breakup of relationships. People described the development of long-term self-sustaining support networks.

Other themes linked the individual and the group or applied to both. These included feeling enlivened with renewed energy, 'the stimulating effect

Table 8.1 Facilitative factors for group relational depth

Process	*Discussion*
The discussion on Sunday started with whether to do an experiential exercise or have more in-depth input from me. This initial focus was dropped and replaced by the appropriate expression of realness by the counsellor. People were fully engaged; fully present and felt stung when interrupted.	The day was about congruence, so I, as the facilitator, had declared the conscious intent for the day. People, in signing up, agreed, so this intent then became the 'collective intent'. Some people were present, engaged in the 'now'.
'What happened to the suggestion and discussion to do an exercise?' said Mary.	Mary took a risk and spoke out about why the subject had changed. She felt safe enough to be different.
What followed was some of us spoke about 'riding a wave'. Also, there was talk about our different perceptions of how the focus had shifted from 'whether to do an experiential exercise' to 'appropriate expression of realness' to 'this process now'. We began to understand the differences. A new 'wave' was growing.	This became an 'event', on which the group focused. There was a safe, trusting culture within which we explored our differences. Again people were engaged and present. People felt uplifted – thus the metaphor of riding a wave.
Then Mel threw in angrily: 'I must be in a different group, all this talk of riding waves. I feel jerked around, I was engaged discussing congruence and it's been interrupted.'	This time, Mel took the risk and was willing to voice his difference.
I offered: 'I can hear your anger and am glad you're telling us that you're in a different place than those of us "on the wave".' He hesitated and then replied: 'I'm glad too; normally I'd be sulky and difficult.'	A 'good enough' empathic, accepting response from me was confirmed by Mel's reply where he made himself more vulnerable and open, by authentically revealing his normal pattern. He's let go of being concerned about how he is received.
Mary, who had initially broken the first thread, said: 'It was as if this time, I was riding both threads, I felt a connection to both.' This seemed to facilitate Mel in exploring deeper, realizing his difference from Mary: 'When I am expecting something to happen, I become really disconcerted when what is planned is changed ... I'm really seeing for the first time how attached and rigid I can be.'	If Mel had been stuck in his rigid 'self', he might have heard Mary's expression of her experience as an interruption; however, his openness enabled Mary's truth about the different threads to facilitate Mel. It is as if Mary's truth connects to the truth within Mel (a resonance or flow?) so that he discovers how attached and rigid he can be. Mel took interpersonal risks (moving outwards) and intrapsychic ones (moving inwards).
The group was attentive in a warm, caring, understanding way, valuing Mel's honesty and openness to his unfolding process. On talking through how one thread had been dropped in favour of another thread, the group had united around this third thread. The conversation that followed was energized, people really listened, different opinions were expressed and questioned with sensitive curiosity and embraced, so that a shared understanding developed from everybody's contribution.	This connectedness, or resonance between Mel, Mary and me facilitated Mel in opening his 'conditioned self' and becoming more fully himself and more connected within the group. The group responded warmly to Mel and Mel responded warmly back, a 'collective resonance', Mel felt he belonged and the group felt engaged and enlivened. The depth and breadth of this conversation and the ability to explore differences non-defensively led to a warm, mutually enhancing connectivity, which allowed shared meaning to grow from a generative dialogue in the group.

of presence begets presence'; a greater degree of trust and cohesion within the group, a bringing people together; a shared resonance as people's boundaries became more semi-permeable, 'a communion' or 'bonding', a 'group consciousness'. 'We are all tapping a group intelligence' illustrates this 'unity from multiplicity'; a heightened sense of the potential of groups and of the potential of one's self in a group. The person feels more whole as a individual, while simultaneously feeling taken up into the group as a larger whole. This is 'multiplicity in unity'. Working more effectively, making decisions easier, realizing how embracing diversity, being our different selves creates creativity.

Within these reported outcomes and their significance, there can be seen tentative first steps towards world-centric values, including an ability to think together and to collaborate. However, concerns were also expressed. One concern related to participants not being sufficiently grounded in their 'own sense of reality' (MacMillan, 2004), whether inflated, as with a grandiose or megalomaniac experience, or regarding a loss in selfhood. The free will of the individual can be subordinated to the group culture, as with a bee within its colony, a person in a crowd, or in response to an authoritative and charismatic leader, as can occur with a disciple within a cult or within a nation with a megalomaniac leader.

The significance of the 'feel-good' experience and sense of 'kinship' for some groups meant the desire to maintain it could prevent the exploration of difficult and contentious issues, as these may create conflict in the group and destroy the sense of community. Scott Peck (1990, p. 88) uses the concept of 'pseudo-community' if a group appears cohesive when this is based on pleasantness and superficial agreement: 'Pseudocommunity is conflict-avoiding: true community is conflict-resolving.' It was also experienced that a 'burgeoning sense of initial connectedness' was 'temporary or relevant only to that situation or topic'. 'It seldom developed to a deeper shift in relationships', or acted as a 'stepping-stone for creating other kinds of outcomes'.

Drawing the research findings together

On the whole, this research did seem to find that mutually enhancing connectivity was experienced during the reported incidents of relational depth in groups. As with Mearns and Cooper's (2005) definition of relational depth, a culture of realness, prizing and understanding each other facilitated this process. In a group, this connectivity and resonance among its participants has a co-creative, multiplier effect that allows people to both open to themselves and to others. Often, this facilitated them to fully differentiate themselves as individuals, at the same time as experiencing a sense of community and of being part of the whole, being 'one'. This was sometimes described as a non-possessive 'love' and experienced as energizing. The group was lifted into wiser, more effective and creative functioning. Better decisions were made and people were more motivated to take action. More research will be needed to deepen our understanding of these processes.

Future possibilities: an evolutionary opportunity

The evolutionary task identified earlier involved a shift away from fragmentation and lack of concern for others and the earth towards developing relational capacities and world-centric values. From the research findings into group relational depth, the mutually enhancing and co-creative connectivity experienced sometimes in groups could be seen as part of this process.

During the research, people recounted knowing themselves better and deepening who they were as an individual, at the same time as feeling a sense of union and being part of the whole. These two characteristics resemble the two seemingly contradictory properties of a 'holon' – a concept developed by Arthur Koestler (1967). A holon's nature is to be both a part at one level and a whole at a different level. As each new level of complexity is reached, emergent properties appear. Consider words (the parts) becoming a sentence (the whole). The sentence is at the next level of complexity and the meaning of the sentence, as a whole, is different from the individual meanings of each word. This new meaning of the sentence can be considered as the emergent property.

For individuals and groups, this would mean a person self-asserts to become a fully differentiated individual – 'a whole at the level of the individual', while also integrating with other individuals to become part of a group – 'a part at the level of the group'. This dual ability is like the heads and tails of a coin or the two faces of the Roman god Janus – to be both *for your self* and *for the group* simultaneously. The individual connects up, becomes coherent, like a whole person version of congruence (Wyatt, 2004). The resultant alignment with their potential and their ability to actualize become the emergent properties. The group connects up and within this mutually enhancing connectivity opens to something larger than itself, which creates a creative space for the generative flow of the formative tendency. The emergent properties are more world-centric values, a collective wisdom, which facilitates more shared meanings, cooperative and deliberative processes and collaborative action.

This dual capacity highlights a difference between individualism and individuality that may be at the core of the evolutionary task of the 21st century. Individualism comes from the 'conditioned self' or the 'small sense of self', which weakens social bonds, whereas 'individuality', the connected up, fully differentiated self, allows people to join together to become groups and assemblies of people who take account of each other and the natural world. Maybe this dual capacity is facilitated by experiences of group relational depth? If this is the case, then facilitating experiences of group relational depth could become a cultural therapeutic that helps to address our evolutionary task.

As our Western culture has been primarily focused on the individual, the facilitator needs to develop sensitivities and capacities so they are able to observe, intuit and sense the connectivity within a group, its social processes and its wholeness, including its generative flow. Maureen O'Hara and John Wood (2004) suggest that facilitators 'tune into the seen and unseen flow in group attention, focus and energy'. By opening to others, attuning to the group and to the generative flow, we become morally engaged and ethically responsible. This is in stark contrast to the separation often experienced between people, families and society. Here no obligation is felt towards others. This is the poor social bonds and the 'selfish society' that Sue Gerhardt (2010) referred to. This relational ethical stance is similar to Levinas's notion of responsibility. The 'I', by responding from an ethical stance to the 'other', opens and transcends from 'self-consciousness' to a responsible and ethical interpersonal way of being (Schmid, 1998).

Facilitation, then, becomes person-centred and group-centred. By sensing both individual and social processes, a cooperative inquiry into the living process of the whole group, its generative tendency and that of each individual can occur. This can facilitate the mutually enhancing and co-creative connectivity of group relational depth, which lifts individuals and groups to experience this dual ability of becoming fully differentiated individuals at the same time as becoming part of a whole.

Conclusion

The research into group relational depth provided wide-ranging evidence of mutually enhancing and co-creative connectivity. The experience of authenticity, of prizing and being prized, and of genuine shared understanding, which can grow to feel like a 'non-possessive love', seems to soften the rigidity of the 'conditioned self'. This enables participants to both feel more fully themselves and to open and connect and become morally engaged with each other, allowing the group to work together for the good of all its members. A sense of union and wholeness is created.

Group relational depth may have the ability to be an antidote to the underlying fragmentation and deep embedded fear inherent in our society, and it offers some hope when considering the intensifying social, political, economic and ecological challenges. Developing the dual capacity of the differentiation of the individual and the ethically responsible and collaborative, relational nature of the collective seems to be part of our evolutionary task. I propose that experiences of group relational depth both clarify the evolutionary task and are part of the process. They are capable of acting as a cultural therapeutic that draws forth the necessary sensitivities, waiting at the edge of our psyche, which can develop world-centric values, collective wisdom and collaborative action.

References

Baldwin, M. (1987) Interview with Carl Rogers on the use of the self in therapy. In M. Baldwin and V. Satir (eds) *The Use of Self in Therapy* (pp. 45–52). New York: Haworth Press.

Barnes, B., Ernst, S. and Hyde, K. (1999) *An Introduction to Groupwork: A Group-analytic Perspective*. Basingstoke: Macmillan – now Palgrave Macmillan.

Berry, T. (1999) *The Great Work: Our Way to the Future*. New York: Bell Tower.

Coulson, A. (1999) Experiences of separateness and unity in person-centred groups. In C. Lago and M. MacMillan (eds) *Experiences in Relatedness: Groupwork and the PCA* (pp. 167– 80). Ross-on-Wye: PCCS Books.

Gerhardt, S. (2010) *The Selfish Society: How We All Forgot to Love One Another and Made Money Instead*. London: Simon & Schuster.

Koestler, A. (1967) *The Ghost in the Machine*. Bungay: Chaucer Press.

Lago, C. and MacMillan, M. (eds) (1999) *Experiences in Relatedness: Groupwork and the PCA*. Ross-on-Wye: PCCS Books.

Lipton, B.H. and Bhaerman, S. (2009) *Spontaneous Evolution: Our Positive Future and a Way to Get There From Here*. London: Hay House.

O'Hara, M. and Wood, J.K. (2004) Transforming communities: person-centered encounters and the creation of integral, conscious groups. In B.H. Banathy and P.M. Jenlink (eds) *Dialogue as a Means of Collective Communication* (pp. 105–36). New York: Kluwer Academic/Plenum Publishers.

MacMillan, M. (2004) Who am I and who are all those other people? In D.W. Bower (ed.) *Person-Centered/Client-Centered: Discovering the Self that One Truly Is* (pp. 64–80). Lincoln, NE: iUniverse.

Mearns, D. and Cooper, M. (2005) *Working at Relational Depth in Counselling and Psychotherapy.* London: Sage.

Rogers, C.R. (1957) The necessary and sufficient conditions of therapeutic personality change. *Journal of Consulting Psychology*, 21(2), 95–103.

Rogers, C.R. (1978) *Carl Rogers on Personal Power: Inner Strength and its Revolutionary Impact.* London: Constable.

Rogers, C.R. (1980) *A Way of Being*. Boston: Houghton Mifflin.

Schmid, P. (1998) 'Face to face': The art of encounter. In B. Thorne and E. Lambers (eds) *Person-centred Therapy: A European Perspective* (pp. 38–52). London: Sage.

Scott Peck, M. (1990) *The Different Drum*. London: Arrow Books.

Thorne, B. (1991) *Person-centred Counselling: Therapeutic and Spiritual Dimensions.* London: Whurr.

Wheatley, M. (2002) *Turning to One Another: Simple Conversations to Restore Hope to the Future*. San Francisco: Berret-Koehler.

Wood, J.K. (1999) Towards an understanding of large group dialogue and its implications. In C. Lago and M. MacMillan (eds) *Experiences in Relatedness: Groupwork and the PCA* (pp. 137–66). Ross-on-Wye: PCCS Books.

Wyatt, G. (2004) An exploration of 'holonic shifts' in groups and its possible human ecological significance of transforming culture. Dissertation submitted for Masters in Human Ecology, Centre for Human Ecology, Edinburgh.

Wyatt, G. (2010) A window into an interconnected world. *Self and Society*, 28(2), 5–24.

9

Client–therapist diversity: aspiring towards relational depth

Colin Lago and Fevronia Christodoulidi

This chapter explores the challenges and complexities faced by counsellors and psychotherapists in achieving relational depth when working with clients from different and diverse communities. Taking the working definition of relational depth by Mearns and Cooper (see Introduction, this volume), the reader will be steered through a landscape of relational barriers that can stand in the way of satisfactory 'transcultural' therapeutic progress. In short, the first part of this chapter sets out to seriously question any possibility, whatsoever, of the emergence of relational depth within multicultural settings. We thus begin with a somewhat questioning, pessimistic attitude.

A quite different, indeed positive stance is assumed in the latter sections of this chapter. Following this presentation of an alternative view, some brief case studies of the occurrence of relational depth will then be introduced and several hypotheses concerning the optimization of conditions for good relational contact will be drawn.

The introduction of diversity into a relationship immediately contributes to the complexity of that relationship and to the potential in that relationship for non-understanding, for judging the other, for seeing the gap posed by difference. Such difference and diversity inevitably mitigates against the possibility of establishing relational depth.

A note on difference and diversity

In 2004, the Equality and Diversity Forum of the British Association for Counselling and Psychotherapy (BACP) produced a working definition of the concepts and ventured a listing of those groups deemed to be 'different' and 'diverse' within society. Extracts from this document are included below:

> Our commitment to diversity is a principled stand which recognizes, values and responds to the natural diversity of human life and experience and does not view difference from the majority culture as inherently pathological or problematic. This requires the application of a critical perspective to unspoken or unexamined norms, as well as a commitment to social inclusion and to treating people with fairness and respect.

The statement continues: 'It requires recognition of power, privilege, disadvantage and oppression and challenges notions of supremacy' and proceeds to name, more specifically, those who might fall within the term 'diverse':

> There are particular groups which are privileged in U.K. society. These groups represent the often-unexamined norm from which 'difference' is defined.
> For example:
> *Advantaged/Norm* includes white people, heterosexual people, able-bodied people, men and people of working (income generating) age.
> By contrast:
> *Disadvantaged/different* includes black and minority ethnic people, lesbian, gay and bisexual people, disabled people, women, young people/older people/unemployed people ...

Lago (2010) refers to Moodley and Lubin (2008), who cite these last categories as the 'big 7 stigmatized identities – race, gender, sexual orientation, class, disability, religion and age.

Diversity and difference are relational phenomena

In moving from the categories of diversity as cited by Moodley and Lubin (above) to the broader considerations of the BACP document, we are taken from a point of view that difference and diversity equate to the broad description of those from specific minority groups in society to the radical realization that, effectively, difference and diversity are profoundly relational phenomena. This is wonderfully exemplified in the following quote by Marion Corker (in Lago and Smith, 2003, p. 45):

> What Jennifer was saying was that she accepted who she was, including the deaf part of herself. Her experience of disability came from expectations placed on her to conform to the common stereotype of deafened [sic] people and assumptions that her deafness must be the most important aspect of her life. She said later: 'I wouldn't experience being deaf at all if they allowed me to continue being who I am. Really, the deafness belongs to them.'

Thus, within a 'multicultural' counselling/psychotherapeutic relationship:

- The client is normally seen as the person of difference/diversity.
- However, and critically, both client and therapist are 'different' from and to each other.
- Where the therapist hails from the majority group in society and the client hails from a 'minority' group, the 'power' imbalance between them is amplified.
- The extraordinary range of possible therapeutic pairings that could occur are vast, and thus the potential for interpersonal differences and misunderstandings considerable.
- Additionally, the perceptions of the client from the therapist's perspective are likely to be profoundly affected by the 'prejudicial milieu' in which the therapist has been acculturated and the stage of 'counsellor identity development' the therapist has achieved (Ponterotto, 1988). Similarly, the client's perceptions of the therapist will be affected by a whole range of similar factors, familial, historic, contextual and so on.
- A particular complexity may also emerge where the therapist themselves hails from a different cultural/linguistic origin, for example France or Iran, and has trained as a therapist in, say, the UK. The overlay of differing and perhaps competing philosophies and ways of being they, themselves, have to deal with can be particularly confusing.
- In therapeutic situations where interpreters are required, the additional persona of the interpreter to the therapeutic relationship, although desirable and necessary for linguistic fluency and understanding, can also increase the complexity of the relational dynamics in the interview room. Might the occurrence of relational depth be almost impossible to achieve in this scenario?
- The multicultural/transcultural therapy scenario is further complicated by the addition of the supervisor into the professional dynamic. For example, who is the supervisor? What are their cultural, linguistic, theoretical origins? How sensitive are they to the issues of diversity? These are critical questions that can impact negatively upon the therapeutic dyad (see, for example, Lago and Thompson, 1997).

Quoting again from the BACP (2004) definition of diversity (see also Tuckwell, 2002; Ryde, 2009; Lago, 2006a; Lago and Haugh, 2006):

> Consideration also needs to be given to unconscious or unacknowledged notions of supremacy linked with advantaged/privileged groups. For example, an unexamined notion of white supremacy can lead to a situation where white cultural values, and the state of being white, are imagined to be the norm, and any variation from this norm is automatically viewed as problematic or pathological. This sense of supremacy can be evidenced in prejudice, stereotyping, discrimination, exclusion, which can occur at an individual, organizational/institutional and societal level.

Any and every therapeutic dyad does not exist within a power vacuum. In its simplest form, for example where both client and therapist hail from similar cultural, familial, gender and sexual preference positions, the role power of the therapist still differentiates between the two. Where there are also differences in dominant group therapist/minority group client pairings, particularly where the client hails from one of the 'big 7' stigmatized identities (see above), then the 'dichotomization of power' (Rosen and Walker, 2004) becomes considerable and represents not only an ongoing challenge to the success of the therapeutic work but also to the very possibility of achieving relational depth at all.

In short, we are left with two critical questions: Can a therapist, coming from the 'majority' group within society, truly and empathically indwell in the minority group client's experiencing and views of the world, particularly if those views are alien to the therapist's? And, in relation to the specific focus of this chapter, can a therapist and client, both hailing from quite different 'cultural' origins, achieve moments of relational depth? Our brief answer to both is 'no' and then 'yes'. And ultimately 'only if'.

We have already begun to evidence the negative view above, that is, that relational depth across difference is not easily possible. In the next section, we introduce many more potential lived differences between client and therapist; differences, we contend, that will mitigate against the occurrence of relational depth.

Examining the definition of relational depth in the context of difference and diversity

Can a 'state of profound contact and engagement between two people' of diverse origins (Mearns and Cooper, 2005, p. xii) be created? Lago (2006b, p. 53) offers a diagram depicting some 'cultural barriers to communication'. Suggested as a training exercise, trainees are invited to consider the multiple cultural barriers that potentially stand in the way of clear communication in any 'cross-cultural' pairing. Starting the exercise with an imagined pair of people, for example an Inuit and a Bolivian, or a Russian and a Briton, many ideas and hypotheses can be generated. There are 24 different elements of interpersonal perception, culturally determined behaviour and communication styles featured in Lago's diagram. They include, for example:

- interpersonal projections
- positions on morality
- what is deemed as acceptable/unacceptable behaviour
- language differences
- customs and rituals
- gender differences
- nonverbal behaviour
- communication styles.

Each of these elements, in and of themselves, would be sufficient to interrupt any possibility of real communication and meeting occurring. If one adds to this complexity by considering the complex rules surrounding communication described by Casse (1981), you might wonder if anything meaningful at all can occur between persons, let alone persons of difference. Casse (pp. 51–72) posits that:

- Pure communication is impossible.
- We communicate all the time.
- We see things which do not exist.
- We do not see things which exist.
- We perceive differently.

Further barriers to the formation of relational depth in diversity include:

- *Therapist levels of comfort when faced by 'difference':* if the therapist has strong negative feelings towards the group from which the client hails, how might they offer warmth and acceptance? How might they manage their congruence/transparency in relation to the client? What levels of discomfort or judgementalism are disclosed through their nonverbal behaviour, an area we know we can do little consciously about?
- *Client implementation of a 'proxy self' that is protective but distancing* (Lago and Thompson, 1997): this phenomenon may have developed through previous processes and moments in the client's life, resulting in their 'identity-wounding' (Alleyne, 2005) and 'identity traumatization' (McKenzie-Mavinga, 2005, 2009).
- *Race avoidance:* or any aspect of the client's communication and/or identity avoided by the therapist (Thompson and Jenal, 1994; Moodley et al., 2004).
- *Counsellor lack of diversity awareness, sensitivity and cross-cultural capacity* (Knipscheer and Kleber, 2004a, 2004b).
- *Incompatibility of client and counsellor identity developmental stages* (Carter, 1995).
- *Unskilled usage of interpreters* (Tribe, 2011): added to this are the further elements of the interpreter's own level of experience and their capacities and understandings of the process.
- *Contextual dissonance:* negative attitudes conveyed to the client via the therapeutic agency.
- *Therapist use of insensitive and/or inappropriate language.*
- *Therapist capacity for the discomfort of not understanding.*
- One further element to this list might be added the position of *clients who are experiencing complex physical life circumstances*, for example poverty/ illness/lack of basic needs, to the point where their capacity to work psychologically and therapeutically is highly impaired, such as asylum seekers.

The possibility for relational depth across diversity

Notwithstanding these barriers, we contend that moments of relational depth are possible to achieve despite multiple differences, given particular circumstances and conditions. Clemmont Vontress, an eminent American writer within the field of 'multicultural therapy', has always argued that 'counsellors who recognize that commonalities that humans share are apt to be more effective helping all clients than those who focus on perceived differences' (cited in Moodley and Walcott, 2010, p. 11). We will now proceed to present this more positive perspective.

Lost in concentration

Imagine the following scene. Two strangers find themselves sharing a small compartment on a long-distance train journey. One is a well-educated woman from East Asia taking a dream holiday journey across Europe. The other, slightly younger woman is a nun of American origin, travelling to work in a charitable residence in Eastern Europe.

The train draws out of Paris and, although having exchanged a polite 'hello', they become lost in their own thoughts, in reading, perhaps knitting and so on. From time to time, sometimes stimulated by scenes outside the train window, they engage in polite and light conversation. Other passengers arrive and depart at the stations en route.

Time moves on and they begin to acknowledge the endurance element of their differing, although currently loosely shared, journey. The purchase and then partaking of refreshments from a passing tea trolley offers further opportunities for conversational exchange. As time wears on and dusk arrives, the conversation becomes more open and more intimate. Past experiences, family memories, embarrassing moments, shared stories of illnesses all emerge.

As night falls, they prepare the couchettes above their seats to sleep in and change from their day clothes into their night clothes. Sitting together over a late night warm drink, relaxed, contented and deeply appreciating each other's stories and their company, they arrive at a special moment of intimacy, where so much is felt and so little needs saying. This special atmospheric moment, sadly, is rudely interrupted by the train slowing down for the next stop. This seems to give them a slight psychological jolt and the conversation turns to wondering about the name of the next station and if they should be getting to sleep to be rested for the following day.

Despite their apparent differences, these two women journeyed towards a moment of relational depth. They had shared a moment that has now gone but can never be taken away. In the process of the journey, they had become increasingly intimate and revealing in their sharing of stories. Over the hours together, they had become more relaxed, more themselves and more able to let go of their daily 'defence' patterns. They had become more trusting of each other. They liked each other. Each had become more transparent to the other. They had let go of being impatient with the length of the journey; they had let go of what their boss had said to upset them the previous day; they had ceased to worry so much about appearing acceptable, fashionable and so on. They had settled down in this special moment. There was no threat from the other, indeed they would be parting soon. They were more deeply relaxed in themselves and with each other. All external noise and other passenger activities had completely receded in their experiencing. They had, more or less simultaneously, realized that they were learning from each other and from the similarity of their stories, despite huge differences in their origins, cultures, beliefs and so on. They had reached a moment of 'co-absorption', a state of unusual joy, indeed, of altered consciousness.

Does this account offer an accurate depiction of what Mearns and Cooper term as 'relational depth'? And if it does, what factors might we derive from this story and then proceed to hypothesize about the facilitation of such special transformative moments?

What happened?

- A journey, jointly shared.
- A coming together through being together.
- A sense of developing bonding.
- Of coming to trust.
- Of feeling safe and that neither of them had any purpose to achieve or fear of manipulative motivation by the other.
- Consequently being open and present to each other.
- Listening carefully to each other – witnessing each other's accounts of their lives.
- Of sensing being accepted and acceptable.
- Of liking each other.
- A developing sense of feeling deeply understood, combined with an emotional climate of emerging 'togetherness'.
- In this climate, all sense of external noise diminishes and an altered state of consciousness for both participants can be experienced.
- Within this safe and intimate climate, there can be special moments where there is no 'as if', no sense of protective differentiation from the other; they are profoundly within the moment and with-in each other. The moment of relational depth.

Factors that can lead to the experience of relational depth in diverse therapeutic relationships

The above story and subsequent analysis is set within a non-clinical context. In transferring these ideas to the diverse therapeutic relationship, we hypothesize that moments of relational depth are more likely to occur where there is:

- *A conducive context in which both parties meet:* elements that contribute to this climate are interview room location, decoration, warmth, freedom from external noise and comfortable seating.
- *A mutual effort to reduce the 'gap':* Stevens and Holland (2008) specifically addressed, in their research, the question of what one does when counselling across a language gap. We are mindful of having used the term 'gap' rather more broadly at the beginning of this chapter in relation to the complete range of diversities. Nevertheless, their seven suggested strategies, although presented differently to many of the points in this section, constitute an action-oriented approach to addressing this 'gap'. (Briefly, they recommend: identify the gap, acknowledge it, minimize it, maximize the advantages it offers, tolerate it, use your therapeutic skills and work harder.)
- *A quality of attendance to and acceptance of the client:* this can facilitate an emerging reciprocity of relationality between the two.
- *No directive intent from the therapist:* the therapist goes into each session without memory, will or desire (Mearns and Cooper, 2005; Natiello, 2001). The therapist has no intentionality for the therapeutic process, no need to demonstrate expertise, no subjects that they consider must be addressed by the client, no techniques to be introduced with the client and so on.
- *Where there exists a state of readiness in both participants:* an Indian metaphor states that when the fruit is ready, it will drop off the tree and when the ground is ready, it is soft and will receive it without bruising. The therapist's state of readiness, we contend, must not only include their emotional and psychological availability but also be underpinned by their transcultural sensitivity and competence (see Lago, 2010).
- *Conjoint experiencing:* where both therapist and client experience an openness to each other and to the unfolding story.
- *Deep listening:* each paying considerable attention to the other. To be listened to and to feel understood can beget feelings of warmth, acceptance, self-worth, reduction of fear and anxiety, gratitude and feelings of intimacy. In deep states of listening, Jungians assert that in the silence there can also be the emergence of grace and mystery.
- *An active process of co-creation of such moments between counsellor and client:* Another Indian metaphor wonderfully illustrates this unifying process. The metaphor says that where rivers join is a sacred place.
- *Empathic attunement:* between both participants in the dialogue. A deep (seemingly visceral) understanding of the other is experienced.
- *A considerable state of comfort and relaxation, jointly experienced.*

In these circumstances, 'counselling is more like the process of being in love than solving a detective mystery' (Kennedy, 1977, p. 27).

A special moment

A female colleague had been seeing an African client for quite some time. Although her cultural heritage had originated in East Asia, she had been resident in the UK for many years and had practised as a counsellor for over a decade. Some of her work brought her into contact with refugees and asylum seekers. One particular client she saw was a middle aged man who had suffered multiple difficulties in his own life and country of origin, which had led to him seeking asylum in the UK. She reported: 'I somehow disliked him from the very beginning. I experienced him as saying: "I am the man, I'm in charge; you must do what I ask." A real macho man.'

She came to dread each session with this client, and he continued to turn up regularly and on time. And he always wanted to continue with the work – an obvious source of discomfort to the therapist.

The client had chosen a particular interpreter (who, incidentally, the therapist had known for 10 years herself). She both liked and considered him to be a 'lovely man' and, indeed, through unforeseen needs of the agency in which they had had to move room locations three times over the course of the counselling, she had realized how this 'gentlemanhood' of the interpreter had helped her to feel less threatened and safer with this client.

However, the client's style never seemed to change. There was always this heavy negative masculine energy around: 'I've done so many bad things in my life, no one will ever forgive me … but I was told you can help me.' So, he kept coming and the therapist kept trying.

She, however, found it difficult to see what progress was being made and believed that he only really wanted her to work as an advocate for him, to write letters to the Home Office and so on. This was in spite of his assertions that: 'You listen to me. You understand me.' She didn't fully believe it.

The final room they ended up working in had only recently been evacuated and was in a slight state of disarray. There were some pictures on the wall and his chair, quite coincidentally, faced one particular landscape painting, painted as from within a room looking out through the window. On sitting down to begin the interview, he looked at the picture and went very quiet. His manner changed extraordinarily. The therapist said: 'He seemed to have gone deeply into himself. Tears appeared in his eyes. He kept looking at the picture, then at me, then the picture again.'

All three of them (the counsellor, client and interpreter) sat very quietly for an extended period of time. Occasionally, the counsellor just nodded her head a little to signify her presence, her reassurance, and said, soothingly, a couple of times, many minutes apart: 'It's okay.'

Eventually, he began to explain: 'That picture has taken me back to my parent's home, and I suddenly felt the love I have missed, deep inside, and by not saying anything, I know you have understood.' He extended his hand and the therapist let hers lie lightly on top of it. He apologized for crying but repeated something he had said many times before: 'The doctor said you would understand.'

'Thank God,' the therapist explained in supervision, 'that I had the opportunity to see this man through that picture. I was scared to death working with him. Thank goodness he also invited that particular interpreter.'

A moment of triangular relational depth?

Conclusion

The issue of diversity within the counselling relationship can pose a considerable number and variety of challenges to the establishment of a sound working alliance between therapist and client, to the sensitivity and accuracy of their communications, and, ultimately, to the effectiveness of the therapeutic process. We have described some of these barriers to successful outcome and from this cautious perspective, we may appreciate that moments of relational depth might never have an opportunity of occurring. However, our own combined experiences gained as therapists over time suggest to us that moments of relational depth are more than possible when working across diversity and we have demonstrated examples of this, in addition to offering theoretical hypotheses concerning the optimization of such moments.

References

Alleyne, A. (2005) Invisible injuries and silent witness: The shadow of racial oppression on workplace contexts. *Psychodynamic Practice*, 11(3), 283–99.

BACP (British Association for Counselling and Psychotherapy) (2004) *Diversity Policy Statement*. Lutterworth: BACP (out of print).

Carter, R. (1995) *The Influence of Race and Racial Identity in Psychotherapy: Towards a Racially Inclusive Model.* Westport, CT: Greenwood.

Casse, P. (1981) *Training for the Cross-Cultural Mind.* Washington, DC: SIETAR.

Kennedy, E. (1997) *On Becoming a Counsellor*. Dublin: Gill & Macmillan.

Knipscheer, J.W. and Kleber, R.J. (2004a) The importance of ethnic similarity in the therapist-patient dyad among Surinamese migrants in Dutch mental health care. *Psychology and Psychotherapy: Theory, Research and Practice*, 77, 273–8.

Knipscheer, J.W. and Kleber, R.J. (2004b) A need for ethnic similarity in the therapist-patient interaction? Mediterranean migrants in Dutch mental health care. *Journal of Clinical Psychology*, 60(6), 543–54.

Lago, C. (2006a) Upon being a white therapist: Have you noticed? In C. Lago (ed.) *Race, Culture and Counselling: The Ongoing Challenge* (2nd edn) (pp. 198–203). Maidenhead: Open University/McGraw-Hill.

Lago, C. (2006b) *Race, Culture and Counselling: The Ongoing Challenge.* Maidenhead: Open University Press/McGraw-Hill.

Lago, C. (2010) On developing our empathic capacities to work inter-culturally and inter-ethnically: Attempting a map for personal and professional development. *Psychotherapy and Politics International*, 8(1), 73–85.

Lago, C. and Haugh, S. (2006) White counsellor racial identity: The unacknowledged, unknown, unaware aspect of self in relationship. In M. Cooper, B. Malcolm, G. Proctor and P. Sanders (eds) *Politicising the PCA: An Agenda for Social Change* (pp. 198–214). Ross-on-Wye: PCCS Books.

Lago. C. and Smith, B. (eds) (2003) *Anti-Discriminatory Counselling Practice*. London: Sage.

Lago, C. and Thompson, J. (1997) The triangle with curved sides: Sensitivity to issues of race and culture in supervision. In G. Shipton (ed.) *Supervision of Psychotherapy and Counselling* (pp. 119–30). Buckingham: Open University Press.

McKenzie-Mavinga, I. (2005) Understanding black issues in counsellor training. Unpublished PhD thesis, Metanoia Institute, Middlesex University, London.

McKenzie-Mavinga, I. (2009) *Black Issues in the Therapeutic Process*. Basingstoke: Palgrave Macmillan.

Mearns, D. and Cooper, M. (2005) *Relational Depth in Counselling and Psychotherapy*. London: Sage.

Moodley, R. and Lubin, D. (2008) Developing your career to working with multicultural and diversity clients. In S. Palmer and R. Bor (eds) *The Practitioners Handbook: A Guide for Counsellors, Psychotherapists and Counselling Psychologists* (pp. 156–75). London: Sage.

Moodley, R. and Walcott, R. (eds) (2010) *Counseling Across and Beyond Cultures: Exploring the Work of Clemmont E. Vontress in Clinical Practice*. Toronto: University of Toronto Press.

Moodley, R., Lago, C. and Talahite, A. (eds) (2004) *Carl Rogers Counsels a Black Client: Race and Culture in Person-Centred Counselling*. Ross-on-Wye: PCCS Books.

Natiello, P. (2001) *The Person-Centred Approach: A Passionate Presence*. Ross-on-Wye: PCCS Books.

Ponterotto, J.G. (1988) Racial consciousness development among white counsellor trainees. *Journal of Multicultural Counseling and Development*, 16, 146–56.

Rosen, W.B. and Walker, M. (2004) *How Connections Heal: Stories from Relational-Cultural Therapy*. New York: Guilford Press.

Ryde, J. (2009) *Being White in the Helping Professions: Developing Effective Intercultural Awareness*. London: Jessica Kingsley.

Stevens, S. and Holland, P. (2008) Counselling across a language gap: The therapist's experience. *Counselling Psychology Review*, 23(3), 15–24.

Thompson, C.E. and Jenal, S.T. (1994) Interracial and intraracial quasi-interactions: When counsellors avoid discussing race. *Journal of Counseling Psychology*, 41(4), 484–91.

Tribe, R. (2011) Working with interpreters and bicultural workers. In C. Lago (ed.) *The Handbook of Transcultural Counselling and Psychotherapy* (pp. 81–93). Maidenhead: Open University Press.

Tuckwell, G. (2002) *Racial Identity, White Counsellors and Therapists*. Maidenhead: Open University Press.

10

Supervision and relational depth: a companion on the journey

Elke Lambers

This chapter explores how supervision can support the therapist to maintain and develop their capacity to be fully present and available to the challenge of a relationship at depth. Attending to the development of this capacity is a central part of the therapist's developmental process – their 'developmental agenda' (Mearns and Cooper, 2005, p. 136).

Supervision is rooted in a potentiality model: the supervisor accepts the supervisee as a person in process and trusts their potential for growth (Lambers, 2000, p. 197). The supervisor's intention is to create with the supervisee the conditions that facilitate freedom and self-responsibility and it is through the personal encounter in that relationship that both supervisor and supervisee continue to learn and develop. A high level of mutuality, engagement and presence in the supervision relationship invites and stimulates the therapist to explore the depth of their experience with their client, and gives them support and encouragement to go to greater depth within themselves so that they can meet the client more fully in their experience. Supervision does not teach or instruct the therapist how or when to relate at depth to their clients, but the quality of the supervision relationship facilitates the therapist's openness and receptiveness to their client and so supports the development of their capacity to engage at relational depth.

Therapy: the challenge of relationship

This perspective on supervision is not specific to particular therapeutic orientations but is based on a distinct relational understanding of the nature and meaning of the therapeutic encounter: 'The developmental task of the therapist is to become able to offer an engagement [at relational depth] to every client, regardless of their individual difference' (Mearns and Cooper, 2005, p. 136). This statement sets out an enormous challenge. It asks the therapist to make a commitment that goes beyond their immediate relationship with the client in front of them: it states an ongoing commitment to the therapist's ability to stretch and extend their openness and receptiveness to ever new and potentially challenging encounters with future clients.

Every client who comes through the door of the therapy room presents the therapist with a challenge: to enter into a relationship. As the therapist becomes more present and more congruent in that relationship, their client will experience greater freedom and safety, 'so that they can go to particular depths within their own experiencing' (Mearns, 2005). To be able to meet every client in a relationally deep way does not refer to the therapist's skill in dealing with problems or symptoms presented by clients. The therapist seeking to offer a relationship at depth does not use the relationship as a means to treat, cure or change the client's problem. The client's problem is accepted and respected as an expression of their self-experience, but it does not define the person: the therapist remains oriented towards the whole person – not towards the client's specific symptoms or difficulties. As Mearns stated in his keynote speech at the 6th World Conference for Person-Centered and Experiential Psychotherapy and Counselling:

> If we are to remain consistent with our objective to offer an engagement with the client at relational depth, in order to gain access into his or her existential processing, then we should not treat these various client processes as *problems* in themselves. (2004, p. 99)

Psychological and emotional distress can be understood as disturbances of relation, experienced and manifested in relationship with others, including in the relationship with the therapist (Mearns and Cooper, 2005; Barrett-Lennard, 2009, p. 84; Lambers, 2010). The client's way of experiencing themselves and their relationships becomes visible in the therapy relationship. We experience our client's world, their sense of self, their expectation of relationship not only through their story and their reflections on their experience, but also through our direct experience of them. Therapy, then, is not about treating the specific relational or processing difficulty, but the therapist is sensitive and responsive to the client's unique style of processing as it becomes visible in the therapy relationship.

To be able to meet the person fully requires of us the willingness and capacity to meet them exactly as they are in our relationship: with their fear, their need for closeness, their distrust, and the ways they protect themselves. We experience first-hand *what it is like to be them* and, as we do so, we may also find ourselves challenged, threatened and vulnerable, touched in our own sense of existence (Lambers, 2010). In those moments, our need for self-protection may compete with our capacity to maintain a therapeutic perspective. We may want to withdraw, seek to control the relationship, perhaps blame the client: 'she is not ready for therapy' or 'he does not want to change'. Some therapists avoid the challenge of relationship by adopting the role of expert; others choose to work only with clients with whom they feel comfortable. Some form long-standing dependency relationships based on a superficial level of relating.

Relational therapy is about responding uniquely to each unique person, being responsive to all of who they are in the relationship, and about being open to the challenge that we create together in our encounter. Working at relational depth requires an openness not only to all parts and dimensions of the client, but also to all parts and experiences of the therapist in that relationship (Lambers, 2006). 'Relational therapy is best supported by relational supervision' (Lambers, 2006, p. 274).

The role of supervision in the development of the therapist

'Initial training can only prepare the therapist for the challenge of the therapeutic relationship' (Lambers, 2007, p. 375). The trainee or novice therapist needs to integrate in themselves an enormous amount of new personal experience, theory and skills. Listening, responding, being open to the client's experience, and learning to process their experience of the relationship with clients are new therapists' main concerns. The training course provides a supportive environment where the therapist can experience and explore the limits to their acceptance and understanding, but learning to expand and stretch the capacity to engage deeply with an ever increasing variety of people – and with a greater depth of experiencing – remains one of the most challenging aspects of the lifelong learning process of every therapist; it is a central part of the therapist's ongoing 'developmental agenda' (Mearns and Cooper, 2005). Supervision can play an important part in this process of development, both during and after training.

From a relational perspective, each therapy relationship is unique: it is a relationship experienced and shaped by two unique people and the interaction and interplay between them creates the potential for new experience. The more we are prepared to engage fully in the relationship with our clients, the more likely it is we will be affected by them, changed by them, challenged by them.

The following vignette illustrates how a therapist, Jeremy, explores this challenge in supervision:

J: I am struggling with one of my clients. Last week he started to talk about some things he had never mentioned before – I think he was hinting at his attraction to young boys and I think I avoided it completely. I don't know if I can go there with him. How can I empathize with a paedophile?

S: I hear horror in your voice …

J: Horror ... yes, that is a good word. Horror of what may be on his mind or what he may have done, horror at the kind of things I may have to hear, and horror that I can't hear it – horror at myself for not being able to accept him as he is.

S: Such a shocking confrontation with yourself – you look tortured – it seems almost like a crisis for you.

J: Yes. Not almost, it *is* a crisis. I don't know if I can be a therapist at all. Maybe other guys have been wanting to talk about this stuff, and I missed it, or worse, blanked it. And now I have seen it, but I am not sure that I can work with it or that I even want to work with it. I feel out of my depth – I am sure that is what you think too.

S: Jeremy, I would like to see how we can work with this. I understand some of your feelings of shock and horror, but I would like to think we can do more with this difficult experience.

J: I don't know ... I know too much about what abuse does to kids. But I am sad too, I think he really trusts me and now I am letting him down. But how can I work with him? Accept the sinner, not the sin? Could that work?

S: I think you know the answer to that one, Jeremy. But for the record, no, and I could not help you to work in that way. But I see that it seems really hard just now to see the 'person' that you knew before. Something that he has shown you about himself has become a stumbling block, it has tripped you up. And I also hear that you feel sad and disappointed in yourself, as though you don't like what you are discovering about yourself. This is some challenge. You don't seem to have a clear sense just now of how to respond as a therapist – it is like 'your therapist has left the building'. Can we help him find his way back in?

J: (Smiles) Okay. I owe it to my client, and to me. I guess I am still learning and it is scary. Thank you for not letting me off the hook … but I am going to need quite a bit of help, this is new ground for me.

S: I think it may be new for both of us.

Jeremy is powerfully confronted with his fear and revulsion at the thought of entering more deeply into his client's experience; he is also shocked and dismayed at his failure to honour the trust of the client. He is struggling to maintain a therapeutic perspective – his need for self-protection makes him want to close off.

The supervisor acknowledges Jeremy's fear and distress, and also seeks to connect with the 'therapist' in Jeremy. She is compassionate and empathic as well as challenging and congruent. She is clear about her therapeutic values and perspective but does not judge her supervisee for what could be seen as his wish to run away. As Jeremy decides to accept the challenge of relationship with his client, the supervisor also acknowledges the new challenges that she and Jeremy may face in their relationship.

From a developmental and relational perspective, the purpose of supervision is to facilitate the therapist's congruence in the therapeutic relationship, to facilitate their ability to be open to their experience so that they can be fully present and engaged in the relationship with the client. Supervision offers an opportunity to explore and acknowledge how the therapist's unique self, their life experience and their process of development can support the therapeutic process and the therapeutic relationship (Lambers, 2006, p. 273; Patterson, 1964; Mearns and Cooper, 2005; Villas-Boas Bowen, 1986). The therapist's humanity, the experience of the processes that have made us and continue to shape who we are, is viewed as a trustworthy source for relationship (Lambers, 2006; Wosket, 1999). The supervisor is a companion in the supervisee's exploration of the challenges they face in their journey with their clients.

The example above illustrates the supervisor's commitment to the supervisee: she appreciates deeply the supervisee's experience and his struggle, and his response expresses delicately his sense of her presence. Neither supervisor nor supervisee are solely responsible for such moments of relational depth; each is willing to be open and present to their experience of themselves and of each other and each invites and encourages the other. Relational depth is a two-way process.

Working with the developmental agenda

Attention to continuing professional development is an ethical requirement of the therapy profession. Therapists fulfil this requirement by dutiful attendance at conferences, personal development workshops, seminars, sometimes at great expense of time and money. Often, therapists report that these activities have a short-lived effect, usually because they do not offer the continuity of a more sustained development programme, but perhaps also because they have been chosen for practical reasons such as topic, trainer, location or cost, rather than on the basis of the therapist's ongoing assessment of their own developmental needs.

There is always an *implicit* developmental aspect to supervision. It is often the only place where therapists can share their experience, reflect on their work and on the impact it has on them, and attend to personal challenges as well as professional and ethical concerns; all this supports the therapist's ongoing learning and development. The focus in a supervision session is usually on the exploration of issues directly arising from ongoing therapy practice and not much time is left for taking a wider overview of their deeper significance and meaning for the therapist's development. However, supervision could provide an excellent context for focused and *explicit* attention to the therapist's 'ongoing self-curriculum' (Mearns and Cooper, 2005, p. 155), encouraging and challenging the therapist to ask themselves: 'What do I need to work on in my development so that I can offer and encounter at relational depth to every client?' This programme of self-development is led by the supervisee, with the supervisor as a sounding board or, even better, a partner in the process of setting out, monitoring, developing and updating their developmental agenda.

In the following example, we see how Jeremy enlists support from his supervisor in working on his developmental agenda:

> After our last session, I spent some time thinking about myself, where I am as a therapist. I am quite confident now about my ability to connect with my clients and most of them come back regularly and seem to benefit from our work, and that is encouraging. But my experience with this one client has made me think. Am I really open and able to go to a place where my capacity for acceptance is challenged? I was really shocked, not just by what had happened with this client, but at the thought that I had become perhaps too confident, complacent even. I was getting comfortable in my practice – and perhaps I have been keeping myself too safe. The clients I work with are often difficult to reach, but I feel an affinity with them and I like working with them. But I avoid working with some people – women for a start. I find people with strong religious beliefs difficult – I can't get into their perspective at all. And when I have a gay or black client, I go anxiously out of my way to show how open and non-discriminatory I am. So, what does that tell me? It tells me that I don't look past what some people represent for me. In fact, I probably know very little about their world, but I act as though I do. But I hide it very well, especially to myself.
>
> I also realize that I sometimes use charm and humour to avoid dealing with the client's anger and criticism, and I defend myself with the power of my empathy. Pretty incongruent sometimes.
>
> There is probably a lot more I need to work on, but this is plenty to start with. I would like to make a plan for working on these things. I have some ideas already. I am going to join a regular encounter group, a place where I will be challenged to face some of my prejudices and fears and clever ways of protecting myself. I am going to record my therapy sessions and listen to myself more carefully. I am not sure what I can do about my religious prejudice – I will think about that one. And my over-the-top positive attitude to gay and black clients, I think that comes from my need to be seen as powerful and a 'good guy' – my need for approval. So I need to work on being more real, less defensive and controlling. If anything, I need to be less frightened of making a mistake, of not being good enough. I would like to put that on our agenda in supervision. Oh, and I have asked to be given a female client – I can't go on avoiding half of humanity (said with a smile).

Jeremy's specific plan incorporates a variety of elements: self-development and personal growth, systematic monitoring and reflection on practice, actively seeking to challenge what he recognizes as his prejudice and fear – 'broadening the self' that can be offered in the therapy room and 'expanding experience of humanity' (Mearns and Thorne, 2007, pp. 145, 147). What is striking in his statement is that he takes responsibility for his development, and while he is critical of aspects of his work and his way of being, he does this from a place of self-acceptance. Some aspects of his development he will explore outside the supervision relationship, but the presence of the supervisor would be particularly important in helping him to explore how he can bring different dimensions and parts of himself to the therapy relationship, and how his own humanity may be a source of connection with the client. He trusts his supervisor as a companion on his developmental path – it is so much better to have company than to do all this on his own.

Relational depth in supervision

Relational depth in supervision involves a high level of contact and engagement, in which both persons are contributing to a real dialogue around their shared experience in the moment – both of the supervisee's experience of self in relation to the client and of the relationship between supervisee and supervisor (Lambers, 2006, p. 274).

The supervisor

Supporting the supervisee in their ability to relate at depth and to be authentically present (Schmid, 2001) in their relationship with clients 'requires a high degree of presence and authenticity on the part of the supervisor' (Lambers, 2006, p. 274). Working at relational depth in supervision does not make it into an unboundaried relationship, with a blurred distinction between supervision and therapy. In fact, the opposite may be true. When there is relational depth, both people are fully and transparently themselves and the dynamic of the relationship can be openly explored. Each can trust the other and there is no confusion about purpose, nothing hidden about their intentions. There is a high degree of freedom and a deep respect for the individuality and uniqueness of the other. Spence (2006, p. 6) goes even further when he explores the supervision relationship as 'offering love'; paraphrasing Fromm (1957), he suggests that 'in order to love the client, the supervisee must be loved by the supervisor'.

Although the supervision relationship has many of the elements of a therapy relationship, the nature and focus of both relationships are different. In therapy, the client is completely free to explore whatever issues and concerns are around for them. In supervision, the primary focus is on what emerges for the supervisee in their experience of the relationship with the client (Villas-Boas Bowen, 1986; Patterson, 1964). Nevertheless, the supervisee may well experience the relationship as therapeutic. The exploration of the 'unspoken relationship' (Mearns, 1991, p. 118) can provide opportunities for learning about power and about the developing norms in supervision, and, as in any human relationship, areas of personal vulnerability may surface that may have to be negotiated carefully. This kind of 'metacommunication' (Rennie, 1998) can provide an interesting opportunity for safe experimentation with communication about the experience of the relationship. As we know from research into the client's experience in therapy, the experience of relational depth seems to be different for clients and therapists (McMillan and McLeod, 2006; Cooper, Chapter 5, this volume). There is, as yet, no research into the experience of depth in the supervision relationship, but reflection on the unspoken relationship might contribute to our understanding of the experience and meaning of relational depth in supervision.

Just as the relationship in therapy is the vehicle for therapeutic change (Barrett-Lennard, 2009), so too is the relationship in supervision a vehicle for the growth and development of the therapist. The supervisor's consistent, congruent empathy and acceptance create a climate that is both supportive and challenging and communicates trust in the supervisee's ability to take responsibility in the work with their clients, to continuously seek to deepen their capacity for relating at depth. Only if the supervisee feels met, accepted and trusted in the relationship with the supervisor can they open up to the fullness of their experience with the client. To facilitate such openness, the supervisor needs to be willing to be an active partner in the dialogue, engaging with the supervisee in the exploration of their experience without feeling the need to influence or direct how they practise. In the same way as each therapy relationship is the unique creation of therapist and client, the experience of moments of relational depth are deeply personal and unique to the two people in that relationship. It is therefore not possible for the supervisor to direct or instruct the supervisee as to how they should conduct the therapy relationship, to teach the supervisee how to achieve such moments of meeting at depth, or to monitor or evaluate their ability or success in doing so. In the words of Villas-Boas Bowen (1986, p. 296): 'the function of the supervisor is to create the atmosphere that will enable the supervisee to find his or her own style of being a therapist'.

The supervision relationship offers a powerful model for the therapeutic relationship. There may be moments of relational depth, but also moments of painful misunderstanding and struggle for connection. The experience of each other's humanity supports both supervisor and supervisee in the development of their openness and presence in therapeutic relationships.

The supervisee

Supervision is essentially an adult relationship between colleagues, where both parties are responsible to each other. In her reflection on the experience of supervision, Gibson (2004, p. 36) describes this very well as feeling 'very grown up in a way that I don't do in therapy' and 'more responsible for myself in a supervision session'. In my experience, therapists who actively engage with their developmental agenda acknowledge the importance of supervision. They can articulate what they need from their supervisor and are prepared to explore their experience with clients in depth; they are willing to show themselves and be seen, even in moments of vulnerability and doubt. In such a supervision relationship, the supervisor is welcomed as a companion whose perspective is valued, not feared, and the supervisee is an active partner who openly contributes to the development of the relationship. The supervisee knows best what it is they need to attend to in their own development, but the outside perspective of the supervisor can help them to identify possible blind spots and encourage them to challenge themselves more. The supervision relationship provides a unique learning opportunity, not only through reflection on the experience of the relationship with the client, but also through exploration and reflection on the experience of each other in the supervision relationship. The experience of being met in the supervision relationship facilitates the supervisee's ability to be open to all dimensions of their experience in the relationship with the client and enhances their capacity to meet their clients more fully and deeply.

The power and impact of the supervision relationship is vividly described in the following extract of the personal reflection by a supervisee at the ending of her supervision with me. We had worked together for two years. She had taped every session and would often listen to the recording on the bus home or on the way to meet me. We stopped when I retired from my practice. Her statement was a real gift to me:

- Theoretically, I learned so much from having issues explained and discussed in practice, like the threads of theory that run through Rogers' process conception, hence my client's ability to work out issues for themselves and to know at the end of the day what is best for them personally.
- I learned not to be put off by 'who' the client is and see them as a 'person' in distress and seeking support.
- I learned to separate complex issues brought by my clients and not get confused.
- I learned to appreciate at a deeper level the courage it takes for people to seek help and the courage it takes to continue even when exploring issues becomes unbearably painful. Also, for me to respect my client's decision to stop, and for me to stop beating myself up over the 'disappearing' client.
- I learned to go with angry clients and not to try and appease them or replace their anger with something else.

- I learned the value of listening but also 'hearing' at a deeper level and be aware of 'missing' crucial statements, particularly with the angry, aggressive or belligerent client or the client who continually externalizes.
- To see beyond the obvious in clients has been huge for me. Really huge.
- I learned in supervision to be aware of my judgmental and critical side and keep it in check which has been very, very rewarding.
- I also experienced in supervision the great feeling of being challenged in a supportive, totally gentle way, a far cry from the aggressive and critical challenge which I was wary of.
- From my clients, via supervision, I have learned so much about myself.
- I became aware of my own tendency to patronize my clients at times.
- I became aware of some of my own prejudices which block me from seeing my client as an individual.
- I learned how my tendency to diagnose can block my empathy big time by concentrating on goals and outcome.
- I learned how crippling incongruence can be in supporting my client's process and in building our relationship. This has been the biggest challenge for me, how I experience myself in that relationship with my clients. I have been missing a lot of what has been going on between my client and myself but now have a more heightened awareness of this and these other issues.
- I appreciated the trust my supervisor placed in me to be aware of, and deal appropriately with, my own personal circumstances.
- In conclusion, I felt totally held, respected as a person and valued as an individual by my supervisor. This is the way I would aim for my clients to feel at the end of our work.

I am grateful to my supervisee who gave permission to share here her experience of our work togeher. These reflections illustrate the power and impact of the supervision relationship, both in terms of professional and personal development.

There was room for exploration of theory, of questions arising from the relationship with clients, of personal issues and of the relationship between supervisee and supervisor. In order to facilitate moments of relational depth, therapists do not have to be perfect (Knox and Cooper, 2010, p. 255). It is sometimes through our mistakes, our own vulnerable humanity that we can connect deeply with another person. The greater awareness of the supervisee's self-experience in the relationship with clients has enabled her to be more open to her clients, more sensitive and accepting of their processes, able to meet each client with energy, resilience and courage.

Mearns and Cooper (2005, xii) define relational depth as: 'a state of profound contact between two people in which each person is fully real with the other, and able to understand and value the other's experience at a high level'. What a fitting description of relational depth in supervision.

Conclusion

In the same way that each therapy relationship is the unique creation of therapist and client, the experience of moments of relational depth are deeply personal and unique to the two people in that relationship. Supervision does not teach or instruct the therapist how or when to relate at depth to their clients, but the quality of the supervision relationship facilitates the therapist's openness and receptiveness to their client and so supports the development of their capacity to engage at relational depth: 'Relational therapy is best supported by relational supervision' (Lambers, 2006, p. 274).

The supervision relationship offers a powerful model for the therapeutic relationship. A high level of mutuality, engagement and presence in the supervision relationship invites and stimulates the therapist to explore the depth of their experience with their client, and gives them support and encouragement to go to greater depth within themselves so that they can meet the client more fully in their experience. In such a supervision relationship, the humanity that is at the core of the therapeutic relationship can be fully acknowledged and celebrated (Lambers, 2006, p. 275).

References

Barrett-Lennard, G. (2009) From personality to relationship: Path of thought and practice. *Person-Centered and Experiential Psychotherapies*, 8(2), 79–93.

Fromm, E. (1957) *The Art of Loving*. London: George Allen & Unwin.

Gibson, D. (2004) On being received: A supervisee's view of being supervised. In K. Tudor and M. Worral (eds) *Freedom to Practise: Person-centred Approaches to Supervision* (pp. 31–42). Ross-on-Wye: PCCS Books.

Knox, R. and Cooper, M. (2010) Relationship qualities that are associated with moments of relational depth: The clients' perspective. *Person-Centered and Experiential Psychotherapies*, 9(3), 236–56.

Lambers, E. (2000) Supervision in person-centred therapy: Facilitating congruence. In D. Mearns and B. Thorne (eds) *Person-Centred Therapy Today: New Frontiers in Theory and Practice* (pp. 196–211). London: Sage

Lambers, E. (2006) Supervising the humanity of the therapist. *Person-Centered and Experiential Psychotherapies*, 5(4), 266–76.

Lambers, E. (2007) A person-centred perspective on supervision. In M. Cooper, M. O'Hara, P.F. Schmid and G. Wyatt (eds) *The Handbook of Person-Centred Psychotherapy and Counselling* (pp. 366–78). Basingstoke: Palgrave Macmillan.

Lambers, E. (2010) Whose problem is it? Understanding disturbance as challenge in relationship. Public lecture delivered at Strathclyde University, Glasgow.

McMillan, M. and McCleod, J. (2006) Letting go: The client's experience of relational depth. *Person-Centered and Experiential Psychotherapies*, 5(4), 277–92.

Mearns, D. (1991) On being a supervisor. In W. Dryden and C. Feltham (eds) *Training and Supervision for Counselling in Action* (pp. 116–28). London: Sage.

Mearns, D. (2004) Problem-centered is not person-centered. *Person-Centered and Experiential Psychotherapies*, 3(2), 88–101.

Mearns, D. (2005) How I work as a person-centred therapist. Public lecture at Kansai Counseling Center, Osaka, Japan.

Mearns, D. and Cooper, M. (2005) *Working at Relational Depth in Counselling and Psychotherapy*. London: Sage.

Mearns, D. and Thorne, B. (2007) *Person-Centred Counselling in Action* (3rd edn). London: Sage.

Patterson, C.H. (1964) Supervising students in the counseling practicum. *Journal of Counseling Psychology*, 11, 47–53.

Rennie, D.L. (1998) *Person-Centred Counselling: An Experiential Approach*. London: Sage.

Schmid, P. (2001) Authenticity: The person as his or her own author. Dialogical and ethical perspectives on therapy as an encounter relationship. And beyond. In G. Wyatt (ed.) *Rogers' Therapeutic Conditions: Evolution, Theory and Practice*, vol. 1, *Congruence* (pp. 213–28). Ross-on-Wye: PCCS Books.

Spence, S. (2006) The amateur supervisor: Supervision as an offer of love. *Person-Centred Quarterly*, August, 1–6.

Villas-Boas Bowen, M. (1986) Personality differences and person-centered supervision. *Person-Centered Review*, 1(3), 291–309.

Woskett, V. (1999) *The Therapeutic Use of Self*. London: Routledge.

11

Experiencing relational depth: self-development exercises and reflections

Mick Cooper

Since the publication of *Working at Relational Depth in Counselling and Psychotherapy* by Dave Mearns and myself (Mearns and Cooper, 2005), I have developed a range of exercises to help counsellors and psychotherapists explore and develop their capacity to relate to their clients in depth. These exercises, of course, are not a 'how to' guide on making relational depth happen: by their very nature, moments of relational depth cannot be contrived. Rather, they are an invitation to explore experiences of relational depth (as 'moments'; see Chapter 1, this volume), and to consider ways in which this experiencing might be facilitated or inhibited. Although the exercises are oriented towards counsellors or psychotherapists with a background in person-centred therapy, I have found that they can also be helpful for therapists of other orientations.

For the purposes of this chapter, most of these exercises are described for readers to try out on their own, ideally in some quiet and private space. Exercise 5, however, does require a partner; and for each of the exercises, I have suggested how they might be undertaken with other people. This might be colleagues in the counselling field, such as fellow practitioners or students, as part of a supervision group, or on a training course. A version of this chapter written specifically for trainers, with additional notes on how these exercises might be delivered in a group format, is available at pure.strath.ac.uk/portal/.

Each of these exercises has the capacity to evoke powerful emotions. It is important, therefore, to only undertake the exercises that you feel happy to try out, and if you do them on your own, do make sure there is someone available for you to debrief with, should the need arise.

1. Reviewing relational connections

Aim
To raise your awareness of how everyday relational interactions may affect your mood.

The exercise
1. Reflect on the relational encounters that you have had this morning. This may include:
   - 'Real' others: for example your partner, the cat
   - 'Imaginary' others: for example someone you were having a conversation with in your imagination.
2. Ask yourself:
   - What was the quality of the connection like with that person? For example good, bad, indifferent
   - How did that impact on you? For example 'depressed me', 'energized me'.

Dyad/group variation
Pair up with someone and take 10 minutes each to explore the questions above.

Reflections

Through this simple exercise, people generally notice how much of an impact relational encounters can have on their feelings and way of being. An argument with their partner, for example, sets them off on a bad mood; a cuddle with their son that morning gives them a warm glow. This highlights how our experiencing is not closed or cut off from others, but intrinsically connected to other people in the world. As Heidegger (1962) and other intersubjective thinkers have put it, our being is always a 'being-in-relationship'.

2. Experiencing relational depth

Aim
To help you develop an awareness of the experience of relational depth.

The exercise
Explore the following question: 'If you were experiencing an in-depth sense of connection with another person right now, that is, experiencing relational depth, how would you know it? For example:

- What would you be feeling in yourself? For example 'exhilarated', 'vulnerable'
- What would your experience of the other person be like? For example 'They would seem very open'

- How would the relationship be experienced? For example 'A real sense of cohesion'
- What would the atmosphere be like? For example 'A sense that something magical is taking place'.

In reflecting on this, you may find it helpful to think about times in which you have experienced a deep sense of connection with another person (not necessarily within a therapeutic relationship) in your life. What was it like?

As an additional/alternative exercise, try expressing your experience of relational depth through drawing, painting or some other creative medium, such as poetry.

Have a look at the review of research findings on the experience of relational depth (Chapter 5, this volume). Do your own experiences match?

Dyad/group variation
Take 15 minutes with a partner, and ask yourselves: 'If *we* were experiencing an in-depth sense of connection with each other right now, how would *we* know?'

Reflections

I have facilitated this exercise many times in groups, and I am still struck by how frequently the same words or phrases come up to describe this experience of in-depth relating; for example, mutuality, synchronicity, trust, stillness, openness, safety, warmth, equality, no need for words, aliveness, sense of time standing still, feeling in your stomach, a tingling all over. Also, some great idiosyncratic descriptions always come up; for example, soupiness, walking on the edge of falling in love, a feeling of holding each other's hearts, reading each other without words being spoken. For me, it really helps to affirm my belief that, although it is by no means clear what moments of relational depth are, there is something 'there', something that many of us seem to experience, and something that is worthy of further exploration.

3. A life without relational depth

The basic assumption underlying this exercise is that, for many of us, good interpersonal relationships are central to our psychological wellbeing (see Means and Cooper, 2005, Ch. 2), and that interpersonal disconnections, as well as intrapersonal ones, can be a primary source of psychological distress.

Aims
1. To help you explore the relationship between relational depth and psychological wellbeing.

2. To help you develop your ability to empathize with clients who may be experiencing isolation and a lack of in-depth relating in their lives.

The exercise

In a quiet space, sit or lie comfortably, and close your eyes. Imagine what it would be like to live a life without any in-depth connections to others. How would it feel? What would your life be like? In asking yourself these questions, you may find it useful to think about times in your life where you have experienced such an absence.

As with the previous exercise, you may find it useful to express your perception/experiencing of a life without relational depth through some creative medium, such as drawing.

As a follow-up exercise, ask yourself this question: How much do you agree or disagree with the statement: 'Chronic disconnection from others is the primary source of psychological distress' (Jordan et al., 2004). Consider this particularly in relation to clients you are working/have worked with and yourself.

You may also find it interesting to ask yourself: How is it that relational disconnections might emerge in the first place, particularly if people have a natural propensity to relatedness? (See Mearns and Cooper, 2005, Ch. 1.)

Dyad/group variation

In a group context, after conducting the visualization, you can share your experiences/perceptions with a partner, and then go on to discuss the questions above.

Reflections

Doing this exercise for myself, it always strikes me how painful it is to think about a life without connection. I remember a time in my early twenties, travelling through Greece, when I had not had any meaningful connection with anyone for a few days. I was aching with pain – a real deep, desperate yearning – and was approaching anyone who looked like they might talk a bit of English to try and establish some connection. So a life that is consistently like that, for me, is almost too awful to contemplate, and many people who do this exercise seem to come to the same conclusion. But I do think that, for some of our clients, that is the reality of their lives – a deep, painful, aching sense of isolation and disconnection – and as therapists, who may be used to fairly deep connections with others in our lives, it might be easy to forget that not everyone exists in this way.

Interestingly, when doing this exercise, some people may say that they can also see the positive side of a life without any connections: a sense of freedom, liberation, not being tied down to anyone. And, indeed, in a small number of instances, participants have said that this is pretty much what their current life is like, and that this is a personal choice, which feels okay. Obviously, it is important to value such contributions, and not to work from the assumption that relational depth is, de facto, a good thing. I think Martin Buber (1958), the great relational philosopher, puts this very well when he says that we will always have times when we experience the world in relatively disconnected, I-It ways. Indeed, these times can be very important and necessary. But when that is all we have, when there is a total absence of I-Thou moments of connectedness, then we can really struggle.

When I have facilitated this exercise with person-centred therapists, subsequent discussions tend to pivot around the question of whether psychological distress is primarily caused by disconnections with others, or by disconnections with one's own self. Almost invariably, we come to the conclusion that the two are so interlinked that either, or both, could be the starting point for psychological difficulties. I do tend to argue, however, that in classical person-centred developmental theory (for example Rogers, 1951, 1959), the emphasis is very much on *intra*personal splitting – between the self-experience and the self-concept – with very little said, explicitly, about the potential damage that a lack of *inter*personal relating can do. Indeed, in classical person-centred theory, the role of the Other is primarily as the one who *disrupts* our natural, organismic growth (through conditional positive regard); and this contrasts with other relational models of development (for example Bowlby, 1979), which speak much more explicitly about a human need for others. Another way I have put this is to say that, from a relational perspective, there is something that we need for our wellbeing that only others can provide – what Hycner (1991, p. 61) has termed a 'deep soul-nourishment'. So, from this perspective, it may not be enough for us just to like ourselves, we *need* other people to like us: positive regard is not a secondary, learned need (Rogers, 1959), but a fundamental ingredient of a satisfying and meaningful existence. For me, Martin Buber (1988, p. 61) puts this beautifully, when he writes:

> The human person needs confirmation because man as man needs it ... Sent forth from the natural domain of species into the hazard of the solitary category, surrounded by the air of chaos which came into being with him, secretly and bashfully he watches for a Yes which allows him to be and which can come to him only from one human person to another. It is from one man to another that the heavenly bread of self-being is passed.

This can, then, lead on to a discussion of how person-centred practice, from a relational depth perspective, might differ from a more classical approach (for example Merry, 2004; Rogers, 1942). How I tend to think about this is as follows: if we assume that the principal source of psychological distress is intrapersonal disconnection, as a consequence of the existence of conditional positive regard (Rogers, 1959), then it makes absolute sense that the most healing thing we can do is to provide our clients with an unconditionally positively regarding context, in which they can begin to 'put themselves back together again'. However, if psychological distress is also understood in terms of real, in-the-world splits between self and others, then establishing a specific, person-to-person connection also becomes a key element of helping some clients back into health and wellbeing. This is a subtle distinction but, for me, it is like the difference between providing a 'crucible' for clients to do their work, versus providing a more immediate, person-to-person encounter (see Figure 11.1).

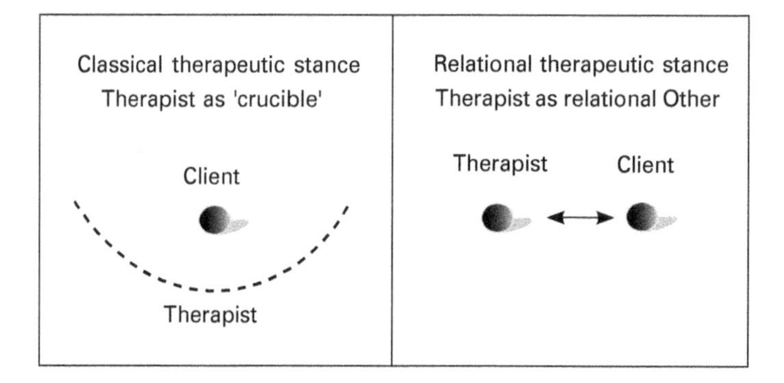

Figure 11.1 Classical and relational therapeutic stances

What does this mean in terms of actual practice? For me, a relational way of being person-centred, in contrast to a more classical one, may mean:

- bringing more of my own experiences or perceptions into the encounter with the client
- being less of a mirror and more of an actual other with different views and beliefs
- moving away from a therapy that is wholly oriented around an 'empathic understanding response process' (Freire, 2007) towards one that might involve a variety of different forms of engagement – asking questions, probing, giving input, maybe even offering advice – depending on what particular clients seem to want at particular times
- moving beyond a neutral, nonjudgemental 'acceptance' of the client to a more active, intentional prizing of their being-in-the-world: not just a 'however they experience the world is fine', but a deep relational affirmation of their being in all its uniqueness (see Chapter 2, this volume)
- being willing to share with a client my genuine care or concerns for them (see Chapter 2, this volume).

But are these differences really meaningful? It is at this point in workshops that I often find myself in lively disagreement with person-centred participants. Some feel that I am caricaturing the classical person-centred approach, and that they would do all these things anyway. Some simply cannot see what the distinction is all about. Others, though, do get a sense that there is a subtle shift of emphasis here; and that while it is by no means an either/or dichotomy, there is some spectrum of person-centred practice that ranges from a more 'holding', nondirective stance to a more active, dialogical one – and that different clients do best with different emphases at different points in time. Indeed, I know for myself that since studying and writing about relational ideas, I have become a different kind of therapist: more 'just myself' with my clients, more relaxed and informal, less 'precious', more willing to just 'get stuck in' with a client and do whatever might seem helpful at that particular point in time.

4. Strategies of disconnection

This exercise is a way into exploring the question of how we, as therapists, might be able to deepen our relationship with our clients. The theory behind this exercise comes from the work of Judith Jordan and colleagues (Jordan et al., 2004), mentioned above. It starts with a paradox: evidence from the child and developmental psychology field (see Mearns and Cooper, 2005, Ch. 1) makes it is clear that human beings want, and are able, to engage deeply with others from the first moments of life. But then, how is it possible that so many of us can become so chronically disconnected from others, with all the psychological difficulties that can follow? Jordan et al. answer this paradox by suggesting that we may develop 'chronic strategies of disconnection'. These are ways that we may have developed of protecting ourselves from hurts in early close relationships that then become fixed and sedimented, such that we carry on protecting ourselves from intimacy even when, as an adult, that relational depth may actually be very healing. A young girl, for instance, is teased by her mother for wanting closeness and intimacy; so she learns to withdraw from connection, perhaps by removing herself physically, perhaps by detaching herself in her own head. And, as an adult, she continues to withdraw physically or psychologically from the possibility of closeness with others, even when those encounters could provide her with exactly the deep soul nourishment that she so desperately craves.

So this exercise invites you to think about your own chronic strategies of disconnection, and it goes on from this to invite you to think about whether any of these strategies may be relevant in your therapeutic work. For, without doubt, we will bring into the therapeutic work who we are, and if we have ways of disconnecting from relationships in our everyday lives, there is a strong possibility that these may also turn up in our clinical work.

A personal example: as a child, if I got hurt or upset by my family, I would threaten to leave home and go sit outside the front door of our flat for what seemed like ages (although probably only five minutes or so), before boredom or hunger would set in and take me back inside. As an adult, I can still tend to deal with personal hurt by withdrawing, and by walking away from situations when, in fact, I would often be better off addressing the problem and trying to re-establish connection. And I can also see how this is sometimes played out in my therapeutic practice. For instance, if a client tells me that they want to end therapy, I am sometimes very quick to agree with them that it is the best thing to do, and that it is 'really fine' with me, rather than inviting them to spend a bit more time exploring their feelings. Essentially, what seems to happen here is that I feel a bit rejected or hurt, and I deal with it by quickly withdrawing from the situation, rather than giving things a bit more time to be worked through, and for a connection to be re-established.

Aim

To help you develop an awareness of what might get in the way of you relating more deeply with others, and particularly your clients.

The exercise

1. Reflect on this question: 'What are your chronic strategies of disconnection?' That is, what are the ways that you, in your life, pull away from deeper relating with others, when to remain in connection might actually be more rewarding? For example, do you withdraw mentally, use humour, avoid physical closeness, become compliant, stop listening, become very formal.
2. Reflect on this question: 'To what extent might these strategies of disconnection also be present in your therapeutic work?' For example, if you use humour to distance yourself from people in your everyday life, are there also times when you do this with your clients? If none of these strategies are present, what might be other ways in which you disconnect from clients in the therapeutic encounter?

Dyad/group variation

With a partner, take 10 minutes each to explore your general strategies of disconnection (question 1, above). Once you have both done this, explore together how manifested these strategies might be in your therapeutic work (question 2, above).

Reflections

It is important to emphasize that this exercise encourages you to consider *chronic* strategies of disconnection: things that you do, systematically, to pull away from deeper relating to others, and which are potentially redundant or unhelpful. So, it is not about things that you do to keep yourself safe from destructive or harmful relationships, but ingrained and automatic patterns that may get in the way of you obtaining deeper, more satisfying levels of relating.

In my experience, some people who do this exercise are really struck by how commonly their chronic strategies of disconnection are carried over into the therapeutic relationship, while others find very few parallels at all. Of course, both answers are totally appropriate.

From data that Rosanne Knox and myself are currently analysing, it seems that the five most common strategies of disconnection that therapists (mainly person-centred practitioners and trainees) use in their *lives* are as follows (in approximately descending order):

- Mental withdrawal: for example 'Thinking about something else at the same time as talking to someone'
- Physical avoidance: for example 'Send emails instead of speaking'
- Silence/quietness: for example 'Go "mute" for a while'
- Humour: for example 'Make a joke'
- Aggressiveness: for example 'Express irritation/anger/frustration'.

However, the five strategies of disconnection that were rated as being most present in their *therapeutic work* were as follows (again, in roughly descending order of relevance):

- Rescuing: for example 'Doing over helpful'
- Other focus: for example 'Being a good listener but not sharing'
- Hiding/invisibility: for example 'Quietly disappearing'
- Intellectualization: for example 'Stay in the head rather than go to the feelings'
- Conflict avoidance: for example 'Avoid challenging others'.

It would be interesting to see if therapists from other orientations also tended to disconnect from their clients in these ways.

On the basis of this research, Rosanne Knox and I have developed a short questionnaire that can be used by people to reflect on their chronic strategies of disconnection (see Appendix at end of chapter). The instrument is yet to be validated and finalized, but the version presented here may still be a useful tool for helping to think about your own strategies of disconnection: both outside and inside the therapeutic encounter.

5. Developing embodied empathy

This exercise *does* need to be conducted with a partner. It is based on the concept of 'embodied empathy', a term I have used (Cooper, 2001; Mearns and Cooper, 2005) to describe a form of interpersonal engagement that goes beyond a purely cognitive, or even affective, understanding of someone's world towards a full-bodied resonance with their being. I might experience, for example, a tightness in my stomach as a client talks about a particularly frightening situation, or a pressure on the top of my head as they describe the stresses they are under. As with relational depth, embodied empathy does not seem to be something that I can *make* happen, but it may be something that therapists can be more or less open to and, as the research would suggest (see Chapter 5, this volume), it seems to be an important ingredient of a relationally deep encounter.

Aims

1. To help you develop your capacity to empathize with your clients in an embodied way.
2. To help you appreciate the value of, and develop a trust in, your own embodied experiences in relation to clients.
3. To help you become more relaxed and spontaneous in your practice.

The exercise

1. With a partner, decide who will be the talker and who will be the listener.
2. The talker should talk for around 10 minutes about an issue of current concern that has some emotional content, that is, there is some emotion there, but not so much that it needs a more extended period of talking through.
3. The listener should do the following:
   - First, sit yourself as comfortably as possible. Let yourself be as relaxed as you can, and don't worry about anything you have been taught about how to sit or look when you are counselling.
   - As the talker starts to talk, try and let yourself 'breathe in' what they are saying. Give yourself time to resonate, at a physical level, with what the talker is expressing. Just notice what you are feeling physically.
   - Try not to worry about what you are going to say. In fact, *try not to say too much at all*, aside from brief interjections like 'mm', 'aha' and so on.
   - The one time you should respond in depth is if you feel some physical sensation in response to what the talker is saying. For example, you might experience an aching in your shoulders or a sense of numbness throughout your body, and you should share this with the talker, for instance: 'As you describe that argument, I can feel a real tightness in my chest.' Don't worry if it seems totally out of place, just give it a go.
   - You may not feel any physical resonance for the whole period, and that is fine. Just don't say too much.
4. Swap roles and repeat.
5. Take 10 minutes or so to discuss this experience:
   - How did it feel to listen in this way?
   - How did it feel to be listened to in this way?

- To what extent did the physical sensations that you reflected match what the client was experiencing?

Reflections

Some people seem to find this exercise really interesting and helpful, while others, quite honestly, don't. It often seems to be most helpful for individuals in the initial stages of counsellor training, and particularly where they are experiencing a pressure to work in a relatively formulaic, unspontaneous way, for example 'sit upright', 'reflect', 'don't ask questions'; or where they are really worried about how they 'should' respond to their clients. Such participants have said that they find this exercise really liberating, helping them feel much more enthusiastic about their work as counsellors, or counselling skills practitioners. On the other hand, some trainees, as well as some more experienced practitioners, find the practice in this exercise quite restrictive and unnatural. It is important to emphasize, therefore, that this exercise is just about *trying something out*, and is not a mandate on how you should practise from here onwards.

When this exercise does work for people, they can be really surprised at how accurately their own bodily experiences mirror those of the clients. This can help them to trust, more fully, their own felt reactions to clients, and to draw on them more fully in their therapeutic work, thus deepening their level of relating. My favourite feedback, however, was from a Danish psychologist who, at the end of a relational workshop day, wanted to say how much she had liked this embodiment exercise. Unfortunately, she didn't get her English quite right and so said to me, in front of a large group of her colleagues, 'I very much like your body.' The fact that she had been offering psychoanalytic interpretations throughout the day made it even funnier!

6. Interpersonal perception: factors that facilitate, and inhibit, connection

This exercise is probably best conducted in a group context, although it has the potential to be quite challenging – as well as very rewarding. In my experience, it tends to be most helpful for groups of participants who have had previous interactions with each other, for example students on the same diploma training course or colleagues in a local counselling network, and where there is an opportunity for ongoing processing of what emerges from it. It is essential that participants in this exercise, if done in a group, have had some basic training in therapeutic or personal development work, such that they are able to hear feedback in a nondefensive way, and to share it in a way that is 'owned' and noncritical.

The exercise is based on the premise that it is not just the things we intentionally do, whether consciously or 'unconsciously', that get in the way of us connecting with others and our clients (as in our chronic strategies of disconnection, above). Also, there may be things about us that are simply there, perhaps just by chance, that make others more wary of connecting with us. For example, over the years, I have come to realize that my physical presence – as a fairly broad man, with dark features and a fairly deep voice – can lead people to feel quite intimidated, even when, actually, I might be feeling quite frightened or vulnerable myself. In fact, I have even had the experience of specifically saying to people – fellow trainees in a personal development group, colleagues – that I am feeling scared and vulnerable, and them refusing to believe it because of something in how I am coming across. So, in developing our capacity to connect with others, it may be quite important to have a sense of how others experience us (our *metaperceptions*; see Cooper, 2005, 2009), such that we can try and address any aspects of ourselves that inhibit contact. Of course, this does not mean that we should change who we are but simply being aware of it, or perhaps finding ways to compensate for it, may be of value; for example, I might try to communicate my vulnerabilities more fully.

Aims

1. To help you develop your awareness of aspects of yourself that might make others, including clients, wary of making contact with you.
2. To help you develop your awareness of aspects of yourself that might make others, including clients, drawn towards making contact with you.

The exercise

1. Reflect on, and write down, those characteristics of you that might make people drawn towards connecting with you, and those that might make them wary of connecting with you.
2. You may then want to check this out with someone who knows you, such as a colleague in the counselling field or a fellow trainee, to see if they actually do experience you in this way, or whether there are other things that actually draw them towards, and make them wary of, connecting with you. Try to find someone who you can trust to respond in a sensitive way, but also who will be open enough to articulate anything that might make them more wary of connecting with you (see guidelines for feedback, below).

Group variation

1. Form into groups of four. As far as possible, try to go into groups with people you have had some prior interaction with, but not people you know extremely well.
2. On a piece of A4 paper (landscape orientation), create a three by four grid (that is, draw two horizontal lines, and three vertical lines, equally spaced apart) (see Figure 11.2). In the top row of the second to fourth column, have the name of each of the other group members. In the left-hand column of the second row, write: 'Perceptions of this person that make me want to

connect with them'. In the left-hand column of the third row, write: 'Perceptions of this person that make me wary of connecting with them'.

3. Now, take 10 minutes, and for each member of your group write down, in the relevant parts of the grid, what makes you drawn to, and wary of, connecting with them. In doing so, bear the following in mind:
   - Be clear that what you are writing down is your experience/perception of this person, and not some objective assessment. So, it is not about telling someone what their personality or character is 'really' like, but about 'owning' your personal perception or experience of them, with an acknowledgement that someone else might experience them in a very different way.
   - Find a good balance between being honest and being sensitive. You will be asked to share these perceptions with the other person (although, of course, you don't have to), and given the limited time frame for the exercise, it is important that you don't open up a whole set of issues that cannot be dealt with in the given time span. On the other hand, the more honest you are with someone, the more useful this is likely to be.
   - If you have had no contact with someone, write down your first impressions.
4. Now, pair up with one of the members of your group, and one of the pair should take 10 minutes to share with their partner, and discuss, the perceptions of them that make them drawn to, and wary of, connection with them. Now take 10 minutes to do this the other way round.
5. Now pair up with another member of your group and repeat Step 4 (this should take 20 minutes per pair). Repeat again with the final member of your group.
6. In a large or small group, discuss this exercise (maybe 30 minutes or so). What did you learn about yourself?

	Ishtar	Zak	Molly
Perceptions of this person that make me want to connect with them			
Perceptions of this person that make me wary of connecting with them			

Figure 11.2 Example grid for interpersonal exercise

This exercise can also be undertaken in threes. Just adjust the grid accordingly, that is, three columns instead of four, and take 10 minutes or so, in turn, for each person to receive feedback from their partner(s).

Reflections

When this exercise is conducted in a group or with pairs giving feedback, it is essential to remember that the task is to write down how you *perceive* or *experience* others, and not to be making judgements or assessments of what the other person is *actually* like. When I ran this exercise with a group of Greek therapists, one of the women exclaimed: 'But how can I tell someone that they are an idiot.' I re-emphasized to her that the exercise was about really owning one's perceptions and experiences, and not making judgements about someone else. 'Oh,' she responded, 'so I should tell them that I *feel* they are an idiot.'

Interestingly, the kinds of perceptions that people have of others that make them wary of contact are often things that, on the surface, might seem quite positive; for example 'clever', 'knowledgeable', 'beautiful', 'experienced' or 'confident'. Sometimes, though, it seems that these perceptions can leave a person feeling intimidated or inferior. Participants also commonly state that they feel wary of contact with another person because they are worried that that person will judge them or think they are 'silly'; or because they experience someone as very open, honest and direct. On the other hand, the perception of another person as 'withdrawn', 'shy' or 'nervous' can also lead to a wariness about contact. Two physical features that come up quite often as making people wary of contact are someone being tall, and wearing glasses. 'Male' also seems to come up a lot, as does age differences, although these factors might be particularly related to a counselling context. Interestingly, too, participants often note that the features that make them wary of contact with someone are also the features that make them drawn towards contact, for example someone's perceived intelligence or their attractiveness.

Conclusion

Of course, the above exercises are just a few of the ways in which the experience of relational depth can be explored. They do, however, provide the basis for a fairly substantive exploration of the phenomenon, and one that seems to have proved relatively engaging and informative for many workshop participants over the years. For readers who might hope to come away from these exercises knowing how to 'create' relational depth with their clients, they will prove disappointing; but as a few small steps on the journey towards a greater understanding of – and capacity to engage in – in-depth relationships, they have the potential to be some useful stimuli.

Appendix **Chronic strategies of disconnection: a reflective tool** (Cooper and Knox, v2)

Chronic strategies of disconnection are patterns of behaviour that people develop to protect themselves from hurt or anxiety in close relationships, but which may now be redundant: that is, they tend to do them automatically, when it may, in fact, be more beneficial for them to stay in closer connection with another person.

Reflecting on your own experience of close relationships as an adult and times in which you feel hurt or anxious, to what extent do you tend to use the following strategies to disconnect from others (when you might be better off staying in connection)? Once you have completed this reflect on which strategies, if any, might be present in your therapeutic work.

	Not at all	*A little*	*Moderately*	*A lot*
Immersing yourself in activities (e.g.,TV)	0	1	2	3
Being busy	0	1	2	3
Distracting yourself	0	1	2	3
Talking a lot	0	1	2	3
Being aggressive to others	0	1	2	3
Acting in an arrogant way	0	1	2	3
Criticizing others	0	1	2	3
Being cold or prickly	0	1	2	3
Ending contact with people	0	1	2	3
Being controlling	0	1	2	3
Pushing others away	0	1	2	3
Feigning disinterest: that you don't really care	0	1	2	3
Being overly formal or polite	0	1	2	3
Keeping things at a superficial level	0	1	2	3
Using humour or laughter	0	1	2	3
Avoiding communication with others	0	1	2	3
Isolating yourself physically from others	0	1	2	3
Physically avoiding people	0	1	2	3
Using drugs or alcohol	0	1	2	3
Daydreaming	0	1	2	3
Withdrawing emotionally	0	1	2	3
Intellectualizing	0	1	2	3
Mentally shutting down, 'going into your head'	0	1	2	3
Not joining in with things	0	1	2	3
Becoming tired or going to sleep	0	1	2	3
Avoiding conflict	0	1	2	3
Being compliant, appeasing	0	1	2	3
Not expressing your wants	0	1	2	3
Being closed in your body language	0	1	2	3
Changing the subject	0	1	2	3
Avoiding eye contact	0	1	2	3
Not listening	0	1	2	3
Becoming quiet or silent	0	1	2	3
Focusing attention on others	0	1	2	3
Rescuing: being overly helpful to others	0	1	2	3
Being independent	0	1	2	3
Trying to hide or make yourself invisible	0	1	2	3
Criticizing yourself	0	1	2	3
Feeling sorry for yourself/'playing the victim'	0	1	2	3

References

Bowlby, J. (1979) *The Making and Breaking of Affectional Bonds*. London: Routledge.

Buber, M. (1958) *I and Thou* (trans. R.G. Smith) (2nd edn). Edinburgh: T & T Clark.

Buber, M. (1988) *The Knowledge of Man: Selected Essays* (trans. M. Friedman and R.G. Smith). Atlantic Highlands, NJ: Humanities Press International.

Cooper, M. (2001) Embodied empathy. In S. Haugh and T. Merry (eds) *Empathy* (pp. 218–29). Ross-on-Wye: PCCS Books.

Cooper, M. (2005) The inter-experiential field: Perceptions and metaperceptions in person-centered and experiential psychotherapy and counseling. *Person-Centered and Experiential Psychotherapies*, 4(1), 54–68.

Cooper, M. (2009) Interpersonal perceptions and metaperceptions: Psychotherapeutic practice in the inter-experiential realm. *Journal of Humanistic Psychology*, 49(1), 85–99.

Freire, E. (2007) Empathy. In M. Cooper, P.F. Schmid, M. O'Hara and G. Wyatt (eds) *The Handbook of Person-Centred Psychotherapy and Counselling* (pp. 194–204). Basingstoke: Palgrave Macmillan.

Heidegger, M. (1962) *Being and Time* (trans. J. Macquarrie and E. Robinson). Oxford: Blackwell.

Hycner, R. (1991) *Between Person and Person: Towards a Dialogical Psychotherapy*. Highland, NY: Gestalt Journal Press.

Jordan, J.V., Walker, M. and Hartling, L.M. (eds) (2004) *The Complexity of Connection: Writing from the Stone Center's Jean Baker Miller Training Institute*. New York: Guilford Press.

Mearns, D. and Cooper, M. (2005) *Working at Relational Depth in Counselling and Psychotherapy*. London: Sage.

Merry, T. (2004) Classical client-centred therapy. In P. Sanders (ed.) *The Tribes of the Person-Centred Nation: An Introduction to the Schools of Therapy Related to the Person-Centred Approach* (pp. 21–44). Ross-on-Wye: PCCS Books.

Rogers, C.R. (1942) *Counselling and Psychotherapy: Newer Concepts in Practice*. Boston: Houghton Mifflin.

Rogers, C.R. (1951) *Client-Centered Therapy*. Boston: Houghton Mifflin.

Rogers, C.R. (1959) A theory of therapy, personality and interpersonal relationships as developed in the client-centered framework. In S. Koch (ed.) *Psychology: A Study of Science* (pp. 184–256). New York: McGraw-Hill.

PART III

Related Perspectives

12

Dialogue as the foundation of person-centred therapy

Peter F. Schmid

Friedrich Nietzsche (2000) once stated that we only hear the questions we are able to answer – a sentence that should melt in a psychotherapist's mouth, a profoundly important challenge for therapy. Psychotherapy that has to do with understanding others would make no sense, if Nietzsche, with his almost solipsistic statement, was right. It points to a crucial question for all therapists who want to get beyond an understanding of therapy as a behaviour or value-imposing psychotechnique.

I am convinced that the only way to overcome such self-entanglement is to understand the human being as a dialogical being, that is, as a *person*. Therefore, psychotherapy must be understood as dialogue – an anthropological stance intrinsic to the person-centred approach (PCA).

The PCA has been facing this epistemological challenge since its inception. Person-centred psychotherapy has undergone major developments in recent decades. Following Carl Rogers' groundbreaking intention to understand the client as the centre of the therapeutic relationship, this approach, on the one hand, stresses the view of the client as active self-helper, and, on the other hand, the therapist is seen as actively responding to the person of the client – being both with and counter to the client (Schmid and Mearns, 2006; Mearns and Schmid, 2006).

In this chapter, I will argue that 'dialogue' is not only much more than the general understanding this term implies, but also that it has a specific, profound, yet often misunderstood meaning, and characterizes the very essence of person-centredness. I will present an outline of the basic anthropological, epistemological and ethical foundations and therapeutic and political consequences of this understanding of the paradigm by trying to clarify what a genuinely dialogical understanding of person-centred therapy (PCT) means. This will, I hope, provide a philosophical underpinning of developments that are associated with 'therapy as encounter', 'person-to-person therapy', 'relational depth', 'client-centred relational therapy', 'dialogical approach' and so on, as was clearly demanded by Mearns and Cooper (2005, pp. viii–16).

In order to do so, I shall, first, look at the development of PCT towards a balanced 'substantial-relational' understanding. Then I will sketch the current view on some essential characteristics and basic terms of PCT following these lines. Finally, I will discuss what the fundamental dialogical nature of PCT and psychotherapy in general means for theory and practice.

Being and becoming a person: the development of PCT towards a balanced substantial-relational understanding

In the past 20 years or so, the PCA in general, and PCT in particular, witnessed the rise of what is now seen as a relationship-oriented theory and practice: a growing emphasis on the relational dimension of psychotherapy and counselling, highlighting relationship, encounter, intersubjectivity, mutuality, relational depth and the societal aspects of therapy (Cooper et al., 2007). This is in line with a growing emphasis on the importance of relationship in the world of psychotherapy as such. The development was also characterized as a shift from a 'one-person-centred therapy' to a 'two-person-centred therapy' (Cooper, 2007).

Rogers

This development can be traced back to Carl Rogers (1902–87) who, in the course of his lifetime, increasingly drew attention to 'congruence' or 'genuineness', and, accordingly, came to view his client-centred therapy as an encounter relationship (Rogers, 1962a). In the almost 70 years since its inception, the PCA has been further developed by Rogers and by his colleagues. This reflects Rogers' demand to never stop exploring and researching one's experiences and to refrain from canonizing a certain stage of his writings or the theory as it stands. Of course, this has led to different interpretations, strands of thinking and schools or 'tribes' within the 'nation' of person-centred and experiential therapies (see the overviews in Sanders, 2004, 2007), as has happened with all other schools of therapy.

In the years after its birth, client-centred or, as it was called originally, 'nondirective therapy' was mainly concerned with not interfering in the client's process of actualizing their own potential. Hence the focus of these 'newer therapies' (Rogers, 1942, Ch. 2) was on what the therapist should not do (compared to traditional therapeutic approaches): a primarily 'nondirective' stance. After this, the emphasis and research focused on what the basic attitudes of the therapist should be in order to facilitate a client's growth – the 'client-centred' period of the development, with the statement, exploration and investigation of the necessary and sufficient conditions for therapeutic personality change (Rogers, 1957). Two of the major criticisms PCT was confronted with were (and sometimes still are) that the PCA is seemingly an individualistic approach and that the centre of attention is on the therapist despite the trademark 'client-centred' (see the discussion in Schmid, 1994). However, if we look at Rogers' own further developments of the PCA, these arguments fail completely. With the spotlight on the relationship between client and therapist, Rogers began to understand 'psychotherapy as encounter' (Rogers, 1962a), and with the concentration on the client's work in therapy, the client was more and more seen as an 'active self healer' (Bohart and Tallman, 1999) in a facilitative relationship. Thus, the name 'person-centred' was also fully justified in its anthropological-philosophical notion (see below). In this chapter, I will also show that a dialogical understanding was already implicit in Rogers' conception and practice.

Further developments

After Rogers, multiple strands came about, partly trying to combine person-centred ideas with other orientations, and partly developing the core concept of the actualizing person to further improve person-centred thinking and doing. This led different scholars and therapists, coming from different perspectives, to develop a genuine person-centred, bipolar (or multipolar) model of psychotherapy, where both (or all) persons involved are the focus of reflection, forming a process of co-creating the therapeutic process. I have been developing an understanding of 'therapy as the art of encounter' and 'dialogue' from 1989 (Schmid, 1989, 1991, 1994, 1996, 1998b, 1998c, 2000, 2006a, 2007). This development has also been spearheaded by Dave Mearns (1996) and Mick Cooper (Mearns and Cooper, 2005), by Godfrey Barrett-Lennard (2005) and others (for an overview, see Schmid and Mearns, 2006, p. 177; Schmid, 2007, p. 40). Therefore, we can currently truly speak of a *dialogical understanding of the PCA*.

These scholars, different as they are in some ways, have all claimed not to be adding something new, but rather trying to deepen both the understanding of the person-centred anthropology and the practice of the person-centred relationship. Their detailed anthropological and epistemological investigations of the past few years have brought about a significant theoretical and practical development of PCT, in particular providing a better understanding of its central conceptions. In this understanding, relationship is *essential* to the human being. The concept of 'encounter' has now gained acceptance and become established (see Schmid and Mearns, 2006, p. 177; Cooper, 2007). It is the state of the art of genuine PCT. It marks a change of paradigm not only within the PCA, but also within psychotherapy and counselling generally.

Substantial differences to other orientations

Interestingly, other psychotherapeutic orientations have been running parallel in developing their self-understanding – albeit not referring to Rogers and the PCA. It might be stated in astonishment, amusement and ironic pride that therapists of all orientations increasingly refer to both a relationship-oriented understanding of psychotherapy and a serious trust in the autonomous position of the individual, thus reframing their theories towards the stances pioneered by Rogers. This is true, for example, of self-psychology and intersubjective psychoanalysis, and trends towards a relationship-oriented conception can also be seen in behavioural and systemic approaches. Furthermore, new dialogical therapies have arisen (for details, see Schmid and Mearns, 2006), and there is growing empirical support (Cooper, 2004).

All in all, the mainstream approaches in psychotherapy have acknowledged that relationship is important for, and in, psychotherapy. Beyond this, for many schools, the emergence of an examination of the relational dimension of the person and the respective nature of psychotherapy has led to a considerable shift in the understanding of psychotherapy and personality development.

Although the development within the PCA has been in line with this parallel development, in many strands of psychotherapy it has been qualitatively different. In most cases, the relationship was and is only 'used', seen as a means or precondition (for example a 'working alliance') for doing the actual therapeutic work on or with the client. Not so in PCT, where the understanding of relationship is different from its understanding in other orientations. According to the image of the human being in PCT, what it means to be in a therapeutic relationship is consequently fundamental to the process and considered in depth.

The development towards the focus on the nature of the relationship has sometimes been understood as a one-sided relation-centred stance. But, on the contrary, an understanding based on encounter (dialogical) philosophy clearly rejects a biased, individualistic interpretation. Thus, it becomes obvious that both independence and interrelatedness, that is, being from and for oneself on the one hand ('substantial', that is, literally 'achieving a standing position from below, standing on one's own feet') and being from and in relationship on the other ('relational', interconnected), refer essentially to one and the same human nature (Schmid, 1991, 1994, 1998b). We only view and experience it as different aspects because we look at it from different perspectives. To regard the human as a substantial-relational being is what is meant by saying *the human being is a person*. A genuine understanding of the PCA emphasizes both the uniqueness and capabilities of the individual and the unavoidable connectedness of the individual-in-relationship.

If you do not consider the relationship to be a means or even a method to use – as many therapy schools do – but as a fundamental characteristic of human existence, then it follows that psychotherapy must be seen in the light of dialogue, which marks an essential paradigm shift for psychotherapy that ultimately can be expressed concisely with the statement that 'psychotherapy is dialogue or it is not psychotherapy' (Schmid, 2006a, p. 251).

The state of the art in understanding the core terms: essential foundations of PCT as a dialogical approach

What follows is a brief summary of the core terms that characterize the principal advancements towards a dialogical understanding.

The dialectical understanding of the person

Philosophically, the PCA is grounded in the conviction that the most adequate image of the human being that has been developed so far in the history of humankind is to regard them as a 'person', hence the name of the approach. This means that the human being is intrinsically and dialectically both substantial and relational: being from oneself and thus autonomous, *and* being from relationship and thus interdependent with others. Human beings have an innate capacity, need and tendency to develop on their own *and* in relationships. Both autonomy and interrelatedness constitute the one human nature. In Carl Rogers' (1958) terms: the human being is motivated by the actualizing tendency as the inner force and resource to lead one's own life out of one's own capabilities, which can only be tapped if the individual is facilitated by a special kind of relationship (see below).

Thus, the two essential dimensions of person-centred anthropology, of being a person, are 'independence' and 'interconnectedness'. To be a person depicts an understanding of the human being as a 'substantial-relational being', autonomous *and* interdependent, characterized by self-responsibility *and* solidarity. This image of the human being is the essential conclusion of the process of reflection about ourselves in the European tradition during more than two millennia, from Jewish and Greek peoples via Muslims until today (Schmid, 1991, 1994, 1996, 1998a, 1998b, 2007).

In particular, a deeper understanding of the relational dimension of personhood within the paradigm has been achieved, whether you term it 'relationship therapy' (Rogers, 1942, following Jessie Taft, 1933), 'interpersonal' (Rogers, 1962b), 'person to person' (Rogers and Stevens, 1967), 'encounter approach' (Schmid, 1994), 'meeting at relational depth' (Mearns and Thorne, 2007) or 'dialogical' (Schmid, 1996, 2006a). (For details, see the bibliography in Schmid and Mearns, 2006, pp. 177–8; the 2006 special issue of *Person-Centered and Experiential Psychotherapies* on relational depth, 5(4); Cooper et al., 2007). Such an image of the human being, with its profoundness, radicalism and dialectical balance of substantiality and relationality, can only be found in a genuine person-centred approach and is the foundation of the identity of this approach to therapy and the state of the art of genuine PCT in theory and practice today.

The dialectical nature of the relationship as encounter

If a person enters a relationship with another as a person, this is termed an 'encounter relationship'. To encounter means 'to be touched by the essence of the opposite' (Guardini, 1955). The term 'encounter' denotes a relationship where the other person is not regarded as an alter ego, but is met as truly being an 'Other'. This means that I cannot simply meet and understand the experience of another person through me and my experiences. The attitude rather is to open up, genuinely accept and empathically try to comprehend what the partner in the relationship is going to disclose. This marks a far-reaching epistemological paradigm change, because it means that I no longer draw conclusions from the way in which I experience the other person or understand their experiences, thus putting them into my categories, but instead open up to what the Other is going to disclose and wants to be understood.

Therefore, we no longer follow an epistemology of 'egology' – a term coined by French philosopher Emmanuel Levinas (1957, p. 189) – taking as its starting point that which is already known. Instead of trying to understand itself by itself, we act upon an epistemology of transcendence, of 'alterity' (that is, otherness), where the movement goes from the Other to me. The respective epistemology can correctly be named a 'Thou-I relationship', because it has its origin in the opening up of the 'Thou'. The Thou precedes the I – a basic stance for the way of understanding in PCT, possible only through the authentic attitude of unconditional positive regard and empathy (Schmid, 1994, 1998c, 2002, 2003, 2006a).

The fundamental We

Carl Rogers (1962b) was convinced that 'the interpersonal relationship' is 'the core of guidance'. As early as 1939 (p. 197) he wrote, in the context of child guidance, that 'the relationship between the worker and the parent is the essential feature'. This 'encounter person to person' – as he described the psychotherapeutic enterprise – is the core of an 'intersubjective, co-creative process of personalization', of becoming a person (Rogers, 1961). Therapy therefore springs from a 'fundamental We' (Schmid, 2003); its nature is to co-respond to the situation the client finds themselves in. This also means that therapist and client are co-responding to the relationship they find themselves in, in the very moment of their being together. So, they are co-creating the relationship out of mutual encounter. The client's contribution to this fundamentally dialogical process is to actively make use of their inherent capacity to make the acknowledgement and empathy of the therapist work (Bohart and Tallman, 1999). The therapist's contribution is to be present.

Presence as the elementary therapeutic attitude

'Presence' – from the Latin *praeesse*, meaning 'to be fully there' – is the existential foundation and deeper meaning of the well-known, but often superficially misunderstood core conditions of 'authenticity', 'acknowledgment' and 'comprehension' (to use Buber's terms) (see Geller, Chapter 13, this volume). The therapist's task is to realize these continuously and in any given situation, thus responding to the challenge of the relationship in its concrete context. This provides a climate of safety, trust and respect for the client, enabling them increasingly to face themselves and embark on a path of development. In this view, Rogers' (1957) carefully elaborated basic attitudes are considered to be three dimensions of one fundamental attitude towards life: presence (Schmid, 1994, 2002) – *the* core condition of encounter, of being-with and being-counter (Schmid and Mearns, 2006).

The dialectical nature of the actualizing process as personalization

As persons – in the meaning of person outlined above – we are not only in relationship, we *are* relationship (Schmid, 2002, 2004). In-depth investigations (Schmid, 2008a) of the origins of the idea of the actualizing tendency reveal that the idea of an actualizing tendency – with its roots and parallels in the classical doctrines of *energeia* (actuality) and *dynamis* (potentiality) by Aristotle and Thomas Aquinas – is in itself a dialectic principle. According to them, the potential can never become reality without an efficient cause (*causa efficiens*); it needs something or somebody from the outside to become what it can become – in personal terminology, it needs an other, another thing or person.

For the understanding of personality development, this means that life is the actualization, the realization of the given possibilities, the potency, which needs an 'influence' from outside, that is, somebody else, another human being. *This is the foundation of the essential importance of relationship* – surprisingly also from a substantial viewpoint, that is, regarding the person in their unique individuality. Although the actualizing tendency is a tendency inherent in the individual, the presence of the other is needed to make it work. The relational and the substantial are not independent dimensions but two sides of the same coin. With the very idea of actualization, 'the Other' is inevitably connected. We have indeed moved on from the 'self-centred period' of the so-called humanistic movement with its numerous self-terms, like self-development, self-determination and self-realization. We cannot even think of a person without thinking of their relationships.

The actualizing tendency, therefore, must be seen as a dialectical axiom. It is wrong to think of it only as an enclosed inner force of the individual. *It must also be regarded as relationship-oriented and therefore a social construct.* In human beings, its specific *human* quality turns out to be a 'personalizing tendency', characterized by freedom and creativity (Schmid, 1994, 2008a).

So the PCA finds itself in a tradition that appreciates the possible in the same way as the real and therefore does not reduce the person to what can be found obviously and superficially.

These few characteristics can serve as a basis for the investigation of the meaning of dialogue in PCT.

The fundamental dialogical nature of PCT: psychotherapy means to enter dialogue

Increasingly in recent years, the word 'dialogical' appeared to describe the theory and practice of this viewpoint. 'Dialogue' is a word that has many different meanings. Therefore, we need to have a closer look at some authors and their interpretations.

What is discussed as 'dialogical' in PCT?

A short review of what has been written about a 'dialogical approach' may shed light on how it is understood. There are quite different notions of 'dialogical'.

In many streams in Germany, a much more technical understanding of *Gesprächstherapie* prevails and is discussed. To give an example: Finke and Teusch (2007a, pp. 228, 250, 2007b), two German psychiatrists, generally consider the relationship in PCT as 'dialogical', in the sense of aiming at communicating and understanding. They contrast a dialogical relationship with an alter ego relationship and argue for an integration of the person-centred and positivist medical model thinking. Thus, they think that, in addition to 'the dialogical', a functional pragmatic relationship (bringing back an understanding of the traditional role of therapist and client) is necessary in order to meet the criteria of the current scientific paradigm. Without the latter, it would only be a 'practice of dialogical philosophy with therapeutic intention', but not 'psychotherapy' (Finke and Teusch 2007, p. 228). You may find many others who think like this, for example Germain Lietaer (2008, p. 35), who writes about a 'dialogical working alliance'.

In my opinion, their stance is an obvious contradiction; in their opinion, this is a necessary standpoint of an approach that wants to be taken seriously in our scientific-oriented world.

A sharply different understanding can be found in the *Dictionary of Person-Centred Psychology* by Tudor and Merry (2002, p. 41). In defining 'dialogue', they use a quote by Hycner (1993, p. 51), when they say that dialogue means 'a conversation between two or more persons' that 'requires two persons entering in a genuine relationship with each other'; thus it may be viewed both as a *precondition* for therapy and *the therapy itself.* Bohart and Tallman (1999, p. 129) spoke of 'dialogical processes, when some clients want more than empathic listening, namely feedback. They may particularly find a mutual, co-constructive dialogue in which ideas are traded back and forth to be rewarding and useful.' From the standpoint of the client as an active self-healer, the therapist should see what they are doing as dialoguing and not as intervening: 'Co-constructive dialogue means there is a back and forth, where a therapist's thoughtful response is evaluated and responded to by the client in an equally thoughtful and intelligent manner' (Bohart and Tallman, 1999, p. 129).

Tudor and Worrall (2006, pp. 241–2) understand dialogue in the context of mutuality and co-creative relating: 'Dialogue is the practice and mutuality is the outcome. Dialogue implies a conversation or exchange between two (or more) people.' They argue that through 'dialogue, client and therapist acknowledge each other's voices and co-create the meaning of what they hear. It is the visible outworking of the philosophy and theory.' They also stress their view that the mutuality in therapy is not symmetrical (a point also made by Murphy, Chapter 14, this volume).

Pete Sanders (2007, p. 112) wrote:

> A dialogical approach to therapy is one that emphasizes or even rests completely on dialogue, that is, the co-created relationship between the helper and the person helped. This is different from the 'traditional' phenomenological approach of client-centred therapy wherein we look at the separate experiences of the therapist and the client. A dialogical approach is concerned with the 'between'.

Sanders (2007, p. 111) pointed out that the dialogical approach, 'sometimes called "encounter-oriented" approach', is

> not so much a 'school' but the idea that therapy *is* dialogue, *is* relational. It is a restatement that the approach and process of therapy needs to be based *on and in* dialogue and that the 'goal' of therapy is the enhanced relational ability of the client – summarized by the phrase 'healing through meeting'. (emphases added)

Sanders (2007, p. 112) goes on to state that 'a dialogical approach is implicit in the recent work of Godfrey Barrett-Lennard and Dave Mearns, but Peter Schmid has been foremost in bringing an encounter-oriented approach to the family of PC therapies'. My own view here is different: I don't think that I brought the dialogical approach to PCT, rather I unearthed what was already there and elaborated on it. But I agree with Sanders' statement that 'dialogic therapy is not identified with a "school" of therapy' but is a restatement or a renaissance. To found a new school or approach or tribe or whatever was never my intention and still isn't; rather, I aim at a deeper understanding of the underlying anthropology and epistemology, personality theory, psychopathology and theory and practice of therapy that follows from it. I am convinced that Rogers' approach – *the* paradigm change in psychotherapy – is far from being fully sounded out.

Sanders (2007, pp. 112–13) went on to state that 'there are no differences of any substance between classical CCT [client-centred therapy] and the emerging dialogical therapy'. It is 'only through facing the Others and appreciating their uniqueness' that they can 'be free to actualize their potential. Anything else would effectively constitute a limiting condition of worth, either acted out, or implied by our personal philosophy.' Therefore, 'dialogical therapists would pay particular attention to their deep understanding of what it is to be human'.

With the publication of Dave Mearns and Mick Cooper's (2005) book on relational depth, the concept, initially described by Mearns in 1996, became popular in Britain. This is interconnected with the concept of dialogue; however, it has a different focus from my understanding of a dialogical approach, which views PCT – dependent on the notion of person, encounter, dialogue and presence – as the unfolding of a fundamental given: a primary, basic, seminal interpersonal situation. Both Mearns and Cooper and I describe a way of understanding therapy, of 'being with and counter the client' (Schmid and Mearns, 2006), but on different levels.

What does dialogue mean from an anthropological and epistemological viewpoint?

'Dialogue' is a term with specific notions in the history of philosophy. A brief look into the evolving notion of dialogue in anthropology will also help to understand its meaning for psychotherapy (for more details, see Schmid, 2006, 2007, 2009).

Dialogue comes from the Greek *dia*, meaning between or through (related to the Latin 'inter', as in 'intercourse', or French *entretien*), and *logos*, meaning word or meaning, significance So, dialogue literally means 'between' or 'through words'. One might translate it with 'conversation', but also with 'flowing of (or through) meaning'. According to this, dialogue is usually understood as face-to-face conversation, as mutual exchange, characterized by symmetry and equality: a meeting of the one with the other.

The first philosopher, as far as we know, to realize the importance of what happens between two people in a conversation, 2,500 years ago, was Socrates (*c.* 470–399 BC) with his *Dialogues* as reported by Plato. He introduced the systematic use of dialogue as an independent literary form. In all these dialogues, there is an explicit or implicit disagreement, we may say incongruence, and the purpose of the dialogues is to resolve the disagreement. Most of these dialogues break off without a final resolution, as in real life. This serves self-knowledge and the insight that we ultimately know nothing, which does not lead to resignation but to a proactive search for wisdom, ultimately to live a good and truthful life (eu zen).

Socrates' 'maieutic' method (from the Greek *maieutikos*, one who acts as a midwife, the profession of his mother) rests on the idea that truth is already in the human being and only needs to be delivered, to be brought to life. Despite the fact that this is similar to many humanistic viewpoints, dialogue here is understood as a pedagogical instrument, a means to teach, to educate. So, it is no surprise that rational-emotive therapy uses 'Socratic dialogues' as a technique to change irrational assumptions. Thus, Socrates might well be seen as a model for an 'in order to' psychotherapy.

It's a big leap to Martin Buber (1878–1965), the Austrian-born Jewish theologian, and his understanding of dialogue, seen as the underlying idea of most humanistic therapies. For him, the significance of dialogue is not in either partner alone, and not in both together, but in their exchange. Thus, dialogue is what *follows* from 'interpersonality': 'The sphere of the interpersonal is the opposite-to-each-other; its unfolding is what we call dialogue' (Buber, 1961, pp. 275–6). True dialogue is not transmission of information, it leads to a common 'between'; it is participation in the being of the Other. The respective attitude towards the Other is referred to as the 'I-Thou relationship' by Buber.

But this view was also disapproved of and developed further. Emmanuel Levinas emphasized that dialogue is not to merely understand each other, expressing mutual empathy. He suggested that Buber was caught in circularity – in the enclosed circle of the I-Thou. According to Levinas, dialogue is a step beyond the thinking of the one and the other. Dialogue is not the experience of a meeting of persons talking with each other, and it is not a consequence of meeting each other: dialogue is of original immediacy, it is not mediated (Levinas, 1989, pp. 72, 74).

Buber (1978) emphasized that the I-Thou is a 'primary word'. To address another person as Thou, and thus enter dialogue, is not dependent on a previous experience of the Other, and addressing the Other as 'Thou' does not derive from an experience. Dialogue is not a consequence of an experience, it is not the discovery of sociality. On the contrary, *dialogue is an original, primary occurrence*; as Levinas (1989, p. 74) puts it, it is the interpersonal relationship, 'the original sociality' that occurs in dialogue.

So far, Levinas is in line with Buber. But for Levinas, dialogue is not about symmetry, as stressed by Buber, but dissymmetry in the relationship: 'It is precisely because the Thou is *absolutely* different from the I that there is – from the one to the other – dialogue' (Levinas, 1989, p. 76). So, it is the other way round: it is dialogue now that constitutes interpersonality.

The fundamental We is not symmetric We. It is, by nature, asymmetric. When we speak of a Thou-I relationship, the Other comes first: the Other calls me, the face of the Other addresses me, it is a provocation, it 'demands'. Therefore, dialogue constitutes responsibility, solidarity, a commitment. The Thou calls the I into service. Levinas (1986, p. 74) says: 'The Other *orders* me to serve him.' Hence, diacony (that is, service) is not a result of dialogue, it is the fundamental essence of the human relationship (Levinas, 1989; Schmid, 1994, pp. 147–8).

Solidarity (social relations that bind people to one another) is not a second order category deriving from experience, but a basic human condition. Such thinking is the turn from monologue to dialogue, from *thinking about* the other to *addressing* the concrete fellow person. This stance is the willingness and readiness to simply say: 'Here I am' (Levinas, 1986). To be *for* the Other, not simply being *with* them. (Here we can see how close this comes to a basic understanding of the *client*-centred relationship.) Such a dissymmetrical relationship is the origin of ethics. *The I is constituted by their responsibility* to the call of the Other. Nobody can be replaced in facing this unconditional demand.

This radically turns the usual order between self-consciousness and dialogue around: encounter in dialogue is the precondition for self-consciousness and self-confidence. Dialogue is the non-indifference of the I towards the Thou, or, to formulate it positively, an existential given that can manifest and express itself in attention, care, unconditional positive regard. In other words, dialogue is a primary, underlying condition of being human, of being a person, as is love. Levinas prefers to think of philosophy as the 'wisdom of love' rather than the 'love of wisdom' (the literal Greek meaning of the word 'philosophy').

To sum up: dialogue, understood as a fundamental condition of being human, is neither the consequence of an insight nor an action to be taken. Dialogue is a primary fact of and in the human condition, an original occurrence. And so it follows: the human person *is* dialogue. This is more than a well-put statement, because it puts our understanding of our being in the world and with each other on new ground: being in the world is being in dialogue. From a dialogical point of view, persons are not only seen as being in relationships; as persons, they are relationship (Schmid, 2004; Schmid and Mearns, 2006). Persons are dialogue.

What does a dialogical understanding of PCT mean?

This is why Levinas's understanding can be seen as an explication of the stance of person-centred psychotherapy: the client comes first; therapy is for the client, the therapist is 'their deacon', is at their service (Schmid, 2003, pp. 112–14).

Levinas criticizes the so-called humanistic approaches as being not humane enough – still putting the ego in the centre and taking it as standard and the rule for everything. This central position of the ego needs to be replaced by the unconditional demand of the Other. In my opinion, there is some truth in the criticism that not only many forms of humanistic therapy but also those forms of client-centred therapy that are only or mainly concerned with therapists' tasks are forms of 'egology' (a narcissistic philosophy that is only concerned with itself). If the therapist is only concerned with what to do, how to behave, how to realize the conditions, if client-centred therapy mainly consists of investigating the side of the therapist, we might really find ourselves again in the trap of being concerned with ourselves, with therapist-centredness, with egology. But client-centred means that the client comes first and therapy is for the client.

If we take the aforementioned notion of dialogue seriously, then dialogue is not the consequence or the aim of therapy. Rather, *psychotherapy means to 'enter' dialogue* (see below). It is interesting to note that 'enter' has the same root as 'inter' – 'between', the Greek *dia* – and derives from the Latin *intrare*, which means 'go into'. Psychotherapy means to enter – to go into – a room that is already there. Humans have a choice 'to enter', to get involved, let themselves in for dialogue or not. So, a closer look at Rogers' understanding of 'therapy as encounter' reveals dialogue as primary occurrence, and therapy intrinsically as dialogue, as entering the 'challenge of the Other' (Schmid, 2006a). Thus, dialogue is in the very beginning of therapy.

Dialogue is definitely not 'a means in order to …', something the therapist has to achieve or perform, nor is it a precondition, let alone a technique. But dialogue is also more than an expression of equality, mutuality and reciprocity, as we are used to thinking. Understood as an existential category, it does not signify moments of intensive exchange in therapy. It is not a goal or an outcome of therapy; neither is it a comprehensive description of the therapeutic enterprise as such.

Dialogue is 'more': the persons engaged in therapy *are* dialogue. This completely turns around our traditional thinking in psychotherapy. We must not come into dialogue in the sense of achieving it, or making it happen; we must come into dialogue in the sense of coming to what is already there, *we enter dialogue*. Dialogue takes place before the first word is spoken or the first glances are exchanged. We need to realize that there is dialogue, regardless of whether we are aware of it or not. *'In the beginning' there is dialogue* (Schmid, 1998a, 2006b), primary, fundamental, basic, deeply rooted and thus seminal.

Psychotherapy is the unfolding of this dialogue. Therefore, dialogue is not a consequence, but a fundament of community. It is about realizing the preceding common We – in all its dissymmetry. *Therapeutic dialogue is realizing the healing and challenging quality of the essential human We. The restoration of this underlying We is the therapeutic in psychotherapy*. This is done by presence as the realization of the core conditions. Hence, presence is not a precondition for dialogue; rather, it is dialogue that comes to the fore in presence. Presence is an expression of the fundamental 'Here I am'. *To say 'Here I am'* (in the full meaning of being-with and being-counter) *is all that we have to do* – also in therapy. (Here is a profound parallel to the concept of relational depth, see below.)

To encounter a person is to realize, to 'make real', that is, to be aware that you are already in dialogue and to act accordingly in the meeting with the Other. It is only in dialogue that persons are really addressed as persons. Therefore, by definition, a person-centred approach is an approach that unveils the dialogical quality already there. The same goes for the person-centred meaning of therapy: not to *make* something happen with or in the client, not to teach the client to do something or behave in a specific way, not to achieve something, but to be present in the full meaning of the word. Dialogue in therapy is not *bringing* the client or oneself into dialogue; rather, it is unearthing and unfolding the interpersonal quality of what at a first glance might seem one-sided advice-seeking, helplessly being at the mercy of somebody, stuck development, intellectual stammering, refusal of growth and so on.

Dialogue and relational depth

It is essential to clearly distinguish between dialogue as an ontological given (that is, the described intersubjectivity of the human condition), and dialogue as an ontic occurrence (that is, the concrete quality of a certain deep relationship and moments of relational depth). It is important, therefore, to be aware of the distinction between the notion of relational depth as developed by Mearns and Cooper (2005) and a dialogical understanding of PCT, as outlined above, although both are related, even interconnected. While Mearns and Cooper talk about the process of contact and communication, of mutual exchange (what I call presence) and thus about the realization, I talk about the foundations, the image of the human being as a person in substantiality and relatedness. In order to avoid misunderstandings, these two levels must not be mixed up: on the one hand, an ontological understanding of dialogue, as a condition of being in the world, an underlying form of existence (this is where my focus is), and, on the other hand, an ontic understanding as a particular kind of relationship (which is what Mearns and Cooper mean by relational depth). Relational depth – be it a quality of relationship, be it specific intensive moments – may be the outcome of the fundamental dialogical situation, which is a precondition for the possibility of relational depth to occur, although by no means a necessity; it is not a precondition for encounter or dialogue.

Although there is this difference in the perspective and the subject, it goes without saying that both conceptions are interrelated and there are a lot of commonalities in what we are talking about. Mearns (2007, p. 23) puts the core conditions together again and emphasizes their power in combination, which is important in order to overcome a behaviour-oriented, technique-oriented or therapist-oriented ('which conditions must I provide?') understanding of PCT: a stance that views the so-called 'core conditions' as descriptions, or even prescriptions, for parts of the therapist's actual behaviour – what Pete Sanders (2009) called a 'Frankenstein model'.

Dialogue as a primary occurrence, the fundamental dialogicity as an ontological given, requires doing therapy according to such a worldview. It requires being in line with the aforementioned understanding of the person when doing therapy, to be in accordance with it, to correspond and correlate, to 'enter into' the given dialogue, which is a process to unfold, not something to be 'made' or 'constructed' or achieved by certain rules. Dialogue is an 'underlying' (ontological) form of existence, which can be allowed to manifest or be blocked from manifesting (at the ontical level). The concept of relational depth is about what it actually means in practice to allow dialogue (in its ontological, existential meaning) to emerge. It is parallel to the notion of person, a matter of both being and becoming. We are persons and yet we become persons. We are in dialogue and yet we have to ever anew 'go into' it to unfold it, we have to correspond to it in the concrete interpersonal situation, we have to facilitate the already present dialogue to be experienced and to unfold its power. The PCA is the way to do this by being present or encounter at relational depth, that is, by realizing as fully as possible the facilitative conditions, as described by Rogers, thus 'creating' a conducive relationship.

For therapeutic practice, one helpful way might be the concept of 'personal or dialogic resonance', which refers to the echo in the therapist triggered by the relationship with the client – beyond self-resonance and empathic resonance, as an integral expression of the quality of presence offered by the therapist (Schmid and Mearns, 2006); another one might be metacommunication in therapy (Schmid, 2004; Mearns and Thorne, 2007, pp. 133–6).

Objections

The question has been raised whether a dialogical understanding, the concept of relational depth or other related notions of PCT are still client-centred in the original meaning or must be seen as a deviation from the pure doctrine (for example Wilders, 2007, Chapter 15, this volume; see the discussion in the 2006 and 2007 issues of *Person-Centred Quarterly* and in internet forums such as pcintl@listserv.uga.edu). And the more interest that has been generated in this development, the more this has brought up the debate of whether the PCA is in danger of losing its identity by such developments. Is the dialogical perspective 'another diversion', an arbitrary deviation, altering its fundamental assumptions? Must this way of understanding be considered as a betrayal of the very foundations of PCT? Or is the dialogical perspective a genuine, compelling development, an authentic understanding of its original ideas and practice?

Let me respond briefly to some misunderstandings and accusations. A dialogical understanding of PCT does not oppose the fundamental nondirectivity of the therapist (Schmid, 2005) and fully preserves the unique expert status of the client by facilitating their self-directedness. It does not contradict Rogers' (1957) statement of the necessary and sufficient conditions, but fully recognizes the conditions of contact and client perception as central (Wyatt and Sanders, 2002), as opposed to a reduction to three 'core conditions', and it recognizes their intrinsic, existential connection, elaborated in the concept of 'presence' (Schmid, 1994, 2002, 2004; Geller and Greenberg, 2002; Geller, Chapter 13, this volume). It sticks to the concept of the therapist's unintentionality and the unpredictability of the process and stands counter to preconceived methods, techniques and skills (Schmid, 2003). It is fully in line with the actualizing tendency concept, even underlines it as a personalization concept (Schmid, 2008a). It underlines the importance of congruence or authenticity, inasmuch as the therapist feels and acts as a real person in the relationship, not only as an alter ego of the client. As a genuine person, they are 'counter in being with' the client (by being touched, surprised, challenged) to respond to the disclosing of the client in an existential way (Schmid and Mearns, 2006).

The criteria that I enumerated for genuine person-centred confrontation and dialogue (Mearns and Schmid, 2006, pp. 259–62) make it clear that a misunderstanding of congruence, which might lead the therapist to bring in their own agenda or feel that they have 'free licence ... to offer suggestions ... criticize ... or berate clients' (Wilders, 2007, p. 3), is clearly out of the question. Anything the therapist says about themselves or about their experience of the relationship must be deeply rooted in the empathic co-experiencing with the client and the relationship and follow the overall criterion that it springs from 'empathic' or 'personal resonance' (Schmid and Mearns, 2006) and is in the service of the Other.

A dialogical concept stands in contrast to those experiential strands in the person-centred and experiential movement, where the trust is with the experiencing, that is, with the process (as defined, for example, by emotion-focused or focusing therapists); in person-centred therapies, the trust is with the whole person (see also Tudor and Merry, 2002, p. 52) and the experiencing is a dependent variable of the person, not the other way round.

Conclusion

A dialogical understanding of PCT is not a new approach, a new psychotherapy. It is nothing more than a continuation of Carl Rogers' development of a *person*-centred therapy. It is intrinsic in the notion of the term 'person' and Rogers' understanding of it. It is nothing other than a deepening of the understanding of the underlying image of the human being. It informs and enriches the approach. It is a perspective that reveals the power of the approach even more.

I am convinced that a dialogical understanding of psychotherapy will not only prevail in PCT but, in the long run, in all orientations of psychotherapy. Although problem-centred and solution-focused orientations, along with a passion for the invention of sophisticated techniques, seem to prevail at the moment, humanity will finally win through.

Psychotherapy is not a method of repairing problems or fostering personal happiness. That is psychotechnique. On the contrary, from the outlined image of the human being, it follows that it is fundamentally an *ethical* and a *political* task (Schmid, 2012).

The nature of psychotherapy is to respond to the call, to the demand of another person truly as an Other. Client and therapist co-respond to the demand of life, to the relational situation they are in – an *ethical enterprise.* The task of the therapist is to be present, the task of the client is to actualize their potential and thus 'make therapy work' by 'in-forming' the therapist, by actively bringing the therapist in form to relate to and understand the client in order to better understand themselves (Schmid, 2003).

As a counterpoint to Nietzsche's question at the beginning, I conclude with the words of the phenomenologist Bernhard Waldenfels (1994, p. 636): without acknowledgement of the radical otherness of the Other, 'responding wouldn't be what it is, namely a way of speaking and doing that – responding to demands of others – surprises itself'. As an enterprise open to surprise, instead of a practice repeating ourselves over and over, thus forcing the others to repeat themselves even louder, psychotherapy is an enterprise open to surprise and to face the unexpected that can evolve in genuine dialogue.

Note

This chapter is a completely revised version of an invited lecture given at the 5th World Congress for Psychotherapy in Beijing, 2008 (Schmid, 2008b) and a lecture at the 8th PCE World Congress 2008 in Norwich (Schmid, 2008c).

References

Barrett-Lennard, G.T. (2005) *Relationship at the Centre: Healing in a Troubled World.* London: Whurr.

Bohart, A.C. and Tallman, K. (eds) (1999) *How Clients Make Therapy Work: The Process of Active Self-healing.* Washington: APA.

Buber, M. (1961) *Das Problem des Menschen.* Heidelberg: Lambert Schneider.

Buber, M. (1974) *Ich und Du.* Heidelberg: Lambert Schneider; orig. 1923

Cooper, M. (2004) Towards a relationally-orientated approach to therapy: Empirical support and analysis. *British Journal of Guidance and Counselling*, 32, 451–60.

Cooper, M. (2007) Person-centred therapy: The growing edge. *Therapy Today*, 18(6), 33–6.

Cooper, M., O'Hara, M., Schmid, P.F. and Wyatt, G. (eds) (2007) *The Handbook of Person-Centred Psychotherapy and Counselling*. Basingstoke: Palgrave Macmillan.

Finke, J. and Teusch, L. (2007a) Die störungsbezogene Perspektive in der Gesprächspsychotherapie. In J. Kriz and T. Slunecko (eds) *Gesprächspsychotherapie* (pp. 227–32). Vienna: Facultas.

Finke, J. and Teusch, L. (2007b) Using a person-centred approach within a medical framework. In M. Cooper, M. O'Hara, P.F. Schmid and G. Wyatt (eds) *The Handbook of Person-Centred Psychotherapy and Counselling* (pp. 279–92). Basingstoke: Palgrave Macmillan.

Geller, S.M. and Greenberg, L. (2002) Therapeutic presence: Therapists' experience of presence in the psychotherapy encounter. *Person-Centered and Experiential Psychotherapies*, 1(1&2), 71–86.

Guardini, R. (1955) Die Begegnung: Ein Beitrag zur Struktur des Daseins. *Hochland*, 47(3), 224–34.

Hycner, R. (1993) *Between Person and Person: Toward a Dialogical Psychotherapy*. Highland, NY: Gestalt Journal Press.

Levinas, E. (1957) Die Philosophie und die Idee des Unendlichen. In E. Levinas, *Die Spur des Anderen* (pp. 185–208). Freiburg: Alber.

Levinas, E. (1986) *Ethik und Unendliches*. Graz: Böhlau.

Levinas, E. (1989) Dialog. In F. Böckle et al. (eds) *Christlicher Glaube in moderner Gesellschaft*, vol. 1 (pp. 61–85). Freiburg: Herder.

Lietaer, G. (2008) Das klientenzentrierte/experienzielle Paradigma der Psychotherapie im 21. Jahrhundert: Offenheit, Vielfalt und Identität. In M. Tuczai et al. (eds) *Offenheit & Vielfalt* (pp. 17–44). Vienna: Krammer.

Mearns, D. (1996) Working at relational depth with clients in person-centred therapy. *Counselling*, 7(4), 306–11.

Mearns, D. (2007) Regarding Barbara Brodley's critique of Mearns and Cooper (2005). *Person-Centred Quarterly*, 2, 23.

Mearns, D. and Cooper, M. (2005) *Working at Relational Depth in Counselling and Psychotherapy*. London: Sage.

Mearns, D. and Schmid, P.F. (2006) Being-with and being-counter: Relational depth: the challenge of fully meeting the client. *Person-Centered and Experiential Psychotherapies*, 5(3), 255–65.

Mearns, D. and Thorne, B. (2007) *Person-Centred Counselling in Action* (3rd edn). London: Sage.

Nietzsche, F. (2000) *Die fröhliche Wissenschaft*. Stuttgart: Reclam.

Rogers, C.R. (1939) *The Clinical Treatment of the Problem Child*. Boston: Houghton Mifflin.

Rogers, C.R. (1942) *Counseling and Psychotherapy: Newer Concepts in Practice*. Boston: Houghton Mifflin.

Rogers, C.R. (1957) The necessary and sufficient conditions of therapeutic personality change. *Journal of Consulting Psychology*, 21(2), 95–103.

Rogers, C.R. (1958) The characteristics of a helping relationship. *Personnel and Guidance Journal*, 37(1), 6–16.

Rogers, C.R. (1961) *On Becoming a Person: A Therapist's View of Psychotherapy*. Boston: Houghton Mifflin.

Rogers, C.R. (1962a) Some learnings from a study of psychotherapy with schizophrenics. *Pennsylvania Psychiatric Quarterly*, Summer, 3–15.
Rogers, C.R. (1962b) The interpersonal relationship: The core of guidance. *Harvard Educational Review*, 4(32), 416–29.
Rogers, C.R. and Stevens, B. (1967) *Person to Person: The Problem of Being Human.* Walnut Creek, CA: Real People Press.
Sanders, P. (ed.) (2004) *The Tribes of the Person-centred Nation.* Ross-on-Wye: PCCS Books.
Sanders, P. (2007) The 'family' of person-centred and experiential therapies. In M. Cooper, M. O'Hara, P.F. Schmid and G. Wyatt (eds) *The Handbook of Person-Centred Psychotherapy and Counselling* (pp. 107–22). Basingstoke: Palgrave Macmillan.
Sanders, P. (2009) Person-centred challenges to traditional psychological healthcare systems. *Person-Centered and Experiential Psychotherapies*, 8(1), 1–17.
Schmid, P.F. (1989) *Personale Begegnung.* Würzburg: Echter.
Schmid, P.F. (1991) Souveränität und Engagement: Zu einem personzentrierten Verständnis von Person. In C.R. Rogers and P.F. Schmid, *Person-zentriert* (pp.15–164). Mainz: Grünewald.
Schmid, P.F. (1994) *Personzentrierte Gruppenpsychotherapie*, vol. I, *Solidarität und Autonomie*. Cologne: EHP.
Schmid, P.F. (1996) *Personzentrierte Gruppenpsychotherapie in der Praxis*, vol. II, *Die Kunst der Begegnung*. Paderborn: Junfermann.
Schmid, P.F. (1998a) *Im Anfang ist Gemeinschaft: Personzentrierte Gruppenarbeit*, vol. III. Stuttgart: Kohlhammer.
Schmid, P.F. (1998b) On becoming a person-centered approach: A person-centred understanding of the person. In B. Thorne and E. Lambers (eds) *Person-Centred Therapy: A European Perspective* (pp. 38–52). London: Sage.
Schmid, P.F. (1998c) 'Face to face': The art of encounter. In B. Thorne and E. Lambers (eds) *Person-Centred Therapy: A European Perspective* (pp. 74–90). London: Sage.
Schmid, P.F. (2000) 'Encountering a human being means being kept alive by an enigma' (E. Levinas). Prospects on further developments in the person-centered therapy. In J. Marques-Teixeira and S. Antunes (eds) *Client-Centered and Experiential Psychotherapy* (pp. 11–33). Linda a Velha: Vale & Vale.
Schmid, P.F. (2002) Presence: Immediate co-experiencing and co-responding. In G. Wyatt and P. Sanders (eds) *Rogers' Therapeutic Conditions: Evolution, Theory and Practice*, vol. 4, *Contact and Perception* (pp. 128–203). Ross-on-Wye: PCCS Books.
Schmid, P.F. (2003) The characteristics of a person-centered approach to therapy and counseling: Criteria for identity and coherence. *Person-Centered and Experiential Psychotherapies*, 2, 104–20.
Schmid, P.F. (2004) Back to the client: A phenomenological approach to the process of understanding and diagnosis. *Person-Centered and Experiential Psychotherapies*, 3, 36–51.
Schmid, P.F. (2005) Facilitative responsiveness: Non-directiveness from an anthropological, epistemological and ethical perspective. In B. Levitt (ed.) *Embracing Non-directivity* (pp. 74–94). Ross-on-Wye: PCCS Books.
Schmid, P.F. (2006a) The challenge of the Other: Towards dialogical person-centered psychotherapy and counseling. *Person-Centered and Experiential Psychotherapies*, 5(4), 241–54.

Schmid, P.F. (2006b) *In the Beginning There is Community: Implications and Challenges of the Belief in a Triune God and a Person-centred Approach*. Norwich: Norwich Centre for Personal & Professional Development.

Schmid, P.F. (2007) The anthropological and ethical foundations of person-centred therapy. In M. Cooper, M. O'Hara, P.F. Schmid and G. Wyatt (eds) *The Handbook of Person-Centred Psychotherapy and Counselling* (pp. 30–46). Basingstoke: Palgrave Macmillan.

Schmid, P.F. (2008a) A personalizing tendency: Philosophical perspectives on the actualizing tendency axiom and its dialogical and therapeutic consequences. In B. Levitt (ed.) *Reflections on Human Potential* (pp. 84–101). Ross-on-Wye: PCCS Books.

Schmid, P.F. (2008b) Active responsiveness. Person-centered psychotherapy – a dialogical approach. Invited lecture, World Conference for Psychotherapy, Beijing.

Schmid, P.F. (2008c) How person-centred is dialogical? Therapy as encounter: An evolutionary improvement? An arbitrary deviation? A new paradigm? Paper, World PCE Conference, Norwich.

Schmid, P.F. (2009) Beyond question and answer: The challenge to facilitate freedom. Invited paper given at the international conference, Person-Centred Counselling and Psychotherapy Today: Evolution and Challenges, Athens, http://members.kabsi.at/pfs0/pp-athens.pdf (published in Greek).

Schmid, P.F. (2012) Psychotherapy is political or it is not psychotherapy: The actualizing tendency as an essentially political venture. *Person-Centered and Experiential Psychotherapies,* 11, 95–108.

Schmid, P.F. and Mearns, D. (2006) Being-with and being-counter: Person-centered psychotherapy as an in-depth co-creative process of personalization. *Person-Centered and Experiential Psychotherapies*, 5, 174–90.

Taft, J. (1933) *The Dynamics of Therapy in a Controlled Relationship*. New York: Macmillan.

Tudor, K. and Merry, T. (eds) (2002) *Dictionary of Person-Centred Psychology*. London: Whurr.

Tudor, K. and Worrall, M. (2006) *Person-Centred Therapy: A Clinical Philosophy*. London: Routledge.

Waldenfels, B. (1994) *Antwortregister.* Frankfurt/M: Suhrkamp.

Wilders, S. (2007) Relational depth and the person-centred approach. *Person-Centred Quarterly*, 2, 1–4.

Wyatt, G. and Sanders, P. (eds) (2002) *Rogers' Therapeutic Conditions: Evolution, Theory and Practice*, vol. 4, *Contact and Perception*. Ross-on-Wye: PCCS Books.

13

Therapeutic presence as a foundation for relational depth

Shari M. Geller

Therapeutic presence involves therapists being fully in the moment on a multitude of levels, physically, emotionally, cognitively, spiritually and relationally (Geller and Greenberg, 2002, 2012). Therapists' cultivation and ability to be present with their clients provides an invitation to the other to feel met, understood, and to open and become present within their own experience as well as with their therapist, which can allow for moments of relational depth to arise.

In this chapter I propose that therapeutic presence is the foundation for deep relational contact. First, a description of therapeutic presence will be provided as grounded in two studies: a qualitative study of therapeutic presence and a quantitative study whereby a measure of therapists' presence was developed and explored for reliability and validity. A theory of relationship based on therapeutic presence will then be offered, followed by a discussion as to how therapeutic presence can provide the foundation and optimal condition for relational depth to be experienced.

What is therapeutic presence?

Therapeutic presence involves (a) being in contact with one's integrated and healthy self, while (b) being open and receptive to what is poignant in the moment and immersed in it, with (c) a larger sense of spaciousness and expansion of awareness and perception. This grounded, immersed and expanded awareness occurs with (d) the intention of being with and for the client, in service of their healing process (Geller and Greenberg, 2002, 2012).

While this description of therapists' presence is grounded in research (Geller and Greenberg, 2002), we can see some parallels to Rogers' later writings, where he began to allude to therapists' presence as an important quality. A well-known quote by Rogers (1980, p. 129) marks the beginning of his shift in perspective:

> When I am at my best, as a group facilitator or as a therapist, I discover another characteristic. I find that when I am closest to my inner, intuitive self, when I am somehow in touch with the unknown in me, when perhaps I am in a slightly altered state of consciousness, then whatever I do seems to be full of healing. Then, simply my presence is releasing and helpful to the other. There is nothing I can do to force this experience, but when I can relax and be close to the transcendental core of me, then I may behave in strange and impulsive ways in the relationship, ways in which I cannot justify rationally, which have nothing to do with my thought processes. But these strange behaviors turn out to be right, in some odd way: it seems that my inner spirit has reached out and touched the inner spirit of the other. Our relationship transcends itself and becomes a part of something larger. Profound growth and healing and energy are present.

Being in touch with one's self and relaxing into the transcendental core as alluded to by Rogers reflects both the (a) grounded and (c) spacious qualities referred to above in our definition of presence (Geller and Greenberg, 2002, 2012). Further, the aspect of presence as (b) being open and immersed in the moment, attuned to what is poignant, is reflected in the following quote from Rogers, when he was interviewed by Baldwin (2000, pp. 32–3):

> Once therapy is under way, another goal of the therapist is to question: 'Am I really with this person in this moment? Not where they were a little while ago, or where they are going to be, but am I really with this client in this moment?' This is the most important thing.

The client-centred orientation that is at the core of the person-centred approach is reflected in the last aspect of the therapeutic presence definition; that being present is held by (d) the intention of being with and for the client.

Research on therapeutic presence has confirmed the essential and healing qualities of therapists' presence that Rogers began to explicate prior to his death. For example, qualitative interviews with therapists revealed that the inner receptive state of the therapist is viewed as the ultimate tool in understanding and sensitively responding to the client's experience and needs (Geller and Greenberg, 2002). In agreement with this research, Rogers began to see the self as a tool, as noted in his interview with Baldwin (2000, p. 29): 'Over time, I think that I have become more aware of the fact that in therapy I do use my self. I recognize that when I am intensely focused on a client, just my presence seems to be healing.'

Research revealed that this inner receptive state includes therapists' complete openness to the client's multidimensional internal world, including their bodily and verbal expressions, as well as openness to their own bodily experience of the moment in order to access the knowledge, professional skill and wisdom embodied within (Geller and Greenberg, 2012). Being fully present, then, allows therapists to access an attuned responsiveness that is based on a kinaesthetic and emotional sensing of the other's affect and experience as well as one's own intuition and skill and the relationship between (Geller and Greenberg, 2002). Similarly, Rogers reflected that: 'In using myself, I include my intuition and the essence of myself' (Baldwin, 2000, p. 30).

Therapeutic presence allows for a therapist to offer nonjudgemental, highly focused and attuned awareness, with the intent of being in service of the client's healing process. Therapeutic presence also allows the therapist to work at a relational depth and enhance the therapeutic relationship and alliance between therapist and client, a key factor in successful therapeutic work (Lambert and Simon, 2008; Mearns, 1997).

Research on therapeutic presence

A series of studies on therapeutic presence has begun to clarify the nature of this quality and its contribution to building a positive therapeutic relationship (Geller, 2001; Geller and Greenberg, 2002; Geller et al., 2010; Hayes and Vinca, 2011; Pos et al., 2011). In particular, qualitative and quantitative investigations have contributed to the development of a model and a measure of therapeutic presence.

The model of therapeutic presence was developed from a qualitative study with experienced therapists who had either written about therapists' presence or espoused presence as a value in their therapy practice (Geller and Greenberg, 2002). This model includes three overarching categories of therapeutic presence:

1. therapists' *preparation* for presence (in session and in life)
2. the *process* of therapeutic presence (what one does when they are being present)
3. therapists' in body *experience* of therapeutic presence.

The process of therapeutic presence includes three aspects:

1. *being open and receptive* to the client's experience
2. *inwardly attending* to one's bodily resonance with the clients' experience
3. *extending and contact* outwards with the client from this place of receptivity and inward contact.

The experience of therapeutic presence includes the four aspects noted in the description provided earlier:

1. being *grounded* in one's self
2. *immersed* in the moment with the client
3. connected to a larger sense of *expansion*
4. being in service of the client's healing or *being with and for the client*.

A second study was conducted, which involved the development of a measure of therapeutic presence, the Therapeutic Presence Inventory (TPI; Geller et al., 2010). Two versions of the TPI were created: one for therapists about their own presence (TPI-T), and one for clients on their perceptions of their therapists' presence (TPI-C) (available to download from www.sharigeller.ca/publications). While the TPI was initially based on the model, it was further developed and validated through an empirical process of refining the measure and using ratings from expert therapists and theorists who have written about presence. The revised measure was then submitted to two larger psychotherapy studies for investigations of reliability and validity (Geller et al., 2010). Pilot research on the reliability and validity of the TPI-T and TPI-C suggested that both versions of the measure have good reliability, face validity and construct validity, and the TPI-C was demonstrated as having predictive validity.

A central finding in this research is that clients reported a positive therapeutic alliance as well as a positive change following a therapy session when they also felt their therapist was present with them (Geller et al., 2010). There was also a moderate correlation found between therapeutic presence and Rogers' relationship conditions (empathy, congruence and unconditional positive regard) as measured by Barrett-Lennard's Relationship Inventory (1973), suggesting a relationship between therapeutic presence and the relationship conditions and yet a conceptual difference (Geller et al., 2010). Both studies supported the view of therapeutic presence as an underlying condition or foundation to Rogers' relationship conditions. Further studies exploring the relationship of therapeutic presence and empathy, in particular, suggest that they are related yet distinct concepts (Pos et al., 2011), and that presence precedes empathy (Hayes and Vinca, 2011). These findings support Rogers' later thoughts:

> I am inclined to think that in my writing I have stressed too much the three basic conditions (congruence, unconditional positive regard, and empathic understanding). Perhaps it is something around the edges of those conditions that is really the most important element of therapy – when my self is very clearly, obviously present. (Baldwin, 2000, p. 30)

A discrepancy existed, however, between therapists' and clients' ratings of therapists' presence (Geller et al., 2010). Findings from the qualitative study (Geller and Greenberg, 2002) revealed that therapists describe their experience of presence, in interviews, as helping them to feel more connected to clients and more efficacious in their use of responses and technique. Yet findings in the second research study (Geller et al., 2010) indicated that clients don't rate themselves as having a more productive session or more positive alliance when therapists report they are more present; however, clients do rate these sessions and the alliance as positive when they themselves feel their therapist is present with them. It is likely that therapeutic presence only impacts clients if they are experiencing their therapist as present with them.

It is important to note that the latter finding is reflective of psychotherapy research in general (Duncan and Moynihan, 1994; Horvath and Luborsky, 1993; Lambert and Simon, 2008). Clients' experience of the therapist has greater impact than how therapists experience themselves. For example, Rogers came to the conclusion that it is the degree to which the client perceives the therapist as being unconditionally accepting, empathic and congruent that is the main factor for a good therapeutic outcome (Rogers and Truax, 1976). The findings of this study reflect this notion, that it is the degree to which clients perceive their therapist as present that allows them to feel more connected to their therapist, as well as support a positive session outcome.

When we look further at these studies, both from a qualitative and quantitative perspective, we see the emergence of a relational approach to presence. While we began these studies seeing presence as an intrapersonal (within the therapist) experience, we recognize that therapeutic presence deepens into a relational experience (Geller and Greenberg, 2012). Given that therapists' presence has the greatest impact on the therapeutic relationship and session outcome when the client perceives their therapist as fully present, it is possible that the client too is becoming more present with themselves and present with the therapist. This may contribute to a deepening in presence for both the therapist and client, and greater moments of relational depth. The research on therapeutic presence, combined with a theoretical and clinical experience and understanding of the impact of presence, has allowed for an unfolding of a therapeutic presence theory of relationship.

Therapeutic presence theory of relationship

A therapeutic presence theory of relationship proposes that therapists' presence is an essential quality underlying effective therapy, including good session process and outcome, as well as integral in deepening the therapeutic relationship, and allowing for relational depth (Geller, 2009; Geller and Greenberg, 2012). Further, this theory holds that therapists' verbal and nonverbal communication of presence is essential, as clients need to experience their therapist as present for presence to be therapeutic.

As clients experience their therapists' presence, they become more present themselves and with their therapists. As both open and become present with each other, relational therapeutic presence begins to emerge, which refers to the deepening of shared presence that occurs as a function of two (or more) people being fully present with one another. This shared relational presence creates a sense of expansion and higher levels of connectedness, including a reverbatory attunement that is expressed as a flow in the therapeutic encounter.

Therapeutic presence and the emergent relational presence can be healing for the client as they feel met, heard and understood in a way that allows them to become more present within themselves, as well as deeply and mutually present and connected. This allows clients to feel safe and emotionally held while opening to exploring the depth of their experience. Qualitative research on therapists' experience reveals that the cultivation and experience of therapeutic presence is also healthy for the therapist, as therapists tend to experience greater wellbeing, emotional regulation, decreased anxiety, reduced burnout, enhanced internal and interpersonal connection, and heightened vitality (Geller and Greenberg, 2002).

The theory of therapeutic presence purports that the most important guide to a therapeutic response or reflection is to be present, grounded and fully open and receptive to the client from moment to moment. From that place of receiving the client on a multisensory level, therapists tune into their own theoretical, learned, personal and intuitive understanding of the client, and a natural response or direction emerges from within. This encourages clients to feel open, safe and accepting or present with themselves and with the therapist, which allows for a synergistic relationship to emerge, where therapist and client can develop greater mutual presence (or 'co-presence', as termed by Cooper, 2005) as well as I-Thou contact and relational depth.

Therapeutic presence as a foundation to relational depth

We know from the research that therapists and clients can experience moments of relational depth and these moments can be highly significant and memorable, as well as potentially contribute to a positive therapeutic relationship and outcome (Cooper, 2005, Chapter 5, this volume; Knox, 2008, Chapter 2, this volume; McMillan and McLeod, 2006). Given that relational depth has been viewed as a combination of the relationship conditions (Cox, 2009; Mearns and Schmid, 2006) and that therapeutic presence has been demonstrated as the foundation for Rogers' relationship conditions (Geller and Greenberg, 2002; Geller et al., 2010; Hayes and Vinca, 2011), therapeutic presence can be seen as an underlying foundation for relational depth, as well as contributing to a positive therapeutic relationship and process. Schmid and Mearns (2006, p. 276) concur that the 'contribution on the therapist's part is to be present' in allowing for this depth of encounter between the therapist and the client.

Recent research supports this view of therapeutic presence as an underlying factor for relational depth. For example, a qualitative study of clients who experienced moments of relational depth revealed that the majority of clients described their therapists in these moments as being more present and authentic with them (Knox, 2008, Chapter 2, this volume). Further, counsellors working with people who self-harm acknowledged that therapeutic presence helped them to work in a way that allowed for relational depth with their clients (Long and Jenkins, 2010). Also, clients tend to experience relational depth as stemming from an invitation into a genuine deep encounter with the therapist (Knox and Cooper, 2010; Knox, Chapter 2, this volume; McMillan and McLeod, 2006). With therapeutic presence, there is a turning towards the client with all one's being to become open and fully immersed in receiving the other with full acceptance, which cultivates an inner attunement to the client and invites the client (and the therapist) into a deeper relational encounter (Geller and Greenberg, 2012).

It is possible that therapists' presence can invite the client into a safer and more open state of being, which allows the therapist into the clients' inner world and deepens the relationship between (Geller and Porges, 2012). Hence, relational depth can occur through therapists' offering of presence and attunement to the clients' readiness and experience in the moment, as well as the clients' opening and becoming present within and with the therapist.

As therapeutic presence deepens into relational therapeutic presence in the therapist, and the client opens to this present-centred connection, therapists experience a simultaneous opening and contact with a larger state of transcendence (for a discussion of levels of presence, see Geller and Greenberg, 2012, Ch. 7). While relational depth exists in between the therapist and client encounter, relational therapeutic presence is similar to the therapists' experience of relational depth, yet also goes beyond this level of mutual encounter and engagement to touch a larger state of spirituality. Relational therapeutic presence includes therapists being in contact with what is poignant in the self, the other and the relationship, while being held by this larger sense of spirituality or transcendence.

It is theorized that the therapist's presence invites the client to open and become present with their self and their therapist, and as the essence of each person comes into direct encounter with each other, a larger state of transcendence emerges that is healing. This state of transcendence can also be seen as emerging from connectedness and awareness of what presents itself in the here and now (Leijssen, 2009). The client may also experience this state of presence and transcendence but we do not have sufficient research at this point to know or understand the clients' experience in this respect.

The healing that can emerge in relational therapeutic presence is reflected in Rogers' (1980, p. 129) comments about being 'close to the transcendental core ... it seems that my inner spirit has reached out and touched the inner spirit of the other. Our relationship transcends itself and becomes a part of something larger. Profound growth and healing and energy are present.'

While these transcendent and relational dimensions of presence can occur as a result of the connection with the other, it can begin with the therapists' own intention, preparation and practice of presence outside or prior to the therapy hour. Similarly, it has been suggested that relational depth 'cannot be planned in advance, but emerges in unrepeatable contact between persons' (O'Leary, 2006, p. 230). Rogers (1980, p. 19) also noted that 'in those rare moments when a deep realness in one meets a realness in the other, a memorable I-thou relationship, as Martin Buber would call it, occurs'. While it is true that a 'therapist alone cannot create a meeting at relational depth' (O'Leary, 2006, p. 230), and that these moments may be 'rare', as Rogers noted, I believe that therapists' practice and cultivation of presence can allow for greater accessibility to the experience and deepening of therapeutic presence and therefore to the possibility of a profound relational connection and relational depth (Geller, 2009).

Conclusion

In summary, a therapeutic presence relationship theory begins with an essential nonspecific therapist's stance of presence that can help cultivate and sustain relational depth, as well as increase the efficacy of the therapy process for the client, the therapist and the relational encounter. The theory of presence involves therapists cultivating an open and accepting way of being that includes being grounded and yet deeply open and sensitive to the various nuances in the client and in the therapeutic relationship. This stance, originating from the therapist's presence, allows for a deepening in the relationship between, as clients feel fully heard, understood and responded to, and, in turn, this felt understanding invites clients to open to a deeper connection with their therapist as well as generates safety to open and contact their own bodily and authentic experience. Eventual presence within the client may ensue as clients generate self-acceptance, self-compassion and presence within, through their therapist's presence, which, in turn, can release their fundamental tendency towards wholeness and growth. A deepening into relational therapeutic presence can occur in resonance with the clients' openness and receptivity to their presence, and this can then become a mutual opening where relational depth can be experienced between therapist and client. The enhanced sensing that occurs from this shared state of presence ultimately guides the therapist's responses as well as deepens the relationship and the client's healing. In this vein, presence must be present for relational depth to develop, and for therapy to be effective.

In conclusion, I wish to emphasize that practising and cultivating therapeutic presence can allow for therapeutic presence to emerge in session with the client and hence invite the client into a deeper level of encounter through meeting them where they are in the moment. While therapeutic presence can start at the self with therapists' cultivation of presence, it deepens in the therapist through present-centred contact with the other and can provide fertile ground for a mutual encounter and relational depth to occur. While therapists' cannot demand the experience of presence or moments of relational depth to occur, they can create the conditions for presence to be revealed, both within and in the relationship. Presence then can deepen in the therapist, client, and between the two, and an optimal environment is created for relational depth to occur, as well as a release of the fundamental tendency towards healing, growth and actualization.

References

Baldwin, M. (ed.) (2000) *The Use of Self in Therapy* (2nd edn). Binghamton, NY: Haworth Press.

Barrett-Lennard, G.T. (1973) Relationship inventory. Unpublished manuscript, University of Waterloo, Ontario, Canada.

Cooper, M. (2005) Therapists' experiences of relational depth: A qualitative interview study. *Professional Psychology: Research and Practice*, 5(2), 87–95.

Cox, S. (2009) Relational depth: Its relevance to a contemporary understanding of person-centered therapy. *Person-Centered and Experiential Psychotherapies*, 8, 208–23.

Duncan, B.L. and Moynihan, D.W. (1994) Applying outcome research: Intentional utilization of the client's frame of reference. *Psychotherapy*, 31, 294–301.

Geller, S.M. (2001) Therapeutic presence: The development of a model and a measure. Unpublished doctoral dissertation, York University, Toronto, Canada.

Geller, S. (2009) Cultivation of therapeutic presence: Therapeutic drumming and mindfulness practices. *Dutch Tijdschrift Clientgerichte Psychotherapie (Journal for Client-Centered Psychotherapy)*, 47(4), 273–87.

Geller, S.M. and Greenberg, L.S. (2002) Therapeutic presence: Therapists' experience of presence in the psychotherapeutic encounter. *Person-Centered and Experiential Psychotherapies*, 1, 71–86.

Geller, S.M. and Greenberg, L.S. (2012) *Therapeutic Presence: A Mindful Approach to Effective Therapy*. Washington, DC: APA.

Geller, S.M., Greenberg, L.S. and Watson, J.C. (2010) Therapist and client perceptions of therapeutic presence: The development of a measure. *Journal of Psychotherapy Research*, 20(5), 599–610.

Hayes, J. and Vinca, J. (2011) Therapist presence and its relationship to empathy, session, depth, and symptom reduction. Paper presented to the Society for Psychotherapy Research, Bern, Switzerland.

Horvath, A.O. and Luborsky, L. (1993) The role of the therapeutic alliance in psychotherapy. *Journal of Consulting and Clinical Psychology*, 61, 561–73.

Knox, R. (2008) Clients' experiences of relational depth in person-centred counselling. *Counselling and Psychotherapy Research*, 8(3), 182–8.

Knox, R. and Cooper, M. (2010) Relationship qualities that are associated with moments of relational depth: The client's perspective. *Person-Centered and Experiential Psychotherapies*, 9(3), 236–56.

Lambert, M.J. and Simon, W. (2008) The therapeutic relationship: Central and essential in psychotherapy outcome. In S.F. Hick and T. Bien (eds) *Mindfulness and the Therapeutic Relationship* (pp. 19–33). New York: Guilford Press.

Leijssen, M. (2009) Psychotherapy as search and care for the soul. *Person-Centered & Experiential Psychotherapies*, 8, 18–32.

Long, M. and Jenkins, M. (2010) Counsellors perspectives on self-harm and the role of the therapeutic relationship for working with clients who self-harm. *Counselling and Psychotherapy Research*, 10(3), 192–200.

McMillan, M. and McLeod, J. (2006) Letting go: The client's experiences of relational depth. *Person-Centered and Experiential Psychotherapies*, 5, 277–92.

Mearns, D. (1997) *Person-centred Counselling Training*. London: Sage.

Mearns, D. and Cooper, M. (2005) *Working at Relational Depth in Counselling and Psychotherapy.* London: Sage.

Mearns, D. and Schmid, P. (2006) Being-with and being-counter: Relational depth: The challenge of fully meeting the client. *Person-Centered and Experiential Psychotherapies*, 5, 255–65.

O'Leary, C.J. (2006) Carl Rogers: Lessons for working at relational depth. *Person-Centered and Experiential Psychotherapies*, 5, 229–39.

Pos, A., Geller, S.M. and Oghene, J. (2011) Therapist presence, empathy, and the working alliance in experiential treatment for depression. Paper presented to the Society for Psychotherapy Research, Bern, Switzerland.

Rogers, C.R. (1980) *A Way of Being.* Boston: Houghton Mifflin.

Rogers, C.R. and Truax, C.B. (1976) The therapeutic conditions antecedent to change: A theoretical view. In C.R. Rogers, E.T. Gendlin, D.J. Kiesler and C.B. Truax (eds) *The Therapeutic Relationship and its Impact: A Study of Psychotherapy with Schizophrenics* (pp. 97–108). Westport, CT: Grennwork.

Schmid, P. and Mearns, D. (2006) Being-with and being-counter: Person-centered psychotherapy as an in-depth co-creative process of personalization. *Person-Centered and Experiential Psychotherapies*, 5(3), 174–90.

14

Mutuality and relational depth in counselling and psychotherapy

David Murphy

The field of counselling and psychotherapy has seen a *relational turn* (Mitchell, 2000), with all the major approaches now acknowledging the important role of relational aspects of therapy (Leahy, 2006). Mearns and Cooper's (2005) theoretical development of 'working at relational depth' has been a welcome contribution and further challenges the 'old paradigm' view of a *unilaterally* created therapeutic relationship, in which the therapist is considered to be 'providing' the relationship 'for' the client. Despite these favourable shifts, research into the therapeutic relationship has tended to focus on the therapist as the active agent and the one responsible for changes made by the client. This is a deterministic and somewhat outdated conceptualization of the therapeutic process. However, the relational turn has brought with it the 'new paradigm'. Whereas the unilateral perspective neglects the role of the client as an active embodied agent contributing to their own change process (Bohart and Tallman, 1999), the relational perspective recognizes a *bidirectional* and *mutual* process. More importantly, the unilateral view of the therapeutic relationship denies recognition of the client's contribution in the mutual generation of a therapeutic relationship.

Relational depth theory stands counter to this and, in contrast, challenges the therapist-centric thinking at the heart of the unilateral view. Instead, relational depth theory supports a bidirectional view of the therapeutic relationship, evidenced in recent studies which have shown that both clients (Knox, 2008; McMillan and McLeod, 2006) and therapists (Cooper, 2005; Knox and Cooper, 2010; Mearns and Cooper, 2005) have experienced moments of relational depth (see Cooper, Chapter 5, this volume; Knox, Chapter 2, this volume; Macleod, Chapter 3, this volume). The research evidence supporting relational depth is growing; however, a consistently reported, but underacknowledged finding is the concept of 'mutuality'.

This chapter will explore the proposition that mutuality is a (the?) core therapeutic process at the heart of relational depth experience. While mutuality as a therapeutic concept can refer to many things (see Aron, 1996 for a full analysis of the concept in psychotherapy), for the purpose of this chapter, I am referring to the mutual generation and perception of the therapeutic relationship conditions of empathy, unconditional positive regard and congruence. Formulating mutuality in this way, I suggest, is most relevant to the discussion of relational depth, and captures Rogers' (1957) six necessary and sufficient conditions being fully operationalized. Of course, the therapeutic relationship has always been a bidirectional phenomenon. However, a positive consequence of the relational depth research has been to bring this into the foreground. If we can welcome and embrace these developments, we can further develop our knowledge and understanding of how therapy works. In the sections below, I first build the theoretical case that the concept of 'mutuality' is at the heart of relational depth experience in psychotherapy, and, second, I will present the evidence from recent relational depth research studies to show how mutuality is central to the experience of meeting at relational depth. Throughout this, I will link the arguments to some of Rogers' own thoughts and statements about mutuality, and conclude that relational depth is implicit to, but not defining of, person-centred therapy, implying that mutual experiencing of the therapeutic conditions represents a successful process/outcome to psychotherapy.

Mutuality as a core underlying construct of relational depth

Relational depth was described by Mearns and Cooper (2005) both as a form of enduring relationship and as an event, or moment, embedded within the broader concept of the therapeutic relationship. First, in taking the perspective of the enduring relationship, Mearns and Cooper (2005) suggest that relational depth involves increasingly congruent communication and that when the relationship has reached this point, transference has been surpassed. The relationship is characterized as 'each person is fully real with the Other, and able to understand and value the Other's experiences *at a high level*' (Mearns and Cooper, 2005, p. xii, emphases added). This both reflects and is consistent with Rogers' (1959) process outcome model of therapeutic change and the development of a deepening and more authentic relationship over the course of therapy. Whether we can ever truly consider transference to be totally absent from the relationship is a complex issue, and I am not convinced of the utility of formulating transference as a dichotomous variable – being either present or not. However, in proposing that transference is not the primary feature in the communication between client and therapist, we can focus on the *realness* between client and therapist within the relationship. The authentic encounter in relational depth is similar to the presence of high levels of mutual genuineness described by Greenson (1967) and later by Gelso (2002) in the concept of the 'real relationship'. Hence, relational depth shares with mutuality a concern with genuine authentic encounter. Proctor (2010) argues that mutual authentic relating involves trusting that the client is communicating their needs as they are perceived, rather than interpreting client behaviour as manipulative or pushing at the therapeutic boundaries. In this sense, and in line with the assertion by Mearns and Cooper (2005) that transference is surpassed, we can see how meeting at relational depth, and in relationships defined by mutuality, the relationship is not based on interpretive strategies. Rather, at the level of enduring relationship, the relational process becomes more concerned with both client and therapist's engagement in mutually respectful and authentic dialogue.

Mearns and Cooper (2005, p. xii) also present the concept of relational depth at the level of moment-by-moment experience and note that, during moments of relational depth, client and counsellor meet in 'a state of profound contact and engagement'. This is similar to Stern's (2004) notion of 'moments of meeting', a concept derived from the earlier work of Pine (1981), which referred to experiences of 'intense moments' within the mother–child relational dyadic system. Stern (1985) suggested that experiencing intense moments of affect between infant and carer plays a significant role in the organization of memories about relational encounters. That is, we learn, in part, how relational encounters will be worked out through experiencing moments of intense affects. So, when a memory of a relational experience is evoked, the accompanying affect that was experienced at the time the memory was first laid down is also recalled. In person-centred terms, these relational memories form part of the self-structure and our capacity to process experience. This means that interpersonal relational experiences of moments of intense affect (I term this 'interaffectivity') can be either growth facilitating or growth inhibiting. Intense interaffective states that are threatening to the maintenance of the organism can be perceived, or subceived, as potentially traumatic. The significance of this for meeting at relational depth is that, during therapy, when non-threatening intense interaffective states are co-created, such as those involved in a moment of mutual encounter and relational depth, the therapeutic relationship provides an opportunity for healing and growth. In these intense relational encounters, the self-structure is being re-authored, and relational experience within our self-structure and relational memories are reorganized, transformed or modified, contributing to a more resilient emergent self-structure with enhanced processing capacities and increased self-awareness.

Meeting at relational depth involves the synergy of relational components as a 'gestalt comprising the core conditions in high degree and in mutually enhancing interaction' (Mearns and Cooper, 2005, p. 36). This suggests that mutual client–therapist *interaction* is the central focus, rather than the focus being on what *either* the client *or* the therapist individually brings to the encounter.

The concept of mutual and reciprocal experiencing of the conditions is also referred to in the theory of person-centred therapy. Rogers, in his public dialogue with Buber, suggested that moments of significant change within therapy could be characterized by the client and the therapist's mutual experience of the therapeutic conditions:

> in the moments where real change takes place ... in the sense that ... I am able to see this individual as he is in that moment ... and he really senses my understanding and acceptance of him. And that I think is what *is* reciprocal and is perhaps what produces change. (Rogers, quoted in Cissna and Anderson, 2002, p. 143)

The above quote captures how the conditions are conceived as mutually present in therapy. Proctor (2010) suggests that we can also consider the 'ethic' of mutuality within person-centred therapy. In addition to mutuality as an ethical way of being in relationship, we can also consider the associated behaviour that outwardly demonstrates this ethical way of relating towards an other. One way of doing this is through mutuality of the client and therapist being actively engaged in the creative generation and exchange of genuine empathic understanding and unconditional positive regard, both of and for one another. Mutuality in this sense is the enactment of each person's inherent relationality. When client and therapist are engaged in mutual encounter, they each experience the therapeutic conditions of and for the other. Schmid (Chapter 12, this volume) puts it thus: 'This also means that therapist and client are co-responding to the relationship they find themselves in, in the very moment of their being together. So, they are co-creating the relationship out of mutual encounter.'

The mutual experience of the therapeutic relationship conditions does not necessarily require that client and therapist experience the therapeutic conditions to the *same degree*. Proctor (2010) acknowledges the commitment within the person-centred approach to dismantling the structural distribution of power within society and identifies that client and therapist experience inequity of role power. However, to present mutuality only in terms of 'equity', or in presenting the power inherent in the roles of therapist and client as a barrier to mutuality, is important but offers a different view on the concept of mutuality. Mutuality is not the same as 'quantitative equity' (Aron, 1996). Rather, both client and therapist experience and perceive the therapeutic conditions to *some* degree for and of each other. It is the bidirectionality of the process that makes it mutual, not the extent that each person quantitatively experiences something. In his public dialogue with Buber, Rogers (in Cissna and Anderson, 2002) acknowledged the difference in role power that therapist and client possess. He agreed that when viewing the relationship from the outside, there is always an inequity inherent in role power. However, grounding his argument in, and commenting from, the phenomenological lived experience of being *inside* the therapeutic relationship, Rogers maintained the view that mutuality was possible and that each person's experience has equal *validity*, even if not equal in quantity.

The roles of client and therapist in therapy are clearly different. This difference is significant for our understanding of both the development of mutuality and meeting at relational depth. With regards to mutuality, and in referring to equity, Buber considered the therapist is 'providing' something for the client, and concluded that this creates an inequity within the therapeutic relationship. Buber suggested that the roles occupied by client and therapist preclude the therapeutic relationship reaching mutuality (Cissna and Anderson, 2002; Aron, 1996). However, Mearns and Cooper (2005) have suggested that meeting at relational depth is similar to the 'I-Thou' relationship. Buber (1958) suggested that the conditions for an I-Thou encounter and to reach mutuality require *non-purposeful* relating. Consequently, if the therapeutic relationship is purposeful, that is, if the therapist sees as part of their 'role' that therapy has a predefined purpose to make something specific happen, then mutuality and relational depth are not possible.

In person-centred therapy, there are no predefined goals to be achieved. Relational depth, in my view, is not a specifically desired outcome within the therapeutic relationship. In contrast, some therapeutic approaches adopt a utilitarian/purposeful view of the therapeutic relationship. For example, cognitive behavioural therapy and psychoanalytic therapy both consider the therapeutic relationship to serve a particular purpose, that is, to act as a context in which it is believed that the active interventions can be applied, for example homework tasks and transference interpretations respectively. Mutuality and relational depth require non-purposeful relating, as the I-Thou relational stance demands, so utilitarian approaches are less likely to provide an opportunity for mutuality and relational depth. Aron (1996), writing from the psychoanalytic perspective, agrees with Buber and suggests that mutuality, as Buber and Rogers considered, was not possible in psychotherapy. However, in agreement with Rogers, it is more probable that mutuality arises in approaches that consider the therapeutic relationship as 'an end in itself', rather than in utilitarian terms where the relationship is considered as a means to an end.

In mutual relations the focus of the client and therapist can also be different. Take, for example, an occasion in which both client and therapist experience empathy for the other. While both experience empathy, the 'target of empathy' (Grant, 2010) differs according to the perceiver. In mutual empathy, the therapist's target for empathy is some aspect of the client's experience or the main point they are trying to communicate; whereas the client's target might be the therapist's attempt to empathize with the client *and/or* the therapist's experience of empathy for the client. In this sense, it can be argued that clients hold both a focus on their emerging congruence *and* an intersubjective awareness of the therapist (see Knox, Chapter 2, this volume).

The client's experience and intersubjective awareness of the therapist place mutuality at the centre of relational depth. Mearns and Cooper (2005, p. 46) support this in stating: 'The therapist knows the client; the client knows that she is known; the therapist knows that the client knows that she is known.' I would also add to this statement that 'the client knows the therapist knows that the client knows that she is known' and so on, ad infinitum.

It is interesting here to consider who is 'holding' who as their primary focus in a mutual encounter or meeting at relational depth. In discussing relational depth, Schmid (2006) insightfully reversed Buber's 'I-Thou' relational stance to become 'Thou-I', giving primacy to the other. However, doing this maintains viewing the therapeutic relationship from the therapist's perspective and doesn't truly reflect a relational perspective within meeting at relational depth. Can the client also respond to the call of the other (Levinas, 1996), and hold a Thou-I stance, or is this not even desirable? This question is important, for if we view the client as inherently relational, and take that to respond to the call of the other is to be a full and active human being, then not allowing this means we deprive the client the opportunity for meeting with full mutuality by only viewing and acting within the therapeutic relationship from the therapist's perspective.

Sayre (2005) has argued that it is never preferable for the client to hold the therapist as the distinct other – Thou-I – and, as an alternative, has suggested that the client might be encouraged to consider an other from outside the therapeutic relationship in order to learn about their interpersonal relations. However, if this is considered in the context of mutuality and returning to the example of empathy used above, a combination of both these views is possible. Placing mutuality as the foundation for a meeting at relational depth, the therapist might hold a Thou-I stance while, in accommodating McMillan and McLeod's (2006) view of relational depth, the client holds an I-Thou relation. Thus, the relationship is mutual yet different, as each has the client's emerging expression of congruence as their primary focus, yet each is also relating to the other in the moment with full mutuality.

Relational depth research and mutuality

So far in this chapter, I have been making a theoretical case for mutuality as a core process in meeting at relational depth. In addition, a number of empirical studies support this and the findings are outlined below. Cooper's (2005) small-scale qualitative study found that therapists experienced their clients as highly transparent and reciprocating their therapist's acknowledgement. This finding suggests that clients go beyond merely *perceiving* the therapist as empathic and accepting towards them, and actively *experience* their relationship with the therapist, requiring the client be engaged in a process of mutual empathy.

Knox (2008) also showed that mutuality was a core element within the experience of relational depth. Following analysis of data collected in interviews with clients, a theme 'relationship' emerged and a subcategory of 'mutuality/co-reflectiveness' was formed. A later study by Knox and Cooper (2010) reported a number of themes from client accounts of experiences of relational depth. Themes indicated that clients perceived therapists as 'offering mutuality'. Under this theme, specific accounts described the therapist as not using power, empowering the client, and of showing their own vulnerability. Although the theme here is presented as supporting mutuality as a core element in relational depth, this might present a slightly different interpretation of the term 'mutuality'. By its very nature, mutuality cannot be offered by one person to the other. Rather, mutuality is created through the interaction *between* the client and therapist.

Research has explored the effect of experiencing the therapeutic conditions from the client's perspective and as being *provided* by the therapist (Haugh and Merry, 2001; Bozarth and Wilkins, 2001; Wyatt and Sanders, 2001). However, far less attention has been given to the contribution clients make (Bohart and Tallman, 1999). McMillan and McLeod (2006) reported that the client's experience of relational depth is different to that of therapists. Their findings suggested that the client's experience appears more closely related to a sense of emerging congruence. Additionally, while therapists experience a deepening of relational connection, clients experience relational depth in terms of their own growth (McMillan and McLeod, 2006). McMillan and McLeod's (2006) findings indicated that clients don't have the therapist as a focus when meeting at relational depth. This challenges the notion of mutuality as a core element of relational depth. Interestingly, Knox (Chapter 2, this volume), on the other hand, found two types of encounter in relational depth. First was a 'face-to-face' encounter, where the attention of both client and therapist was on each other, and, second, a 'side-by-side' type of encounter where the attention of both was on the client. This finding more clearly supports the notion of mutuality as a central concept to relational depth and links back to the aforementioned notion of 'Thou-I' and 'I-Thou' relating.

Knox and Cooper's (2010) study attributed a significant role to mutuality, as clients are reported to actively express their clear *perception* and *experience* of their therapist in the moment of relational depth. Additionally, clients reported experiencing their therapists' experience of them, supporting the view that both client and therapist are engaged in mutual empathy. Jordan (2000) proposed that mutual empathy is a necessary aspect within the therapeutic relationship that enables the client to receive (via perception and subception) the impact they have on the other/therapist.

Rogers (1959) proposed the concept of clients experiencing unconditional positive regard for the therapist. The client's acceptance of the therapist grows as a central element, enabling the therapeutic relationship to develop to its full potential. Knox and Cooper's (2010) study showed clients' and therapists' mutual acceptance and congruence, suggesting that clients were *accepting* of the therapist as *imperfect* and *human*. For clients to experience unconditional positive regard for their therapist is particularly important for resolving ruptures within the therapeutic relationship, or when the therapist makes an inaccurate or unhelpful empathic response. The client's response to their therapist at these moments can be critical and just as important for developing relational depth as those of high contact and engagement. At critical moments, such as when the therapist is 'out of tune' or offers a 'conditional response', the client's capacity for acceptance is crucial for furthering the relationship. As such, ruptures, or points of disagreement or difficulty within the relationship, can be considered as opportunities for mutuality and form part of the process for meeting at relational depth. Wilkins (2000) has described how a therapeutic relationship reached a state of mutuality when he experienced his client's unconditional positive regard for him as the therapist.

Knox and Cooper's (2010) study also reports that clients experience a high degree of *awareness of their own self* and of *accurate symbolization of experience*. This suggests that experiences of relational depth are also characterized by mutual congruence. Additionally, in their research, Knox and Cooper (2010) suggest that the client was *active* and *in control* of their actions. Mutuality requires that both client and therapist have the willingness and openness for mutual encounter. This was supported in a study that looked at mutuality of Rogers' therapeutic conditions within the therapeutic relationship (Murphy, 2010). The study demonstrated that clients actively relate to their therapist and, in addition to experiencing the therapist as empathically understanding, unconditionally accepting and genuine, clients were also perceived by their therapist as being empathically attuned and genuinely unconditionally accepting (Murphy, 2010).

While relational depth research has provided some indication that mutuality is a core concept underlying this phenomenon, research has tended not to look at the way client and therapist experience each other with regards to the same therapeutic encounter. Yet, to truly determine the role of mutuality in relational depth, and specifically the mutual experience of the therapeutic conditions of empathy, unconditional positive regard and congruence, we need to explore these from the client and therapist perspective, basing reports on the same therapeutic relationship *at the same point in time*. In a study testing this 'mutuality hypothesis' (Murphy, 2010), clients and therapists were asked to complete a shortened version of the Barrett-Lennard (1964) Relationship Inventory. Each half of the dyad completed the questionnaire after the first and the third session of therapy to rate their own feelings towards the other and their perception of how the other felt towards them. As a measure of outcome, clients also completed the generic measure of distress using CORE-OM (Clinical Outcomes in Routine Evaluation Outcome Measure) in the first and third sessions in order to assess change over time. This generated a range of perspectives from which mutuality of the therapeutic relationship could be measured and produced some interesting results.

In taking the scores provided by clients at session three, the association between the client's perception of the therapist's empathy, acceptance and congruence and outcome was stronger for those clients whose therapists also rated their clients as offering higher rather than lower levels of empathy, unconditional positive regard and congruence (Murphy, 2010).

These findings suggest that mutual experiencing of the therapeutic conditions is related to outcome, and support Wiggins' (2011) study in which a measure of relational depth was developed that showed the concept of mutuality as significantly associated with both clients' and therapists' reports of the presence of relational depth (see also Wiggins et al., 2012; Wiggins, Chapter 4, this volume). The evidence, it would seem, supports the hypothesis that a core construct underlying relational depth is the process of client and therapist *mutually* experiencing the therapeutic conditions and that this is itself evidence of successful psychotherapy process/outcome.

Conclusion

In this chapter I have looked into the phenomenon of relational depth and suggested that mutuality is a core underlying construct of this experience. In their book, Mearns and Cooper (2005) state that relational depth refers to an experience of the relationship at both the *moment* and *enduring* level of relationship. I suggest this is equally the case for mutuality and that the definition relates more to the level of analysis rather than the phenomenon itself. In his dialogue with Buber, Rogers stated that the relationship could be experienced with full mutuality yet this might last only for a moment. This is highly significant, as it is here in the transcript from Cissna and Anderson (2002) that Buber and Rogers reached agreement – that mutuality could be achieved if only for a moment. In a time where psychotherapy research has invested much by way of demonstrating the effectiveness of one approach over another, relational depth theory shows that we might have more fruitfully continued to focus attention on the relational aspects of therapy. Relational depth theory helpfully requests we (re)turn our attention to relational elements, and mutuality in the therapeutic relationship is but one aspect where further attention and research will prove useful. In turn, relational depth provides a lens through which we can continue to study both 'how' and 'what' the therapeutic relationship contributes to change.

References

Aron, L. (1996) *A Meeting of Minds: Mutuality in Psychoanalysis*. Hove: Analytic Press.

Barrett-Lennard, G.T. (1964) The Relationship Inventory Forms: OS-M-64, OS-F-64 and MO-M-64 plus MO-F-64. Unpublished manuscript, University of New England, Australia.

Bohart, A.C. and Tallman, K. (1999) The active client: Therapy as self-help. In R. House and Y. Bates (eds) *Ethically Challenged Professions: Enabling Innovation and Diversity in Psychotherapy and Counselling* (pp. 258–74). Ross-on-Wye: PCCS Books.

Bozarth, J.D. and Wilkins, P. (eds) (2001) *Rogers' Therapeutic Conditions: Evolution, Theory and Practice*, vol. 3, *Unconditional Positive Regard*. Ross-on-Wye: PCCS Books.

Buber, M. (1958) *I and Thou* (2nd edn) (trans. R.G. Smith). New York: Charles Scribner's Sons.

Cissna, K.N. and Anderson, R. (2002) *Moments of Meeting: Buber, Rogers and the Potential for Public Dialogue*. Albany: State University of New York.

Cooper, M. (2005) Therapists' experiences of relational depth: A qualitative interview study. *Counselling and Psychotherapy Research*, 5(2), 87–95.

Gelso, C. (2002) The real relationship: The 'something more' of psychotherapy. *Journal of Contemporary Psychotherapy*, 32, 35–40.

Grant, B. (2010) Getting the point: Empathic understanding in nondirective client-centered therapy. *Person-Centered and Experiential Psychotherapies*, 9, 220–35.

Greenson, R.R. (1967) *The Technique and Practice of Psychoanalysis*. New York: International Universities Press.

Haugh, S. and Merry, T. (eds) (2001) *Rogers' Therapeutic Conditions: Evolution, Theory and Practice*, vol. 2, *Empathy*. Ross-on-Wye: PCCS Books.

Jordan, J.V. (2000) The role of mutual empathy in relational/cultural therapy. *Journal of Clinical Psychology/In Session*, 56, 1005–16.

Knox, R. (2008) Clients' experiences of relational depth in person-centred counselling. *Counselling and Psychotherapy Research*, 8, 182–8.

Knox, R. and Cooper, M. (2010) Relationship qualities that are associated with moments of relational depth: The client's perspective. *Person-Centered and Experiential Psychotherapies*, 9(3), 236–56.

Knox, R. and Cooper, M. (2011) A state of readiness: An exploration of the client's role in meeting at relational depth. *Journal of Humanistic Psychology*, 51(1), 61–81.

Leahy, R.L. (2006) The therapeutic relationship in cognitive-behavioral therapy. *Behavioural and Cognitive Psychotherapy*, 36, 769–77.

Levinas, E. (1996) *Basic Philosophical Writings*. Bloomington, IN: Indiana University Press.

McMillan, M. and McLeod, J. (2006) Letting go: The client's experience of relational depth. *Person-Centered and Experiential Psychotherapies*, 5, 277–92.

Mearns, D. and Cooper, M. (2005) *Working at Relational Depth in Counselling and Psychotherapy*. London: Sage.

Mitchell, S.A. (2000) *Relationality: From Attachment to Intersubjectivity*. Hillsdale, NJ: Analytic Press.

Murphy, D. (2010) Psychotherapy as mutual encounter: A study of therapeutic conditions. Unpublished doctoral dissertation, available at http://hdl.handle.net/2134/6627.

Pine, F. (1981) In the beginning: Contributions to a psychoanalytic developmental psychology. *International Review of Psychoanalysis*, 8, 15–33.

Proctor, G. (2010) Boundaries or mutuality in therapy: Is mutuality really possible or is therapy doomed from the start? *Psychotherapy and Politics International*, 8(1), 44–58, doi:10.1002/ppi209.

Rogers, C.R. (1957) The necessary and sufficient conditions of therapeutic personality change. *Journal of Consulting Psychology*, 21, 95–103.

Rogers, C.R. (1959) A theory of therapy, personality, and interpersonal as developed in the client-centred framework. In S. Koch (ed.) *Psychology: A Study of Science*, vol. 3 (pp. 184–256). New York: McGraw-Hill.

Sayre, G. (2005) Towards a therapy for the Other. *European Journal of Psychotherapy, Counselling and Health*, 7, 37–47.

Schmid, P.F. (2006) The challenge of the Other: Towards a dialogical person-centered psychotherapy and counseling. *Person-Centered and Experiential Psychotherapies*, 5, 240–54.

Stern, D. (1985) *The Interpersonal World of the Infant: A View from Psychoanalysis and Developmental Psychology*. New York: Basic Books.

Stern, D. (2004) *The Present Moment in Psychotherapy and Everyday Life*. New York: W.W. Norton.

Wiggins, S. (2011) Development and validation of a measure of relational depth. Unpublished PhD dissertation, University of Strathclyde, Glasgow.

Wiggins, S., Elliott, R. and Cooper, M. (2012) The prevalence and characteristics of relational depth events in psychotherapy. *Psychotherapy Research*, 22(2), 139–58.

Wilkins, P. (2000) Unconditional positive regard reconsidered. *British Journal of Guidance & Counselling*, 25(1), 23–36.

Wyatt, G. and Sanders, P. (eds) (2001) *Rogers' Therapeutic Conditions: Evolution, Theory and Practice*, vol. 4, *Contact and Perception*. Ross-on-Wye: PCCS Books.

15

The Person-Centred approach: similarities and differences with relational depth

Sue Wilders

The Person-Centred approach is a unique way of offering therapy. It is based on the radical and unusual concept of an active and engaged therapist trusting and understanding their client, wherever the client's thoughts and feelings take them. The client, not the therapist, is the expert. This is a rarity, when the majority of other models of therapy have the therapist as the expert over the process. This approach is based on the theory of therapy and theory of personality developed by Carl Rogers, crystallized in his paper, A theory of therapy, personality, and interpersonal relationships, as developed in the client-centered framework (Rogers, 1959).

This apparently simple premise of trusting and following the client's process wherever they choose to go and however they choose to present themselves is, I believe, the criterion or benchmark of whether or not a therapist's practice is Person-Centred. The conditions listed below upon which this trust is built are the necessary and sufficient conditions as described in Rogers' (1959, p. 213) theory framework paper:

1. That two persons are in contact.
2. That the first person, whom we shall term the client, is in a state of incongruence, being vulnerable, or anxious.
3. That the second person, whom we shall term the therapist, is congruent in the relationship.
4. That the therapist is experiencing unconditional positive regard toward the client.

5. That the therapist is experiencing an empathic understanding of the client's internal frame of reference.
6. That the client perceives, at least to a minimal degree, conditions 4 and 5, the unconditional positive regard of the therapist for him, and the empathic understanding of the therapist.

Whether and to what extent the developing concept of relational depth meets these conditions and so is within the practice of Person-Centred therapy is of interest to many theoreticians and practitioners.

The ideas around relational depth have, in recent years, captured the imagination of therapists and researchers who are attracted to the idea and meaning of in-depth moments of relating between client and therapist. Since its development, it has mostly been associated with the Person-Centred approach (Mearns, 1996, 1997). It has also been identified as a type of relationship that is present in different models of therapy – not only in the Person-Centred approach (Cooper, 2011; Mearns and Cooper, 2005).

This chapter seeks to investigate the relationship between the ideas associated with relational depth and their impact on the process of Person-Centred therapy. At times, relational depth simply describes a dynamic that occurs spontaneously and can be observed in Person-Centred therapy, whereas at other times and depending on the activity of the therapist, it may subtly alter the therapeutic process towards the therapist's expertism. In considering the inherently nondirective and nonjudgemental practice of Person-Centred therapy, I believe it will become evident here that some ways of thinking about and achieving relational depth are quite different from the Person-Centred approach.

Clarifying concepts and practices

As the hypothesis of relational depth has developed, one area of confusion, I believe, is in the use of the phrase 'relational depth' to describe moments that can occur when Person-Centred therapy is simply being practised as intended (Rogers, 1959). I believe this may be confounding to students of the approach, when existing Person-Centred practices and ideas are presented as if they were developments or enhancements of Person-Centred therapy, potentially leading students to unnecessarily hold an awareness in therapy sessions of opportunities to achieve moments of relational depth (Mearns and Cooper, 2005).

Conversely, and slightly more confusing, some of the concepts and practices used in pursuance of relational depth, which move away from the theory of the Person-Centred approach, are, in my view, wrongly referred to as Person-Centred, or as developments of the Person-Centred approach. Consider this quote, for example, from Mearns and Schmid (2006, p. 256):

> In a previous paper (Schmid and Mearns, 2006) we laid down the basis of person-centred therapy ... We emphasized that it was both alongside the client and in confrontation with them.

The notion of 'being-counter', where the therapist presents their own frame of reference in response to the client (Schmid and Mearns, 2006; Mearns and Cooper, 2005), is, in my view, a good example of an antithetical conflict with the successful practice of the Person-Centred approach of trusting or following and unconditionally accepting the client (Rogers, 1959).

In the past 10–20 years in the UK especially, alongside the various theoretical arguments of what is and isn't Person-Centred, there has been a fragmentation of the depth and breadth of the Person-Centred training process, resulting, I believe, in gaps in understanding and misconceptions of the theory behind the approach. This can lead some students to conclude that the Person-Centred approach is somehow an old-fashioned, shallow, wooden, formulaic and response-led, skills-based therapy.

Although Mearns and Cooper (2005) do warn against using the Person-Centred approach in a formulaic way, they also promote relational depth as the alternative to this, and assert that the emphasis on the therapist experiencing and communicating the core conditions towards the client somehow diminishes the likelihood of a mutual encounter between them (Mearns and Cooper 2005). In Person-Centred therapy, however, it is not the depth of experience which is significant and which mitigates against superficial formulaic responses, but the therapist's congruent experiencing of unconditional positive regard and empathy, and the client's perception of this.

In my experience, and crucial to Rogers' theory of personality (1959), the lessening of conditions of worth, the strengthening of the internal locus of evaluation, the consequent increase in congruence and self-confidence, facilitated by the therapist's unconditional understanding and acceptance, is more likely to bring about an increased engagement from the client in the therapy without any need to 'counter' the client (Mearns and Schmid, 2006) (since to counter would reintroduce conditional valuing to the client), or to seek out or herald moments of relational depth over other moments during therapy.

The designation of warm, acceptant, engaged, congruent therapist behaviour as a description of relational depth behaviour misses the fact that these behaviours will also be present in the Person-Centred therapist during less deep or intense therapeutic experiences.

The Person-Centred approach

Rogers considered his 1959 theory statement as the basis of the Person-Centred approach. However, today, 25 years after his death, there are several offshoots from the approach (focusing, experiential and so on) that accept some part of Rogers' theory and not others, despite the theory being designed to operate successfully as a whole. Writers have referred to various 'tribes' (Sanders, 2004) of the Person-Centred approach, and have designated the practice that is actually consistent with Rogers' theory as simply one of those tribes, giving it the title 'classical'. In my view, this is inaccurate and potentially damaging to the future full understanding and practice of the Person-Centred approach. Person-Centred approach theory radically posits that a reduction of psychological harm occurs when a client is empathically understood in a genuine, unconditionally acceptant way. Such experiences strengthen a client's internal locus of evaluation and experience of self-worth, and is the opposite of what happens when forced to encounter therapist frames of reference. I would argue that those approaches that do not accept the full theory and practice of Person-Centred therapy theory are not so much 'tribes' but different therapies, which, with their various alterations to the theory and practice, also suggest the potential for a variety of unknown outcomes. Bert Rice (2012) wrote about this as follows:

> Most of these offered 'improvements' seem to me to be a step backward rather than a step forward, that is, a compromise of some sort with the directive intent that underlay therapy generally before Rogers turned the field on its head. I am not the only one unconvinced.

Rogers (1959) did explore other ideas and applications of the Person-Centred approach but stayed true to his 1959 theory throughout his own therapeutic career. In 1980, he referred people seeking a complete statement of the approach to his 1959 theory statement. Rogers (1980) and research undertaken into his own therapy practice evidenced that he worked 98 per cent in accordance with his theory (for client-centred analyses of Rogers' response style with real and demonstration clients, see Brodley, 1994, 2001; Brody, 1991; Merry, 1996).

A critical element in the Person-Centred approach is that there is no therapist evaluation of the client; Rogers (1959, p. 208) stated:

> The therapist 'prizes' the whole person of the client. It is the fact that he feels and shows an unconditional positive regard toward the experiences of which the client is frightened or ashamed, as well as toward the experiences with which the client is pleased or satisfied, that seems effective in bringing about change.

Person-Centred therapy offers the opportunity for deep interconnected bidirectional relationships, but these are created through an environment rich in empathy and unconditional positive regard. These deep connections exist not only when the client relates with intensity, but also when they relate in a conversational or presentational style. The Person-Centred therapist genuinely attempts to understand, not only the content, but also the feelings and process of the client. The client is met in their own world, not jolted out of it into the world of the therapist.

In the following extract from Mearns and Cooper (2005, p. 77), rather than the therapist meeting the client Dominic in his world, it would seem that the therapist asks that the client meet him where he, the therapist, is:

Dominic [client]:	Big question. Maybe I'll need another vodka before I answer that.
Dave [therapist]:	Dom, *be* here, be here *drunk*, but don't play fucking games with me.

In another example with the client Rebecca, I believe that the client is again challenged to enter the world of the therapist (Mearns and Cooper, 2005, p. 18). The therapist is open in recounting how he was feeling – 'I felt powerless, silenced, and frustrated' – before addressing Rebecca thus:

> I'm really trying to get a sense of what's going on for you, but I'm finding it hard to engage with, to find a way of communicating something of my sense of it all to you.

This contradicts the idea of congruently experiencing unconditional positive regard and empathy for the client, wherever the client is at, leading to a lessening of conditions of worth and an increase in congruent organismic valuing in the client.

For Person-Centred therapists, the genuine experience of empathic and deep unconditional positive regard occurs with all clients, regardless of the clients' process, content, or depth of experience. Jerold Bozarth (private email communication), questioning the concept of relational depth, states:

> There might somewhere be the question: Who determines when relational depth occurs? That is, relational depth might be experienced in different ways ... for example a client speaking about the weather might be the deepest of relational depth when his/her life might be destroyed by bad crops?

The meaning of congruence in Person-Centred therapy

Despite it being a cornerstone of Rogers' 1959 theory, Mearns and Cooper (2005) describe a therapist's congruent, empathic connection with clients as a relational depth construct and offer this as the counter to working in a caricatured, wooden 'Person-Centred' way. They contrast a picture of incongruent and unengaged Person-Centred therapy with what they describe as meeting at relational depth, as can be seen in the following extract (Mearns and Cooper, 2005, p. 38):

> From the therapist's standpoint, perhaps the most fundamental aspect of a meeting at relational depth is a complete genuineness and transparency in the encounter … Here the therapist is not play-acting the role of 'counsellor' or 'psychotherapist' but is simply being herself in the meeting. So, for instance, the therapist does not adopt the persona of a … blank screen … and neither do they play the part of the overly effusive and ever-smiling caricature of a 'person-centred' counsellor.

Crucially for Rogers, the question of congruence in therapy is completely intertwined with the therapists' actual experience of the therapeutic conditions of unconditional positive regard and empathy, thereby providing a powerful moment-by-moment following and connection with a client; it also assumes the therapist to have a significantly more developed level of self-awareness than a client, who is usually less congruent, more anxious upon entering therapy. This was made clear repeatedly by Rogers' (1959, p. 215) explanation that the six conditions were necessary and sufficient for Person-Centred therapy:

> For therapy to occur the wholeness of the therapist in the relationship is primary, but a part of the congruence of the therapist must be the experience of unconditional positive regard and the experience of empathic understanding.

As an imperfect person, always working towards becoming fully functioning, the congruent experiencing of unconditional positive regard and empathy in the therapeutic relationship is indicative of the level of congruence in the Person-Centred therapist. For the Person-Centred therapist, the therapeutic conditions are a guide, or a measure, to help them in remaining client-centred.

But what does congruence mean in the literature about relational depth? Mearns and Cooper (2005, p. xii) use the term 'real', as in their working definition of relational depth: 'A state of profound contact and engagement between two people, in which each person is fully real with the Other.' What does it mean to be 'fully real' and is such a state truly possible? Might it be possible that 'realness', without the experience of unconditional positive regard and empathy, is, in fact, indicative of therapist incongruence rather than congruence?

In what Mearns and Cooper (2005, p. 9) refer to as a 'dialogical' approach to Person-Centred therapy, they describe therapist congruence as distinct and separate from the necessary and sufficient conditions of Person-Centred therapy, stating of the therapist, 'she is there as a real and genuine human being'.

This imprecise concept of 'realness' includes the possibility of countering or being confrontational to the client (Mearns and Schmid, 2006). Such therapist-framed communications are considered by their advocates as an important part of being 'real' and therefore presumably beneficial for the 'bidirectional' therapeutic experience described by writers of relational depth.

Here, Mearns and Cooper (2005, p. 125) argue that the therapists' frame of reference can be useful in creating the type of process movement that the therapist may consider helpful: 'In terms of facilitating a relationally deep encounter, it may also be valuable to communicate to clients, how much they impact upon us.'

There is an implicit 'expert' stance in any directive decision by the therapist to 'facilitate a relationally deep encounter' and to present the client with the therapist's own frame of reference or 'realness' in order to facilitate a change in the client's process. This contrasts with Person-Centred therapy in which any form of therapist directivity is counter-therapeutic (Rogers, 1959).

Contrasts between the fundamentally relational Person-Centred approach and some ideas about working at relational depth

Mearns and Cooper (2005, p. 9) provide a summary of Person-Centred theory, which is problematic in its understanding:

> If we start from the classical Rogerian (1959) ... it makes absolute sense that the therapist's practice should revolve around the provision of unconditional positive regard to the client.

In this statement, Mearns and Cooper effectively redefine one of the core conditions of Person-Centred therapy (Rogers, 1959, p. 213), that of the therapist's experience of unconditional positive regard, by replacing the word 'experience' with 'provision' of this condition. The importance of this change is that it posits the client as a passive recipient of the actions of an active therapist, which fundamentally alters the nature of the relationship in Person-Centred therapy between the client and therapist. Mearns and Cooper's rewording loses the nondirective bidirectionality that is already inherent in Person-Centred therapy.

In Person-Centred therapy, the experiencing of unconditional positive regard and empathy is an internal (to the therapist) experience. However, although this is an internal experiencing, it is not only an internal experience. The therapist is not intended to live these experiences separate from the client, and this is clear when we consider the sixth condition in the theory, which makes explicit that this is already an interactive relational therapy, as it states that the client must perceive, at least to a minimal degree, the therapist's experiencing of empathy and unconditional positive regard for them (Rogers, 1959).

A bidirectional element is already integral to the therapy because for the client to perceive the therapist's experience, the therapist must relate interactively with the client. How else would the client perceive the therapist's internal experience other than through interaction? The act of perception is not passive, as in Mearns and Cooper's analysis of the client in Person-Centred therapy as a passive recipient of a set of conditions, but requires active engagement on the part of the client. The client actively perceives something of the experience of the therapist. Rogers (1959, p. 199) explained perception as follows:

> For our own definition we might say that a perception is a hypothesis or prognosis for action which comes into being in awareness when stimuli impinge on the organism.

Nondirectivity and the Person-Centred approach

A fundamental difference has emerged between the Person-Centred approach and some of the writings on relational depth in relation to understandings of psychological disturbance and how to remedy this. Mearns and Cooper (2005) and Mearns and Schmid (2006) discuss the use of 'encounter'. Dictionary definitions of encounter include 'to be faced with something difficult to deal with', 'to meet somebody unexpectedly', or as Schmid and Mearns (2006, p. 180) put it: 'encounter means that one is touched by the essence of the opposite'. I would argue that Mearns and Cooper (2005, p. 9) change the whole schema of the theory of Carl Rogers in their thinking:

> If we also hold, however, that human beings have a fundamental need for something more interactive, and that psychological difficulties arise when a person's capacity to engage with others becomes disrupted then this points towards a therapeutic approach in which dialogue and interaction take more centre stage: one in which it is the encounter between the therapist and client, rather than the provision of a particular set of conditions for the client, that is conceptualised as being key to the healing process.

In this counter-style view of therapy, the client exists in a wholly separate sphere from the therapist who, rather than trying to enter the client's world as if it were their own, confronts the client with their own alternative view and experience. Mearns and Cooper (2005, p. 130) stated: 'a therapist's here and now disclosures are more a reaction to, than an empathic response with, her client'. This counter-style view of therapy leads to directive intentions on the part of the therapist, such as 'what you are actually trying to do is to break the non-communicative cycle' (Mearns and Cooper, 2005, p. 102).

In working at relational depth, as described above, the therapist would seem to be aiming to intervene in order to create a result, to move or direct the client, to create a relationship of depth. By contrast, Person-Centred therapy seeks to value all the client's experiences equally, since it is the lessening of conditions of worth and any external locus of evaluation in the client that leads to the development of a more congruent, fully functioning person, as explained by Rogers (1959, p. 208):

> If the self-experiences of another are perceived by me in such a way that no self-experience can be discriminated as more or less worthy of positive regard than any other, then I am experiencing unconditional positive regard for this individual. To perceive oneself as receiving unconditional positive regard is to perceive that of one's self-experiences none can be discriminated by the other individual as more or less worthy of positive regard.

Mearns and Cooper (2005, p. xi) express the view that the client's experiences and process can, in fact, be discriminated towards and evaluated by the therapist as being more, or less worthy:

> When I began to look at the material that was in this 'unspoken relationship' ... I found that most of the *really* important stuff for the client was in there.

Perhaps one signifier of whether an intense therapeutic interaction is Person-Centred is whether there is any directivity on the part of the therapist. For directive therapists, including those seeking relational depth through encounter or counter, the therapists' intent is to create a movement in the client, such as a more intense relationship, or a more 'real' relationship. This holds the potential consequence of the clients' acceptance of the therapists' intent, which is the acceptance of an external locus of evaluation. According to Rogers' theory, this would, in turn, lead to an increase in incongruence of the client, and would therefore, in Person-Centred terms, be counter-therapeutic.

Mutuality and being counter

The writings of Mearns, Cooper and Schmid highlight some fundamental differences with the inherently nondirective Person-Centred therapy (Rogers, 1959), as can be seen in this extract from Mearns and Schmid (2006, p. 260):

> The therapist has the freedom to choose the level of their relationship to the client ... They are free to choose the existential level or a more presentational one.

Ironically, the therapists' choice to relate on different levels of their own choosing does not create the 'mutuality' that it would like to achieve. Instead, it creates a distancing from the client in which each person, client and therapist, exist in separate spheres. Perhaps one intention of the therapist working to create relational depth is for the client to be brought to the level of relating of the therapist. Previous case examples from Mearns and Cooper (2005) would support this view.

Therapists who work in ways that counter the client may experience the difficulties described by Mearns and Schmid (2006, p. 261):

> In the encounter mode there is always a risk ... psychotherapy at the level of relational depth includes the danger of being misunderstood, hurt, rejected, or ignored. This goes for the therapist, but also for the client.

Current research into relational depth would support the view that such an encounter does not necessarily achieve the desired mutuality intended by the therapist. Research conducted by Wiggins et al. (2012, p. 3) found the following dissonance between the experience of the therapist and that of the client:

> The authors suggested that where therapists experience relational depth in terms of the relationship, the client's experience of such is more often about themselves and of a willingness to let go and be free to express themselves with their therapist.

In other words, this is not a meeting in which there is a 'mutual experience' (Wiggins et al., 2012) but two people engaged in their own separate experience. It is possible that the idea of mutuality could have been inspired by Rogers' (1959) Person-Centred condition six – that the client perceives, at least to a minimal degree, the empathy and unconditional positive regard genuinely experienced by the therapist.

However, writings on relational depth take this further, with the expectation that each party, therapist and client, will be 'fully real' (Mearns and Cooper, 2005). This a problematic concept not merely because of the difficulties of determining whether full realness has been achieved, but also because the second of the necessary and sufficient conditions for Person-Centred therapy states: 'That the first person, whom we shall term the client, is in a state of incongruence, being vulnerable, or anxious' (Rogers, 1959, p. 213). If the client were not in this state, they would likely be near to or at the end of their therapy and no longer a client.

In Person-Centred therapy, some degree of what might be described as relational depth does occur naturally as the client differentiates and discriminates between the objects of their feelings and perceptions (Rogers, 1959). However, the client reaches these moments autonomously, facilitated by a radically freeing but connected relationship with the therapist in which the client learns to trust their own process. This can be pragmatically viewed in transcripts and demonstrations by Rogers where clients increasingly move towards greater self-exploration and direction.

The actualizing tendency

Barely mentioned in writings about relational depth is consideration of the concept of an organismic actualizing tendency (Rogers, 1959). Although it is not necessary for therapists to believe in the concept of an actualizing tendency to be able to operate as a Person-Centred therapist, this is the rationale for trusting the client. As Bozarth (1998, p. 28) explains:

> Without trusting in the individual to direct their own life, including their own therapy, it is quite understandable that the therapist may feel some need to control or direct the therapy.

Conclusion

In Person-Centred therapy, there is no counter, however tentatively offered, or conflict for the client to have to assimilate and deal with, or submit to in order to win the approval of the therapist. Instead, there is the opportunity for deep connection between therapist and client, such as that desired by the proponents of relational depth, precisely because the nonjudgemental Person-Centred therapist follows and accompanies the client step by step, breath by breath, thought by thought and feeling by feeling (Rogers, 1959). This leads to the reduction of conditions of worth and a strengthening of client congruence, which brings with it deeper interrelatedness as clients become more self-confident and self-trusting. The Person-Centred approach, when intact, is revolutionary and, in my view, remains far ahead of its time in its execution. The approach stands alone among therapeutic models in wholly trusting the client, one of the only relationships a client can have where growth in a human being is facilitated in this way.

References

Bozarth, J. (1998) *Person-Centred Therapy: A Revolutionary Paradigm.* Ross-on-Wye: PCCS Books.

Brodley, B.T. (1994) Some observations of Carl Rogers' behavior in therapy interviews. *Person-Centered Journal*, 1, 37–48.

Brodley, B.T. (2001) Observations of empathic understanding in a client-centred practice. In S. Haugh and T. Merry (eds) *Rogers' Therapeutic Conditions: Evolution, Theory and Practice*, vol. 2, *Empathy* (pp. 16–37). Ross-on-Wye: PCCS Books.

Brody, A.F. (1991) Understanding client-centered therapy through interviews conducted by Carl Rogers. Unpublished doctoral dissertation, Illinois School of Professional Psychology, Chicago.

Cooper, M. (2011) Relational depth: An author's perspective – Interview with Mick Cooper, at www.onlinevents.co.uk/?s=interview+with+M+Cooper.

Mearns, D. (1996) Working at relational depth with clients in person-centred therapy. *Counselling*, 7, 307–11.

Mearns, D. (1997) *Person-Centred Counselling Training*. London: Sage.

Mearns, D. and Cooper, M. (2005) *Working at Relational Depth in Counselling and Psychotherapy*. London: Sage.
Mearns, D. and Schmid, P. (2006) Being-with and being-counter: Relational depth – the challenge of fully meeting the client. *Person-Centred and Experiential Psychotherapies*, 5(4), 255–65.
Merry, T. (1996) An analysis of ten demonstration interviews by Carl Rogers: Implications for the training of client-centered counselors. In R. Hutterer, G. Pawlowsky, P.F. Schmid and R. Stipsits (eds) *Client-Centered and Experiential Therapy: A Paradigm in Motion* (pp. 273–83). Frankfurt am Main: Peter Lang.
Rice, B. (2012) Person-centred listserve discussion, pcintl@listserv.uga.edu, 27 April.
Rogers, C.R. (1959) A theory of therapy, personality, and interpersonal relationships, as developed in the client-centered framework. In S. Koch (ed.) *Psychology: A Study of Science*, vol. 3, *Formulations of the Person and the Social Context* (pp. 184–256). New York: McGraw-Hill.
Rogers, C.R. (1980) *A Way of Being*. Boston: Houghton Mifflin.
Sanders, P. (2004) *The Tribes of the Person-Centred Nation: A Guide to the Schools of Therapy Associated with the Person-Centred Approach*. Ross-on-Wye: PCCS Books.
Schmid, P. and Mearns, D. (2006) Being-with and being-counter: Person-centered psychotherapy as an in-depth co-creative process of personalization. *Person-Centered and Experiential Psychotherapies*, 5(3), 174–91.
Wiggins, S., Elliott, R. and Cooper, M. (2012) The prevalence and characteristics of relational depth events in psychotherapy. *Psychotherapy Research*, 22(2), 139–58.

16

The transpersonal and relational depth

John Rowan

In this chapter I want to discuss the transpersonal, and to argue that working at relational depth is a spiritual activity, demanding some acquaintance with the subtle level of transpersonal relating. I also want to argue that other approaches from other sources also work at the subtle level, so that working at relational depth links with all these other sources. I find these connections very exciting, as if there were now a large family of therapies all opening up to this level of working. Doing this work, it seems to me, also deepens the whole idea of working at relational depth, making, as it does, a huge impact on the world of therapy. There are two aspects to this. On the one hand, there is the hugely increased interest in the relational aspects of therapy, which has affected the psychoanalysts, the existentialists, the Gestaltists and sundry other people. And on the other hand, there is the much more accurate and specific understanding of the transpersonal realm, which has come from the work of Wilber (2000), Cortright (1997), Ferrer (2002) and others in that field. Many others have commented on the relational question, but far fewer have dealt with the transpersonal side of it, so it is this which forms the basis for this chapter.

What is the transpersonal?

The transpersonal is a level of consciousness where we admit that we are spiritual beings with a soul and a spirit. As we know from the work of Ken Wilber (2000), it is usual to distinguish between the prepersonal, the personal and the transpersonal, and this seems clear enough:

- the *personal* is the ordinary, everyday consciousness with which we are all familiar

- the *prepersonal* is all that comes before that in the process of development, and is well described in developmental psychology generally
- the *transpersonal* is that which genuinely goes beyond the personal into the realm of the sacred, the numinous, the holy, the divine.

This is all well-trodden ground. It has often been pointed out that society helps us to develop out of the prepersonal into the personal, and even helps us through the early development of the personal into the mature ego that is favoured in our society generally. Society does not, however, help us on into the transpersonal. That is something for each person to initiate and take responsibility for. And because society is not interested in the transpersonal, it is a realm that is disputed and subject to warring factions, and often confused with religion (a much more complicated subject).

However, since the founding of the *Journal of Transpersonal Psychology* by Abraham Maslow and Anthony Sutich in 1969, and the formation of the Association for Transpersonal Psychology in 1972, the transpersonal has been studied scientifically, and in 1996 the British Psychological Society founded the Transpersonal Psychology Section, which publishes the peer reviewed *Transpersonal Psychology Review*. This and the publication of a variety of books (for example Cortright, 1997; West, 2000; Wilber 2000; Ferrer 2002; Rowan 2005) based on this work have made the subject respectable and well based.

Distinctions within the transpersonal

Within the transpersonal, there is an important distinction to be made, which is most clearly put by Ken Wilber (2000), who I think is the best map-maker in this area. There are three levels of consciousness within the transpersonal. The first of these is that outlined by Maslow (1987) and which he called self-actualization. We now regard this as equivalent to Rogers' 'fully functioning person', Perls' self as opposed to self-image, Wade's (1996) 'authentic' level of consciousness, and the 'real self' of Winnicott, Laing, Janov and Johnson. This is also sometimes called the 'existential' level of consciousness, and it is the basis of most of the humanistic forms of therapy. But we shall not be referring to that here, because it usually fits better into the everyday traditional approach of the humanistic therapies, including the person-centred approach as most often understood.

The second level of consciousness within the transpersonal is variously called the subtle, the realm of the soul, the superconscious, the heart centre, the intuitive mind, the psychic centre, the *antaratma* and so on. Its distinguishing feature is that it shows forth the divine in the form of symbols and images, which are accessible and reasonably familiar to all. So, it is the realm of the Jungian archetypes (shadow, anima, puer and so on), deities, nature spirits, standing stones, wells, trees, rivers and so on – all things which are accessible to all of us, and which point to the divine if approached in the right way. It is the realm of compassion of a deeply emotional kind; a realm explored so well by Jung (1964) and other Jungians such as James Hillman (1975), and by the psychosynthesis people (Ferrucci 1982), who emphasize intuition and imagery.

The third level of consciousness within the transpersonal is where we are able to give up all the symbols and images, all the comfortable distinctions and divisions, and move into the deep ocean of spirituality, where there are no signposts and no landmarks. This is variously called the causal, the over-mind, the bliss mind, the pure self, formless mysticism, the witness, cessation, the void, big mind and so on. This is less often used in therapy, because it is much harder to attain, and therefore rarer as a resource. It fits better into the realm of meditation rather than therapy. So, within this chapter we shall stay with the subtle.

Relational depth

If we are saying that relational depth is a transpersonal phenomenon, located at the subtle level of consciousness, one of the key features of the subtle level is the phenomenon of 'linking'. Sometimes in the history of psychotherapy, a phenomenon arises that occurs to several people at once, like ripe fruit that drops into everyone's back garden at the same time. It is a situation in therapy where something is experienced that is not empathy, not projective identification, not countertransference and not identification, but can easily be confused with any one of them. Rosemary Budgell (1995, p. 33), in her formal research project, called it 'linking'. She says:

> The experience is described as near fusion, a communion of souls or spirits and a blurring of personal boundaries. To achieve this, both parties have to give up something of themselves while remaining separate. It is not symbiosis but the other end of the spectrum, as described by Wilber (1980). It is the transpersonal sense of relinquishing self. Symbiosis is about being cosy, but this is about working through pain and fear. It is a sacred experience and yet natural and there all the time. It comes from the spiritual or transpersonal realm, being a step beyond empathy and the natural plain.

It is clear from this description that we are not talking about empathy in the usual sense. It has often been emphasized that there is an 'as if' quality about empathy. We try to enter into another person's inner world, but know very well that they are over there and we are over here. This is something different, which goes much deeper into the world of the other person: it is as if it actually overlaps with ours. Tobin Hart (1997) has suggested, however, that it can be regarded as a deeper form of empathy, which he calls 'transcendental empathy'. It is also described in the recent person-centred literature as working at relational depth; as Mearns and Cooper (2005, xii) have suggested: 'It is a state of profound contact and engagement between two people.' I want to go further, and say that it is a transpersonal state, pertaining to the subtle level, and can be best understood as a spiritual kind of consciousness. This means that we can then link it with other work in the therapeutic field more fully and convincingly. One of the main things that has to be done, in this understanding of the matter, is to reproduce in one's own body (as a therapist) whatever the client is describing as going on in their own body. Cooper (2001), for example, uses the concept of 'embodied empathy'. The therapist can get into the same position as the client, and if the client says there is a pain in the middle of the back, the therapist also sets up a pain in the middle of the back. It is in order for the therapist to exaggerate what the client is saying, in order to get deeper into the experience, and to encourage the client to get deeper into the experience. This is also the approach of Alvin Mahrer (1996), who is very explicit about the way in which he does this.

Here again we have linking, this time on a perfectly ordinary, straightforward level. Maurice Friedman has drawn attention to the way in which Martin Buber has talked about 'inclusion' and 'imagining the real'. By inclusion, Buber means a remarkable swinging over to the side of the other with the most intense activity, so that one experiences concretely what the other person is thinking, feeling and willing:

> Inclusion is the extension of one's own concreteness, the fulfilment of the actual situation of life, the complete presence of the reality in which one participates. (Buber, 1985, p. 97)

> I experience ... the specific pain of another in such a way that I feel ... this particular pain as the pain of the other. (Buber, 1988, p. 60)

Friedman (1996, p. 209) makes the point that this relationship of inclusion is not a possession of a spiritual elite:

> On the contrary, it is a gift that every human being has ... Most people imagine that we are imprisoned within our individual experience and find it hard to believe that Buber's imagining the real can actually enable us to make our own what the other experiences.

In the discussions of working at relational depth, it is often stated that this cannot be switched on at will – it has to emerge from the situation. But some of the writers we have been quoting here do not believe this, but rather assume that it is something that can be set up from the start.

In a similar way, James Bugental, who bridges in a unique way the gap between the existential and the humanistic, has introduced some research by Molly Sterling in which the supervisee role-plays the client and the supervisor role-plays the supervisee. Sometimes, a curious thing happened:

> Unexpectedly and suddenly, I lose the ability to maintain the immersion I have been experiencing. The distinctions between 'me' and 'the role-played client' dissolve. It is as though there is a collapse of the separated consciousnesses into one melded experience ... I can't tell which of us is the source of the content I am expressing! (Sterling and Bugental 1993, p. 42)

Bugental speculates that if our deepest nature is manifested by the meld, we may arrive at a rather different picture of our own nature; and he goes on into some transpersonal thoughts.

In the Jungian tradition, Andrew Samuels (1989) is an analyst who has remarked on the way in which the body is involved in this kind of experience. In fact, he has called it 'embodied countertransference'. He says that using the word 'embodied' emphasizes that we are talking here of a physical, actual, material, sensual expression in the therapist of something in the client's inner world. Again, if we have never had this sort of experience, we may find the words hard to understand or to take. But I suggest that all of us who have had experience of working at relational depth have indeed entered this space.

Where it becomes more explicitly transpersonal is when Samuels (1989) says that it takes place in the imaginal world. This imaginal world is an in-between state, where images take the place of language (Corbin, 1969; Hillman, 1975). It is between the conscious and the unconscious, and also between the therapist and the client. Both persons have access to it and can share it. It is the therapist's body, the therapist's imagery, the therapist's feelings or fantasies; but these things also belong to the client, and have been squeezed into being and given substance by the therapeutic relationship. And Samuels (1989) emphasizes that these are *visionary* states, concluding that such experiences may usefully be regarded as religious or mystical. This is the realm which I have called the 'subtle', and also the realm of working at relational depth. Some person-centred people seem a bit reluctant to speak of it as a spiritual experience or as evidence of a spiritual world, but it seems quite obvious to me.

It is common in psychoanalysis today (Stolorow et al., 1987) to recognize that some countertransference reactions in the analyst stem from, and may be regarded as communications from, the patient, and that the analyst's inner world, as it appears to them, is the *via regia* (royal road) into the inner world of the patient; but this goes further in stressing the idea of the *mundus imaginalis* (imaginal world) as shared territory. In person-centred work, this is often mentioned under the heading of 'intuition', and indeed intuition is one of the prime discoveries of the subtle level of consciousness:

> Rogers' years of experience, his deep involvement in the interaction, his insistence on correction as a matter of course, his inability to recall the details of the session – all these suggest his having come to rely on intuitive processes in the mature stages of his work. (Brink, 1996, p. 30)

Similarly, Benjamin Wolman (1986), a psychoanalyst who uses hypnosis, speaks of those times when we become aware of another person's feelings without sensory perceptions and without any possibility of proving or disproving them. He says that such experiences belong in the region of the 'protoconscious'. The protoconscious is not the conscious or preconscious mind, because there things are under control and are available to logic and language. Nor is it the unconscious, because the unconscious is what we are unaware of and cannot simply get in touch with at will. This is not the language of relational depth, but it seems to me that the connection is obvious.

Nathan Schwartz-Salant (1984, pp. 10–11), another Jungian, has spoken in his own terms of this phenomenon, which I am calling 'linking', having to do with what he calls the 'subtle body':

> A realm that is felt to be outside normal time sense and in a space felt to have substance. This space, long known as the subtle body, exists because of imagination, yet it also has autonomy.

He also uses the term 'conjunctio', taken from alchemy, and meaning a joining, such that two become one. Elsewhere, Schwartz-Salant (1998, pp. 185–6) speaks even more deeply of this experience, in discussing a particularly difficult client of his:

> The process is difficult to describe because it exists within an imaginal reality in which one's attention flows through the heart and out toward another person. In the process imaginal sight emerges, a quality of consciousness that perceives the presence of the archetypal level. This sight can be experienced through the eyes, the body or the emotions, but it is a level of perception that gently penetrates in ways that a discursive process fails to achieve. To the abandoned soul, knowledge without heart feels like abandonment. The heart offers a way to connect without violating the soul.

This is an interesting approach, which brings the phenomenon quite convincingly into the Jungian framework. It is clear that he is talking about working at relational depth. This has been spelled out most fully by Nathan Field (1996, p. 71), a London Jungian, who has written extensively on what he calls the 'fourth dimension' of therapy. Here is how he describes it:

> One of the ways in which the four-dimensional state can be experienced is the *simultaneous union and separation of self and other.* I have in mind those moments

> where two people feel profoundly united with one another yet each retains a singularly enriched sense of themselves. We are not lost in the other, as in fusion, but found.

Field speaks movingly of the way in which such an experience has a healing power: 'A totally new *Gestalt* has come into being where separateness and togetherness are simultaneously experienced in all their depth and richness' (p. 73). This sounds like relational depth to me.

This idea is taken up in one of the few discussions of this phenomenon to be found in the psychoanalytic literature. Wilfred Bion was interested in the question of psychic reality. How does an analyst decide how and when to make an interpretation? Bion's answer is that it is through the process of intuition. This involves letting go of the senses. He likened it to the idea of 'negative capability', as explained by John Keats: 'You cannot know psychic reality: you *become* it' (Symington and Symington, 1996, p. 176). This places us squarely in the realm of the transpersonal, or as the Symingtons put it, the mystical. Bion quite explicitly suggests that it is our defences that do not allow us to enter into such mystical experiences.

The pathway by which such an experience becomes possible is through the close relationship with another. Psychoanalysis is the investigation of such a relationship and it attempts to open both partners to the mystical experience. Bion concentrates his focus on those elements that block the two individuals from that experience. The conclusion is unavoidable: that Bion's thinking is geared to facilitating mystical experience (Symington and Symington 1996, p. 178).

It seems clear that the phenomenon of working at relational depth is not a form of identification or confluence. This seems even more clear when we remember that for Freud (1985) identification is something quite primitive. What we are talking about here is not primitive at all, but something sophisticated, which goes beyond the ordinary therapeutic set-up.

Conclusion

The interesting thing is that some people in the transpersonal field feel very strongly that this is not something which can be brought under voluntary control. Rosemary Budgell's (1995, p. 63) research repeatedly found that therapists who had had these experiences did not want to reduce them to something that could be controlled: 'It was a sense of being joined or linked and of something good and healing emanating from another person.' The essence of it for them was that it came unbidden, although this can now be questioned.

It now seems to me that this is a feature of work at the subtle level, as we have described it earlier, and that in fact it would be better to recognize it as such, and place it firmly in the realm of the transpersonal. Tricia Whitehouse

(1999) has done an interesting piece of research among therapists practising in a transpersonal way, and this is certainly the conclusion she reached. Similarly, Jyoti Nanda (2005) did some research with meditators who were also therapists, and found that meditation could often take the therapist into a realm where the normal boundaries were challenged and modified. Mearns and Cooper (2005) have done a marvellous job of naturalizing all these ideas into a person-centred framework, and showing that working at relational depth is not something exotic and extraordinary, but something very accessible to any practitioner willing to open up to these subtle energies.

References

Brink, D.C. (1996) Rogers' therapy cases: Views from within. In B.A. Farber, D.C. Brink and P.M. Raskin (eds) *The Psychotherapy of Carl Rogers* (pp. 55–62). New York: Guilford Press.

Buber, M. (1985) *Between Man and Man* (trans. R.G. Smith). New York: Macmillan.

Buber, M. (1988) *The Knowledge of Man: A Philosophy of the Interhuman* (trans. M. Friedman and R.G. Smith). Atlantic Highlands, NJ: Humanities Press.

Budgell, R. (1995) Being touched through space. Dissertation of School of Psychotherapy and Counselling, Regents College, London.

Cooper, M. (2001) Embodied empathy. In S. Haugh and T. Merry (eds) *Rogers' Therapeutic Conditions: Evolution, Theory and Practice*, vol. 1, *Empathy* (pp. 206–17). Ross-on-Wye: PCCS Books.

Corbin, H. (1969) *Creative Imagination in the Sufism of Ibn 'Arabi*. Princeton, NJ: Princeton University Press.

Cortright, B. (1997) *Psychotherapy and Spirit: Theory and Practice in Transpersonal Psychotherapy*. Albany, NY: SUNY Press.

Ferrer, J. (2002) *Revisioning Transpersonal Theory: A Participatory Vision of Human Spirituality.* Albany, NY: SUNY Press

Ferrucci, P. (1982) *What We May Be.* Wellingborough: Turnstone Press.

Field, N. (1996) *Breakdown and Breakthrough*. London: Routledge.

Freud, S. (1985) *Group Psychology and the Analysis of the Ego*, vol. 12. London: Penguin.

Friedman, M. (1996) Becoming aware: A dialogical approach to consciousness, *The Humanistic Psychologist*, 24(2), 203–20.

Hart, T. (1997) Transcendental empathy in the therapeutic encounter. *The Humanistic Psychologist*, 25(3), 245–70.

Hillman, J. (1975) *Re-visioning Psychology.* New York: Harper Colophon.

Jung, C.G. (1964) *Man and His Symbols.* New York: Dell.

Mahrer, A.R. (1996) *The Complete Guide to Experiential Psychotherapy.* Chichester: Wiley.

Maslow, A.H. (1987) *Motivation and Personality* (3rd edn). New York: Harper & Row.

Mearns, D. and Cooper, M. (2005) *Working at Relational Depth in Counselling and Psychotherapy.* London: Sage.

Nanda, J. (2005) A phenomenological enquiry into the effect of meditation on therapeutic practice. *Existential Analysis*, 16(2), 322–35.

Rowan, J. (2005) *The Transpersonal: Spirituality in Psychotherapy and Counselling* (2nd edn). London: Routledge.

Samuels, A. (1989) *The Plural Psyche.* London: Routledge.
Schwartz-Salant, N. (1984) Archetypal factors underlying sexual acting-out in the transference/countertransference process. In N. Schwartz-Salant and M. Stein (eds) *Transference/Countertransference* (pp. 1–30). Wilmette, IL: Chiron.
Schwartz-Salant, N. (1998) *The Mystery of the Human Relationship: Alchemy and the Transformation of Self.* New York: Routledge.
Sterling, M.M. and Bugental, J.F. (1993) The meld experience in psychotherapy supervision. *Journal of Humanistic Psychology*, 33(2), 38–48.
Stolorow, R.D., Brandschaft, B. and Atwood, G.E. (1987) *Psychoanalytic Treatment: An Intersubjective Approach.* Hillsdale, NJ: Analytic Press.
Symington, J. and Symington, N. (1996) *The Clinical Thinking of Wilfred Bion.* London: Routledge.
Wade, J. (1996) *Changes of Mind: A Holonomic Theory of the Evolution of Consciousness.* Albany, NY: SUNY Press.
West, W. (2000) *Psychotherapy and Spirituality.* London: Sage.
Whitehouse, T. (1999) Experiences of the transpersonal in counselling. Unpublished MSc dissertation, University of Surrey, Roehampton.
Wilber, K. (1980) *The Atman Project.* Wheaton, IL: Quest.
Wilber, K. (2000) *Integral Psychology.* Boston, MA: Shambhala.
Wolman, B.B. (1986) Protoconscious and psychopathology. In B.B. Wolman and M. Ullman (eds) *Handbook of States of Consciousness* (pp. 311–31). New York: Van Nostrand Reinhold.

17

Conclusion: where we go from here

Rosanne Knox, David Murphy, Sue Wiggins and Mick Cooper

In this book, we have explored relational depth using the most recent available evidence and looking through the experience of practitioners in a variety of settings. We have also considered a range of theoretical perspectives on relational depth. But what have we learned along the way, where have we got to and where do we go next?

While the concept of relational depth seems to have relevance across orientations, it also articulates something unique about the person-centred approach. It is, perhaps, surprising that it has taken our field so long to (re) turn attention to this depth of relating between client and therapist, and the relational aspects of therapy as practised and proposed by Carl Rogers. Yet there are so many more areas to explore and understand; so many more questions to be asked and to be researched. For example, there is the question of the matching of clients' and therapists' experiences of relational depth. The chapters of Part I indicate that both do experience a depth of relating, and there is a wide range of emotions and experiences described, some of which seem to be common to both clients and therapists, while others seem peculiar to one or the other (see Chapter 5).

So what are the main issues and tensions with regards to relational depth, and have we managed to deal with these effectively? There remains work to be done in building a clearer distinction between relational depth as a feature of an enduring relationship and as a moment of meeting within the relationship. This is certainly an area for further research and it might yet transpire that these two conceptualizations form part of the same experience, and that what is required are studies to consider these two aspects together. Questions relating to the relationship between these two phenomena also need to be considered. For example, how is a sense of enduring relational depth influenced by the presence of moments of intense contact and relational depth?

And conversely, how does the enduring relationship impact on the likelihood of moments of relational depth occurring? This question has been touched on in Chapter 2, but it seems there is still much to discover about the relationship of these two aspects.

The question of how moments of relational depth might arise is also crucial to the debates around relational depth and nondirectivity. If a meeting at relational depth is actively initiated by the therapist, this would certainly seem to conflict with the nondirective stance of the person-centred therapist. It is an argument made by some within the approach, and it is represented here by Sue Wilders (Chapter 15). However, while John Rowan (Chapter 16), for example, does refer to the concept of 'linking' as something that can be created by the therapist, those more closely aligned with the person-centred approach seem to suggest that relational depth is more like a natural event that occurs as an unintended consequence of the sustained presence of Rogers' ([1957]1990) six therapeutic conditions. More detailed responses by Mearns, Cooper and others can be found in the May 2007 and November 2007 editions of *Person-Centred Quarterly*, and interested readers can find a range of debates around these viewpoints there (Mearns, 2007; Cooper, 2007).

As can be seen from the chapters in Part I, the research to date generally supports the notion that therapists experience relational depth as arising spontaneously, while clients see themselves as the decision makers, remaining in control of the level of relating. This is also consistent with Schmid's description of the client as an active self-helper, where the therapist is seen as actively responding to the person of the client – being both *with* and *counter* (Chapter 16). Yet if an experience of relational depth is not something that is purposefully initiated by the therapist, need we explore it at all? We would echo Mearns and Cooper's (2005) argument that while therapists cannot 'make' a meeting at relational depth happen, it is something that they can prepare for, so that it is a level of connection they are able to engage at, should it be what the client wants.

In looking at relational depth in different contexts with different client groups, the chapters in this book have drawn attention to the possibilities, challenges and particular benefits of relational depth within those particular settings. Eleanor Macleod's study (Chapter 3) shows how seemingly insurmountable obstacles can be overcome, and gives a strong indication of how an experience that frequently carries the description 'beyond words' can be of such immense value to clients with learning disabilities, especially those with limited verbal communication. David Murphy and Stephen Joseph (Chapter 7) have shown how relational depth can create the therapeutic space for posttraumatic growth to occur. The particular relevance for some young people has also been highlighted by Sue Hawkins through her work with young offenders (Chapter 6), bringing to mind Rogers' own work with disaffected boys, during which period much of his theoretical perspective was taking shape.

Of relevance to all therapists working in today's multicultural society, Colin Lago and Fevronia Christodoulidi (Chapter 9) have invited us to think about the potential barriers to relational depth in relationships where the client and therapists come from different ethnic backgrounds, and offer suggestions for ways in which a therapist can mitigate against those barriers. Turning our attention from individual therapy, Gill Wyatt (Chapter 8) has further expanded our focus to embrace groups and extra-therapeutic situations such as organizational, cultural, national and international settings.

We have also looked at how the concept of relational depth might sit with a range of theoretical perspectives, as in Shari Geller's work around therapist 'presence' (Chapter 13), and how this is core to a relationship that allows a depth of meeting. A different view has been offered by John Rowan (Chapter 16) in his proposal that relational depth is something that occurs within the transpersonal realm.

We have tried to engage the reader actively in the debates, research, theoretical perspectives and practice experience around the notion of relational depth. In opening the book with a series of short case studies, we hope that readers might have been able to think about any experiences they may have had themselves, whether as a therapist or as a client. We also hope that therapists might use Elke Lambers' chapter to think about the relevance, potentiality and challenges of relational depth, not just in their role as therapist, but also in supervision, whether as supervisee or supervisor (Chapter 10). We invite readers to engage with the self-development exercises offered by Mick Cooper in Chapter 11, as well as Sue Wiggins' Relational Depth Inventory (Chapter 4), which can be used in both practice and organizational settings.

We hope that this book provides a stimulus for further consideration of in-depth encounters, and that the reader might take away thoughts and ideas that can translate into everyday practice. We hope it might also provide a stepping stone for further research in the field. In a time where so much emphasis is placed on technological and task-oriented facets of therapy, the chapters in this book call for more attention to the relational components. Relational depth provides an opportunity to bring together researchers and practitioners with a shared interest in relational work. It provides us with a concept and set of experiences that can act as a pivotal point around which we can gather together our interests, passions and commitment to what we consider ethical, valuable and effective practice.

References

Cooper, M. (2007) Thoughts and feelings on the relational depth debate. *Person-Centred Quarterly*, May, 14–15.

Mearns, D. (2007) Regarding Barbara Brodley's critique of Mearns and Cooper (2005). *Person-Centred Quarterly*, November, 23.

Mearns, D. and Cooper, M. (2005) *Working at Relational Depth in Counselling and Psychotherapy.* London: Sage.

Rogers, C.R. ([1957]1990) The necessary and sufficient conditions of therapeutic personality change. In H. Kirschenbaum and V. Henderson (eds) *The Carl Rogers Reader* (pp. 219–235). London: Constable.

Index

D